THIS IS MY NAME FOREVER

....

The Trinity
& Gender
Language
for God

EDITED BY
ALVIN F. KIMEL JR.

....

ivp

InterVarsity Press
Downers Grove, Illinois

InterVarsity Press
P.O. Box 1400, Downers Grove, IL 60515-1426
World Wide Web: www.ivpress.com
E-mail: mail@ivpress.com

InterVarsity Press® is the book-publishing division of InterVarsity Christian Fellowship/USA®, a student movement active on campus at hundreds of universities, colleges and schools of nursing in the United States of America, and a member movement of the International Fellowship of Evangelical Students. For information about local and regional activities, write Public Relations Dept., InterVarsity Christian Fellowship/USA, 6400 Schroeder Rd., P.O. Box 7895, Madison, WI 53707-7895.

Library of Congress Cataloging-in-Publication Data

This is my name forever : the Trinity and gender language for God / edited by Alvin F. Kimel, Jr.
    p. cm.
    Includes bibliographical references.
    ISBN 0-8308-1506-6 (alk. paper)
    1. God—Name. 2. Nonsexist language—Religious aspects—Christianity. 3. Feminist theology. 4. Language and languages—Religious aspects—Christianity. I. Kimel, Alvin F., 1952-

BT180.N2 T48 2001
231'.01'4—dc21

                                                                                00-047171

22 21 20 19 18 17 16 15 14 13 12 11 10 9 8 7 6 5 4 3 2 1

19 18 17 16 15 14 13 12 11 10 09 08 07 06 05 04 03 02 01

CONTENTS

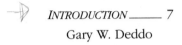

Introduction

Gary W. Deddo

Human address of God has always been a very important matter and one often subject to contention. This has been true across time and religions. Increasingly there has been a cry to change our language about God, especially in Western societies where Christian language has been used in particular to refer to God. Some critics contend that traditional Christian ways of speaking of God have had harmful effects on women. More particularly, they allege that masculine pronouns and masculine images such as Father, Son and King used in reference to God misrepresent God as being male, encourage men to take advantage of women, provide a religious justification for violence done to women and alienate women from the worship of God. These are serious charges.

For the sake of discussion we can formulate these concerns in two questions: (1) Does masculine language for God encourage the abuse of women and the self-justification of men in their violation of women? (2) Does masculine language about God alienate women from true worship?

Often those calling for a reform of language assume that such language serves as a strong factor in creating such harmful situations. It is also often assumed that the elimination of such language is possible and would certainly make a decisive contribution to alleviating wrongful behavior. Furthermore, it is assumed that solving the ethical problem of abuse by altering the practical matter of language is of greater significance than any other concern. Consequently, a consideration of other damaging yet unintended consequences such as spiritual harm to women (or others) or the abandonment of Christian authority and faith are often neglected. These matters are considered of secondary or even of no concern.

The contributors to this volume find the mistreatment of women or of anyone else deplorable, especially when done in the name of the Christian God. Consequently, we are adamantly concerned to provide a genuine solution to the ethically abhorrent problem rather than a pseudo solution that might be ineffectual or even contribute more or even greater harm. This means that our concern for a person's spiritual welfare, as understood within the Christian biblical and theological framework, is of greatest importance. Any alleviation of the ethical problem must be worked out within that framework, not for the sake of the Christian tradition in itself, but for the sake of the spiritual welfare of all persons, whether they share the Christian faith or not.

Of course, this means that biblically grounded theological concerns must be integral to any proposed pragmatic change of language for the sake of greater ethical faithfulness. A concern for the deepest welfare of persons must include a regard for biblical and theological faithfulness as well as ethical behavior. In fact, an essential Christian conviction is that ethical behavior can only truly be grounded and sustained on the basis of a biblically authorized faith. Consequently, careful consideration must be given not only to the problem but to the unquestioned assumptions behind any proposals no matter how seemingly pragmatic, especially those which might have theological, and so faith-affecting, consequences.

Some may regard the biblical and theological focus of this book as evasive of the more pressing issue of the harmful effects that the misuse of reference to God is associated with. Surely, many have argued, there is a simple and straightforward solution: change the language. But as a number of articles in this book imply, this analysis is too simplistic. It begs the question as to whether the language is really to blame and whether a change in language could be made that would change harmful behavior. It also fails to ask whether proposed changes might have other detrimental effects equal to or worse than what is already a troubling situation.

These essays do not assume that language is the cause of abusive behavior nor assume that language can be effectively changed. They do not assume that serious ethical concerns can be solved apart from consideration of biblically grounded theological convictions. Rather, out of concern for a sure and lasting solution to the sinful treatment of women, these assumptions are explored.

Before I summarize the articles that follow, let me suggest that there is one other widely shared assumption that also must be questioned. It lies behind most critiques of traditional Christian language for God and leads to premature proposals for reformation. That assumption is this: abuse of certain language warrants the abandonment of its use. But does it? This is important if the language in question has more than one purpose. It is especially important if its misuse is only incidentally related to a more crucial function.

That Christianity in general terms has been used to justify wrongdoing is not in question. This is a matter of record, and of regret, which ought to lead to a repentance embodied in action by all those who give their allegiance to the Christian faith. However, it should be noted that all religions, true or false, are subject to misuse both by adherents of those religions and by hypocritical impostors perhaps hoping to discredit those religions or to use them for their own ends. World history is replete with examples of leaders manipulating and using religious convictions for their own economic and political ends. It could be argued that the truer the religion, the more susceptible it is to abuse, because the truth in it serves as a cover for the wrong done in its name.

Of course the problem of the abuse of good and true things is not just a problem confined to Christianity or other religions. It is a universal problem facing humanity as a whole in all its existence. This wider issue is of course fully acknowledged within Christianity. The wrongful use of the good things of God by God's own creatures is a primary tenet of

Christian conviction about the perennial fallen state of humanity. It provides the grounds for its conviction of humanity's need for a profoundly transformative salvation. The biblical narrative highlights the misuse of divine privilege, divine names, and even Scripture itself. The pivot of Christian revelation is the misuse, that is, the crucifixion, of the Son of God. The abuse of truth and goodness calls into question humanity, not the proper use of truth and goodness.

As much as we would like for there to be a nonmoral, universal and externally applied solution to the problem of the abuse of truth and goodness, whether in reference to speech about God or any other matter, the human track record, much less the Christian faith, holds no promise for this prospect whatsoever. No change of language itself can solve the inherently moral problem of misuse. Rather, the best guard against misuse would be to recall people to a proper—that is, right—use. The real question, then, must be framed as one of proper use and not abuse of language about God.

Thus the questions noted above should be restated: Does masculine language about God, when properly used, encourage the abuse of women and the self-justification of men in their violation of women? Does such language, when properly used, alienate women from true worship?

The Question of Proper Use and Abuse

A wide variety of critiques and alternative suggestions for language about God has been offered, some much more radical than others. Some are tantamount to rejecting Christianity and its scriptural basis altogether. Others appeal to the Christian revelation as authoritative for Christian faith and call for a modification of the language that seems to comport even more faithfully to that authoritative source than does traditional language. But both groups of critics often seem to accept a relatively similar analysis of the problem even though they may offer distinctive solutions and have divergent views on the ultimate truth of Christian worship and the possibility and reliability of Christian revelation. Neither group of critics has consistently distinguished between proper use and abuse. Rather the focus of both radical and more moderate critiques has been on the abuse; assuming that changing usage, to one degree or another, would prevent or at least diminish abuse. This not particularly feminist assumption perhaps identifies what they have in common and links them both to the larger category of feminist thinking.

This shared assumption has not been helpful in the present debate. For those who wish to maintain a continuity of faith, it has led to a premature judgment on language about God based on an uncritically accepted criterion that assumes that misuse disqualifies proper use. But much more serious is the problem that if no distinction is made between proper use and abuse, then ultimately for both the moderate and radical, the whole of Christianity must be questioned. For no particular language linked with Christianity (and apparently with any other religion) will be found which can actually prevent misuse. Indeed some who originally began with moderate critiques and alternatives from within the framework of Christian conceptions of God have eventually come to repudiate Christianity altogether. Of course, in the end this line of thinking must call into question all merely external pragmatic solutions to our human condition. If we are to confine our critiques to discerning the right language about God, we must be content to inquire as to the right use of language and not into conditions for eliminating the misuse of proper speech about God.

The Essential Issue

If proper use is the real issue, then the primary and first question regarding the critique of traditional language referring to God, upon which all the others must depend, is, Does masculine language itself actually misrepresent the God of Christianity? Until this is decided all other pragmatic and ethical questions regarding the effects of proper use cannot be pursued. If our traditional language does not fulfill this criterion, then it ought to be changed because it misrepresents God, not so much because of other collateral effects. Furthermore, alternative ways of referring to God ought to arise on the basis of a more faithful apprehension of the Christian God, not on the basis of collateral effects upon women or anyone else.

If collateral effects are made the basis of the alternative recommended language, we can have no confidence that it, any more than the traditional language, actually represents God, or at least the Christian God. Consequently alternatives based on any criteria other than the faithful representation of the Christian God cannot for adherents of Christianity warrant any changes in their speech about God. Any critique of a Christian conception of God must be thoroughly grounded in Christian criteria if adherents are to be persuaded to reform. Failing to do this, the alternatives suggested could actually result in the abandonment of Christianity altogether, not in its reformation. So a corollary of the primary question must be, Do the alternatives suggested for replacing masculine references to God truly represent the God of Christianity?

Once proper language about the Christian God is discerned, then the two pragmatic and ethical questions can be fruitfully addressed. (1) Does language, when properly used, encourage the abuse of women and the self-justification of men in their violation of women? (2) Does such language, when properly used, alienate women from true worship? These are second order questions that should be asked by adherents of Christianity in pursuing any critique of speech about the Christian God. They must be asked after giving priority to the primary questions as to whether the Christian God is faithfully represented in traditional or alternative language. But they may—indeed must—certainly then be asked.

It should be noted, however, that if traditional language that faithfully represents the Christian God is then shown also to meet these two secondary criteria of proper use, then no reformation, radical or moderate, is warranted. What would be warranted is a strong calling for the proper use of such language and the proper behavior to go with it.

Of course, if the proper use of Christian language about God fails only these secondary, pragmatic-ethical criteria, then this would lead to further considerations. However, it should be noted that none of them would involve altering the language we use to refer to the Christian God.

If God is faithfully represented by language that, when properly used, is judged nevertheless to be detrimental to women in a way which violates biblical ethical norms, then the real issue is not language about God but a crucial contradiction within Christianity itself. Theology and ethics are apparently at odds. Resolution to this deeper problem might be sought through a reevaluation of the scriptural pattern of language for

God or through a reexamination of the biblical ethic. But changing the language about God would be warranted only if the current language was concluded to misrepresent the Christian God on the basis of its authoritative source.

For if reevaluation of the ethical component revealed that, according to Scripture's own lights, there was no violation of women or misuse of language, then resolution would call either for an adjustment in ethical judgment or for a repudiation of Christian ethics but not for a change in language. The one who judges the Christian ethic to be at fault for not ruling out certain elements of faithful Christian language about God has in effect established ethical criteria external to and independent of Christianity to judge its theological language. Such a one whose primary commitment was to an extra-Christian ethic over against Christian theological language would certainly be sorely tempted to leave Christianity altogether if this commitment did not already constitute its abandonment. Certainly such an extra-Christian critique would have little import for those who regard its ethic and theological language to be in harmony.

One who calls for a change in the language for God on the basis of a purportedly Christian ethic but who believes that language which is faithful to the biblical norm is actually misleading us about God, is calling for not just a change in language but a change in essential faith altogether. Thus, any proposal to alter our language about the Christian God but which aims to do so within Christian bounds must begin and end with the question as to whether our language and any recommended alternatives are faithful to the truth and reality of the God revealed in Jesus Christ according to Scripture. The implications of the secondary order questions noted above, if assumed valid, only can be a call to the proper use of faithful language about God, the exposure of an inner unresolvable tension within Christianity or finally an invitation to abandon Christianity.

Consequently those who are calling for the reformation of our language about God but who intend to remain committed to the Christian worship of God and its scriptural basis will want to do justice in their critique to all four foundational questions listed above. But they will be especially concerned as to whether or not God is truly represented by masculine language and whether such language or any alternatives correspond with the revelatory basis and scriptural pattern they have been given.

However, even if subordinate, there must be a final level of reflection at the pragmatic level as well. Is the language the true source, or at least a key element of the problem? If the problem is misdiagnosed the prescription for cure will surely be off base. So more questions must be addressed: Is the masculine language of Christian worship and piety really a key element in the troubling aspects of women's experience? And if so, would a particular change of language, chosen out of the variety of suggestions made, really effect the healing and reconciliation desired? If satisfactory answers to all of these questions are not found, any proposed solution could just as easily cause harm as great as that experienced in the present situation.

This small collection of essays is meant to address these vital questions—or perhaps I should say, at least contribute to addressing them. The contributors represent a wide spectrum of American Christianity: evangelicals, mainline Protestants and Roman Catholics. While all the contributors are sympathetic to the experiences and concerns of women, the underlying assumption is that the most important question for women *and* men is whether or not our language properly represents the Christian God. The well-being of all persons, not least women, depends ultimately on this.

So several of our contributors make no specific recommendation on what words we ought to use of God today, but rather explore in depth the biblical and authoritative foundations of Christian faith to discern how we might most faithfully speak of God. The first four essays deal with answering this question on the basis of the biblical teaching regarded as providing normative criteria for how we ought to address God. The next two essays treat more general philosophical questions of our knowledge and the nature and function of language within societies. The final three essays take up theological considerations.

In the opening essay Christopher Seitz asks on what basis anyone can legitimately address God at all. On what basis can God be identified and distinguished from anything and everything else? Seitz points out that it is only within the context of the particular people of Israel and of God's activity among them initiating and sustaining their election that any determination can be made as to how God can be properly addressed. Israel is given by God an actual proper name for the One they worship: YHWH. And it is God himself who authorizes Israel to address him at all. This name in particular identifies and differentiates the God of Israel from all other supposed gods. Jesus himself addresses this very same YHWH as his Father, and graciously authorizes his disciples to join him in his filial relationship with YHWH. It is through those appointed disciples of Jesus on the basis of God's original intentions enshrined in the Old Testament story that even those outside of Israel may approach God. Thus, Seitz concludes, how we address God cannot be decided by us on the basis of our perspectives on the metaphorical aptness of a certain term. Through the gracious act of YHWH through the history of Israel, we are given the gift of a personal name: Father, Son and Holy Spirit.

In "The Gender of Israel's God" Paul Mankowski of the Pontifical Biblical Institute in Rome investigates how ancient Israel was taught to grasp and communicate knowledge of God throughout its history, especially in terms of matters related to gender. Was Israel's YHWH understood to be male? Was the God of Israel known to have such a character that would justify the tyranny of men over women and the degradation of those personal characteristics that are often associated with feminine virtues, such as mercy and compassion? Was Israel's God worshiped as a synthesis of male and female sexes and masculine and feminine characteristics?

Mankowski gives us a detailed consideration of Israel's apprehension of God throughout its history by surveying several kinds of information present in the revelation held in trust to it in the books of the Old Testament. He looks carefully at the Divine Name, the associated grammar, the divine titles and epithets, the depiction of YHWH as Father, YHWH as Father of the King, the onomasticon (list of personal names given to individuals) of Israel and also of other nations. He also evaluates the evidence for a female YHWH, especially interacting with the proposal of Phyllis Trible.

Thoroughly engaged with significant research in Old Testament biblical studies, Mankowski finds the picture of YHWH to be a consistent one. "YHWH is God without superior, without peer, without parentage or external origin, without a consort, without offspring. YHWH is also unambiguously 'he' " (p. 35). What emerges in his exploration of the nature of such masculine depiction is that YHWH is uniquely masculine in a way that leaves no room for sexism. The Fatherhood of God is decidedly nonsexual. God is not male. However, there is a proper masculinity about God that incorporates qualities that are often associated in contemporary polemics as feminine. Israel's YHWH is a Father by way of creating, electing and adopting his people without the involvement of a consort. This distinguishes the God of Israel from all foreign deities, whether they be male or female. The God of Israel in his unique transcendent divine masculinity breaks all human projections and self-justifications.

Donald Hook and Alvin Kimel survey feminist proposals for the elimination of the exclusive use of the masculine third-person pronouns in reference to God. They specifically look at the works of Gail Ramshaw-Schmidt, Elizabeth Johnson, Nancy Hardesty, Madeleine L'Engle and Carol Christ. Hook and Kimel argue that given how English grammar functions at present and has functioned down through the centuries, none of the various feminist proposals makes grammatical sense. Instead they foster ambiguities, if not confusion. None has any promise of longevity since certain features of the English language resist change, especially from ideological and overt external pressure. On the basis of their analysis of the nature and function of language, they show that the real solution cannot be found in merely substituting one word for another. No matter what pronouns or substitutes are used, the actual meaning and usage will have to be explained if confusion is to be avoided.

Their contention is that the use of feminine pronouns actually will have the opposite of the intended effect—it will sexualize language about God and still require explanation. If there is confusion as to what the user of masculine pronouns for God does or does not mean, explanation will also have to be provided to indicate that gendered language about God does not mean that God is a sexual being. The decided advantage of masculine pronouns is that they do have a long precedent for carrying nonsexual connotation. Female pronouns do not. So, pragmatically, the feminist proposals are judged incapable of accomplishing what they intend.

The feminist proposals Hook and Kimel look at also are noted to have serious theological problems. The biblical tradition consistently and uniformly indicates that of the two genders available by which we may refer concretely to God, God is depicted as being masculine in a way that transcends biological sexual categories of male and female. The God of biblical faith cannot be referred to as a goddess. This is true even if it is proper to say that God does exhibit both masculine and feminine characteristics or attributes. If that tradition carries normative weight for the knowledge of God, then our language should follow the same pattern. Reinforcing their conclusion is their conviction that referring to God as she or as both feminine and masculine will inevitably sexualize our understanding of God and therefore misrepresent the God of biblical tradition. The use of neutral references would have the effect of depersonalizing our understanding of God, and so be equally misleading. Of course these results would not, in the end, serve the concerns of women either.

Thomas Schmidt surveys the Gospel narratives and finds there a pattern he characterizes as the divine penetration of barriers. He finds this most explicit in the language and images used to refer to the annunciation, the baptism, the death and resurrection and to some extent also in the transfiguration of Jesus. Schmidt also finds corroboration of this theme in Old Testament narratives such as the Song of Solomon and in some rabbinic material. In the New Testament, the calling of Nathaniel, the martyrdom of Stephen and the conversion of Saul exhibit the same pattern. In these key events the God of the heavens is depicted as spatially breaking through into the realm of earth.

While not claiming that the biblical authors were involved in conscious planning of such patterns and allowing that there are limits to the notion of a connecting theme, he nevertheless concludes that there is what he terms "phallocentric" imagery in the New Testament narratives. This imagery cannot be accounted for merely in terms of accommodation to first-century expectations of male messiahs. More likely, he conjectures, they employ "typological imagery commonly (perhaps universally) embedded in human religion and language, especially in Judaism" (p. 105). While acknowledging this pattern he cautions that we in our application can settle for neither a masculine nor feminine gender-based belief system. Rather we should look within the biblical text for egalitarian insights to inform our theology and ethics.

In the following two chapters we turn to philosophical considerations. In his contribution Francis Martin surveys contemporary trends in linguistic philosophy, social criticism and their precedents. He then evaluates some of the trends in feminist hermeneutics and makes a proposal of his own. While guiding us through the complexities of the issues he makes some trenchant critiques of the notions that language and communication must be an exercise of power and that language can only refer to itself. He points out the self-destructive ironies that result if one insists that either case must be true. He holds out the possibility of metacritical and metasocial norms by which to judge our language, communication and social criticism.

Turning to a survey of feminist critical hermeneutics and their approach to Scripture, Martin notes that we should distinguish among reformers who recognize scriptural authority, those who make their own experience and need for emancipation a critical norm, and those who maintain that Scripture is merely another instance of human language referring to itself. He contends that what constitutes "the unity between communicator and recipient is . . . the reality, . . . which is mediated by the words" (p. 129). Given this reality, "knowledge is neither an edifice constructed on inhibiting foundations nor a purely subjective creation whose foundation is the self of the thinking subject" (p. 130).

Most of feminist hermeneutics has drawn upon the competing foundationalisms of either the immanent subject or the principle of the total denial of any extratextual norm. In the end Martin tries to break out of this impasse by taking account of both the subjective and objective aspects of knowing. The subjective aspect must account for the whole person, and any account of person, he reckons, must account for the gender of that person. Gender does not have to dominate the knowing process but can actually contribute a unique "point of view." Masculine and feminine points of view can be regarded as analogically related to one another, as both apprehend a third reality. He holds out the hope that this analogical approach can enable both men and women through their communication with each other to transcend their own subjectivism as they approach the knowledge of the kingdom of God.

William Alston addresses the more general question of how we can speak of God at all, especially when we have no direct sensory contact with God, who is not an aspect of the creation to which we as creatures are limited. Can we speak literally of God? Interacting with the work of antiliteralists John Hick, Gordon Kaufman and Sally McFague, Alston shows us that we can and do speak meaningfully of God both metaphorically and literally. We may do so truthfully when we account for the aspects of the words used which do not apply to God, although they do to us. For example, God may know something. Humans may know something. But because God is God, the way God knows is different from how we know. But both human beings and God may be truthfully said to know. In more technical language we may analogically predicate knowing of God.

Alston acknowledges that such literal speech about God will necessarily be abstract, but in proportion to metaphorical speech it will be more determinate. So, in comparing metaphorical references to God as father and king to literal speech of God in terms of power, sovereignty and majesty, figurative speech is much more open-ended. Although metaphorical reference to God has certain advantages, if we want to make a statement with "definite truth conditions" it is better to use the literal. We can also better pin down the reference of God when we use literal speech.

In a transitional essay between the philosophical reflections and theological considerations, R. R. Reno traces the roots of the assumptions of much feminist theology and shows them to be grounded in the modern tradition of theological and biblical critique beginning in nineteenth century. A comparison of Immanuel Kant (as representative of modern theology) with Rosemary Radford Ruether and Elizabeth Johnson (as representatives of feminist theology) serves to show two shared assumptions. Modern theology and feminist theology share the assumptions that a priori ethical commitments serve as the criterion for judging any theological convictions including those expressed in biblical texts. Second, they share the assumption that traditional speech and the sources of such dogmatic language are suspect and so ought not to be considered authoritative as they are, but must be subjected to radical critique.

Reno notes that this modern critique does not amount to a total rejection of the tradition (for that would be to reject the whole of Christian identity, which many feminists do not want to do). Rather, following modern theological method, a distinction is made between the inner truth or meaning and the outward form or husk, between the general (ethical, for the most part) principles and the particular (theological, for the most part) form of the tradition. These two aspects of the tradition are sorted out on the basis of the general ethical principles that are seen to be buried in the tradition. This entails that the interpreter of tradition and its Scripture must take up an autonomy and freedom over the tradition and its texts. Kant relied upon his apprehension of universal moral duty to do so, while many feminists rely on their feminine experience to provide such prophetic insight.

The problem here, as Reno sees it, is not that of theological innovation, for that is affirmed in classical theological tradition. Rather it is one of relativizing the ultimate authority and disrupting the continuity with the particularity of the biblical witness. Reno argues that critique and theological reformulation are legitimate tasks within the church, but feminism has on the whole undermined itself by making its enabling assumptions those of modern theology. For when the historical particularities of Israel, of Jesus Christ and his atoning work, and of the Christian church and its linguistic forms are robbed of authority, all hope of embodying the life of God in our own particular time and relationships—social and personal—evaporates. If the cross and the crucifixion of Jesus the Son of God incarnated in the womb of Mary cannot serve as real particular reality-determining events, then all we are left with is a generic moralism that must lead and has led to a nihilism or self-love, not to a mutuality or community. The result of this ill-fated alliance will be a violence against "the actual forms of our cohumanity [as men and women]" (p. 188), namely, the finitude of our shared language of text and tradition. And since these are the very concrete conditions of human community, building on such assumptions will end by actually contributing to violence against our neighbors.

In the penultimate chapter Stanley Grenz works through why masculine imagery predominates throughout the biblical text. He surveys a variety of contemporary explanations to account for such imagery, ranging from the more radical critiques to more moderate proposals. He concludes that none of them fully do justice to the biblical record. Although there is a consensus among these theologians that God is not a sexual being of the male gender, he finds their renderings unable to fully account for the decided emphasis on the masculine imagery. This is especially apparent when viewed against the background of an emphasis on female deities and the sexual proclivities of the gods and goddesses revered in the Semitic cultures that surrounded ancient Israel.

Grenz finds a key to the puzzle in the Genesis accounts of the creation of humanity "according to the image of God." There, being created in the image is closely associated with being created male and female. He surmises that "God somehow encompasses what to us are the sexual distinctions of male and female" and that "sexuality, which is an integral part of our humanness, derives its significance from the divine reality" (p. 208). Grenz finds the roots of this insight in the doctrine of the triunity of God. The oneness of God is not a monarchical undifferentiated essence, but rather a triune unity in diversity. The nonsexual social fellowship of the triune persons is the relational reality of God that is reflected in the created sexuality of humanity. Ultimately though, the full reflection of the *imago Dei* is not in the marriage of man and woman, but in the church of Jesus Christ where each member is united to Christ in a way mirroring first of all the marital relation and finally the triune communion itself.

In the final chapter Paul Hinlicky locates the issue of our language about God within the comprehensive framework of rival secular and eschatological conceptions of salvation. He attempts to put the current debate and crisis in the church about rival ways of referring to God in biblical, theological and historical perspective.

Hinlicky counsels acknowledging the legitimacy of feminist concerns within the church because they are inextricably linked to the essential soteriological and eschatological matters of the gospel. Invoking the name of God is inextricable from grasping the true nature of the salvation of this particular God. The gospel is the announcement of the reign of God inaugurated now in the Spirit but to be consummated in the fullness of the coming reign of God.

Apprehension of the true name of God and so the true salvation offered can be approached only on the basis of the transcendent God of Israel naming himself and the community of faith being provided with a faithful access to this self-revelation. Scripture, Hinlicky argues, is shown to provide this access even as it serves to deconstruct all our projections upon God. The key then to the shared ultimate concern of salvation is that God's self-name is given to the church as Father, Son and Spirit. This triune name correlates the nature of this God with our salvation in Christ by the power of the Spirit. The triune God is revealed to be in and through his self-naming a community of divine persons in free and loving relationship. The salvation that comes from this God, then, is salvation into that holy communion of persons who are both united and distinguished as are the Father, Son and Spirit.

Our ethical obligation for reconciliation of men and women is also grounded in the self-revelation of the triune name of God. This saving name is what delimits the boundaries between Christian faith and all other "isms." A God by a different name offers an altogether different salvation. There is saving, reconciling and liberating hope only in the name of the triune God whom we invoke as Father, Son and Spirit. A third alternative would be to cease to speak of God at all. But a God who does not exist or who cannot be named and so known or invoked cannot offer any particular salvation, a future of life in God, or a present ethic at all. Hinlicky concludes that those who are contending with one another within the church can find their reconciliation in the context of the saving name of the triune God.

1

THE DIVINE NAME IN CHRISTIAN SCRIPTURE

Christopher R. Seitz

BIBLICAL RELIGION ALWAYS ASSUMES A PARTICULAR DEITY IS MAKING A claim upon a particular people, and this requires a choice—among several obvious and attractive alternatives—on the part of those claimed. The One God does not reside in essential isolation, only provisionally described by biblical language and statements. "We all worship the same God" is a statement foreign to the Bible's logic.

Seen in this way, the present debates about the "Fatherhood" of God or whether God is to be addressed as "he" or "she" cannot issue into meaningful consensus or "truth" if considered unto themselves. Rather, they are subsets of a more problematic (from the modern standpoint) array of claims about and by the God revealed in Christian Scripture. It is finally the case that *election* is the pivot on which the question of God's "fatherhood" turns. Only with a recognition of Israel's privileged access to God does a discussion of what Jesus calls God and what we should call God follow. Related to election are questions of the *sufficiency of Scripture* to describe God as he really exists, unto himself (or Himself)[1] and toward us. Seen in this way, the modern debate about language for God is not in the first instance a debate about God's character and self.

---

[1]The traditional practice of using capitals to refer to God as "He" obviously sought to distinguish between male human beings and God. That late modern Christians in the West can now view this as an effort to aggrandize being male is obviously a deconstruction of this practice, but that does not make its intention any less compelling or helpful. In fact, it might urge its reconsideration, in that it makes men and women "lower case" without distinction.

Instead, it is a debate engendered by the lack of conviction about either election or the sufficiency of scriptural statements to describe God as revealed to his elected people, first to Israel and by adoption to the church. Moreover, it is a debate about whether Scripture is God's gift to the church, sufficient to describe God as he truly is, enlivened by God's work as Holy Spirit. Indeed, then, any debate over God's "Fatherhood" is absurd if it is detached from a discussion of the Holy Spirit or the nature of the church, as Scripture has set these forth and as they are present realities for Christian men and women.

For this reason, what is at stake in modern debates is not whether God is Father or can be addressed as "he." Rather, what is at stake is whether we are entitled to call God anything at all. The proper question is whether we have any language that God will recognize as his own, such that he will know himself to be called upon, and no other, and within his own counsel then be in a position to respond, or turn a deaf ear. This description of God is fully consistent with the way God dealt with his people Israel in the Old Testament, long before the question of his relationship with others beyond Israel's circle was ever seriously entertained. To raise for serious discussion whether God is "Father" before we have asked whether God is for us or against us, whether God can be known and by whom, whether we can have any meaningful life with God at all, is to threaten offense against the One who purports to be under discussion and assessment.

The Name of the Biblical God

In theory a distinction can be made between two sorts of arguments for revision of biblical language for God (specifically, Father, Son, Holy Spirit). The first is that all human language, including biblical language (and the language of the Jesus depicted therein) is culturally bound and therefore open to revision by subsequent cultures. That is, human language only imperfectly reflects the reality to which it points. The second sort of argument is more restrictive: God has a "name" that refers directly to him, but "Father, Son, Holy Spirit" is not it. Within this latter arena of reflection, one would be less inclined to think that God's Fatherhood, for example, is appropriate because of some essential analogy from the realm of human fathering. Rather, God is "Father in Heaven" because that is what Jesus calls him. If Jesus called him "Mother in Heaven," that then would be the way to call God, whatever we thought about human mothering as distinct from human fathering. "Mother in Heaven" would be the name God responds to when it was used of God.

If it is this more restrictive arena in which biblical language for God operates, then that fact is itself worthy of reflection. The notion that God has a name is a prevalent idea in both the Old Testament and in the cultures surrounding it. Here one can distinguish between the terms *elohim* or *baalim*, on the one hand, and YHWH, Marduke or Asherah, on the other. The former refer to divine beings as a genus, the latter to specific deities. While the former may be used to refer to specific deities, both within the Old Testament and outside it, the latter terms cannot be conjoined. The identity of YHWH, Marduke or Asherah is tied up with a set of narratives which supply content to the individual deity in question, so that who Marduke is, is by definition different than who YHWH is. YHWH is known by reference to what Israel says about him, based on his prior actions with Israel.

The personal name for God, YHWH, is introduced in Genesis 2:4 without any explanation as to how he got that name. I have argued elsewhere that the initial appearance of the personal name YHWH together with the generic Elohim, as this was used in Genesis 1, was intended to ease us toward familiarity with God's personal name, as this was extant even in primeval time.[2] In later narratives (Ex 3, 6), we learn that God makes himself definitively known in the events of the exodus (study the recognition formula—"then you will know that I am YHWH"—as it runs from chapters 5 through 14). The named deity whose name existed from time immemorial reveals who he is in the events of liberation from bondage in Egypt. He gets no new name. The old name is filled with fullest content. In the words of God's self-revelation at Sinai, in the solemn introduction to the Decalogue: "I am YHWH, your Elohim, who brought

---

[2]Christopher R. Seitz, "The Call of Moses and the 'Revelation' of the Divine Name: Source Critical Logic and Its Legacy," in *World Without End* (Grand Rapids, Mich.: Eerdmans, 1998), pp. 229-47.

you up out of the land of Egypt" (Ex 20:2). Here one sees the distinction between a generic and a proper name. Various nations have their various elohim. YHWH is Israel's God, who was made known in bringing Israel out of bondage from Egypt. The narratives tell who this YHWH is; they reflect what this YHWH has done.

The notion that God has a proper name and can be differentiated from other deities with proper names is absolutely clear in the Old Testament. Other gods *(elohim)* lay claims on humanity, but Israel is to have no god *(elohim)* before or beside YHWH (Ex 20:3). Moreover, the character of the name is itself a matter of reverence, since the name really coheres with the God it names (20:7). One cannot therefore malign the name or substitute for the name another name, and somehow leave untouched the deity with whom this name is attached. The very fact that a generic term, elohim, was not deemed satisfactory for describing God or naming Israel's God, is an indication that the proper name YHWH is the name God himself will respond to. There would need to be no concern for God's name, apart from God's self, if in fact such a distinction could be registered in the first place. Concern with revering God's name, such as we find in the Psalms (8:1), would be a form of idolatry if one could hypothetically detach the name from that to which it refers. In the same Ten Commandments in which all forms of idolatry or image making are condemned, the name is specifically discussed (Ex 20:7). Not taking the name of YHWH in vain implies, at a minimum, understanding that YHWH is not an "accident" detachable from a deeper "substance," that is, "God himself."

The Shift to Monotheism

It would seem that the notion that God has a name, a specific set of narratives, and a people whose testimony to him constitute those narratives, would only make sense against a polytheistic backdrop. To name God YHWH is to not call him something else, and it is also to distinguish him from other deities with other proper names, from other people and from other narratives. It is commonplace in handbooks to Old Testament religion to describe a movement from what is called "henotheism" toward what is called "monotheism." The former is reflected in the narratives we have been discussing, and particularly in the Ten Commandments. Other deities exist, but Israel is to cling to its God, YHWH, exclusively. Deuteronomy and the deuteronomistic literature lift this concern to the level of non-negotiable *status confessionis* and the determinative force behind all of Israel's successes or failures as God's people.

The shift to what is called "monotheism" is argued to have taken place with Second Isaiah (the prophet of Isaiah 40—55 working in the early Persian period, c. 550). Theoretically, the elimination of all other gods might render superfluous the proper naming of Israel's YHWH. Yet that never happens in these chapters. While the prophet can be quoted as saying, "I am the first and I am the last; beside me there is no god" (44:6), this remains YHWH's own assertion of his primacy and exclusivity. It is an intramural statement, made by Israel's named deity, that he alone is God. Such a statement is made precisely in the face of a challenge by other peoples and their own religious claims, involving allegiance to Baal and Nebo (46:1), among others. One must carefully distinguish between a claim by YHWH himself to be the only God, and the persistence of other named deities and those who believe in them.

To put this in modern terms, nowhere in Second Isaiah would "monotheism" amount to a practical elimination of all gods but One, such that it could be said, "we all worship the same God." Precisely the opposite is true in these chapters: representatives of other nations "will make supplication to you, saying: 'God is with you only, and there is no other, no god besides him' " (Is 45:14 RSV). That is, they will make the same sort of claim Israel was commanded to make in the Ten Commandments, that against the rival claims of other gods, YHWH demanded sole allegiance. Now that claim is emboldened with the assertion, that other gods are in fact only illusions. This is not a sublime monotheism capable of differentiation from a more concrete henotheism—rather, it is henotheism of a particularly potent stripe. The other elohim that continue to demand allegiance from humanity have detachable names and detachable existences—to the degree that YHWH insists they do not exist at all and envisions a time when representatives of the nations will make the confession once enjoined of Israel only.

The other obvious fact is that while in Isaiah 40—66 YHWH asserts his own uniqueness and exclusivity, nowhere does this lead to a practical elimination of polytheism. The pressure in the late literature of the Old Testament is therefore not toward a sublime expression of monotheism, but toward an anticipation that soon all nations will come to recognize Israel's named God YHWH as God alone. Ezra-Nehemiah and Daniel focus particularly on the confession of foreign rulers—or the consequences of lack of recognition—of YHWH as God Most High, while other literatures of the period depict in irenic (Zech 8:23) or more stringent terms (Zech 14:16-19) the necessity of seeing Israel's named God as God of all creation, worthy of worship and praise. The same holds true for YHWH's own people, who fight among themselves and against the righteousness of YHWH and his servants (Is 56—66).

Modern Monotheism and Accidental Polytheism

Before moving into the New Testament to see how this specific naming of God is handled, a brief reflection on the significance of the Old Testament for the modern question of proper language for God is in order.

The notion that there is only one God has ironically led in the modern period to a curious quasi-polytheism. Because this one God is thought to transcend all human expressions, not to mention names, of "him" (scare quotes are required and illustrate the dilemma), and because the many different forms of religious belief and language among Christians are still thought to point to the selfsame reality of "God" (here scare quotes are actually appropriate), we have a theoretical monotheism conjoined to a functionally polymorphous religiosity, summarized nicely by the phrase "we all worship the same God."

As we have seen, frequently in scholarly treatments one is led to believe that faith evolves or develops in respect of "monotheism," theoretically and functionally. That is, Israel's faith, if it is described as monotheistic, is said to have developed toward this, away from something else. If this could actually be demonstrated, it might be the case that the Bible could be used to defend the sort of monotheism with the capacity to relativize all human language about God—that is, a monotheism in which it could be said, "we all worship the same God." This is what has occurred in certain—largely Western, affluent—sections of

Christianity. As we have seen, however, there is in fact very little distinction to be made between condemning the worship of other gods—acknowledging their existence within systems of belief and practice—and saying that such gods are in fact no gods at all. These are simply variations of henotheism.

To reject the existence of other gods is not thereby to bring an end to religious beliefs in them or halt their capacity to gain allegiance. This still remains an intramural claim, without any rational basis such as would commend general assent from the disinterested. This claim is made by Second Isaiah only on the basis of an appeal to a history of YHWH's dealings, in time and space, with his own people. One either accepts that evidence or rejects it, especially if it is a history not one's own.

Perhaps the greatest single irony of modern liberal Christianity in the West is that its most self-confident minimal statement (a monotheistic faith) is precisely what has created a functional and widespread polytheism. Because it is claimed that all human language only imprecisely names "the One God who alone is," rival languages, symbol systems, and root metaphors are all tolerated under the umbrella of Christian monotheism, because all of these point beyond themselves to "the One God" who supposedly can never be named. The metaphors can be heaped up, one upon another, in a manner even somewhat more elastic than was true in clearly polytheistic systems. Yet what the Old Testament remains most committed to, at the late period as much as at the early, is the exclusivity of the one named deity, YHWH, who is to be the sole object of worship by his own elected people and, eventually, by all creation. His name is never absorbed, but exalted, preserved, revered, just as are the narratives which tell who he is and what he intends for his own people and for all creation. It is against this backdrop that the New Testament takes both its bearings and its point of departure.

From YHWH to Father

As the Old Testament canon began to take final shape, the divine name gradually ceased to be vocalized. How this happened is unclear. Why it happened involved a number of factors, but chief among them was the sense of the name's sanctity. Fear of the name's defilement led to various means of circumlocution ("the Name"; "the Eternal"; "the LORD"). Note that these began not as abstractions in search of something definite but as the opposite: glosses on a known and specific name that were intended to serve as the name's more cautious or deferential point of reference. Moreover, they only functioned in a system where the rules were quite clearly known; whenever the circumlocutions were employed, they referred to the proper name of Israel's God, YHWH. In other words, this was not a move toward abstraction for its own sake but a purely functional "shorthand" meant to honor the name, not replace or improve on it.

It is striking that so complete was this convention that nowhere in the New Testament does the proper name appear, except perhaps by allusion, for example, "before Abraham was, I am" (Jn 8:58 RSV), a clear reference to the *ehyeh asher ehyeh* of Exodus 3:14 and other such statements. As this example illustrates, it is the appearance of Jesus as Son of God, and not just the retraction of the divine name, that permitted this sort of highly volatile allusion. That is, on the few occasions where allusions appear in the New Testament, they appear in conjunction with Jesus rather than with the God with whom he claims special relationship.

A cursory reading of the Gospels reveals that Jesus most frequently refers to God as Father ("the Father"; "your heavenly Father"; "the Father who sent me"; "our Father in heaven"). A similarly cursory reading of the Old Testament would show that, in fact, this is a fairly rare way to refer to the named God, YHWH (Is 63:16). On the other hand, it is quite customary for God to refer to his own people as "son" or "sons." The title— if that is not too strong a term—plays a specific role in respect Israel's Anointed One (*mashiah*), as in Psalm 2: "He said of me [David], 'You are my son, today I have begotten you' " (v. 7 RSV). Even so, from surveying the Old Testament we would gain no special picture of Israel's kings in terms of their own language for God, as involving the term *Father*. In the Old Testament the filial relationship is described *from God's perspective*, hence the overwhelming preponderance of "son" over "Father" as descriptive of the divine-human relationship.

This preponderance changes in the New Testament. Two things can be said about this. Most obviously, the term *Father* emerges into greater

usage independent of anything in the milieu which would suggest a particularly culture-bound usage that could or should then be open to revision;[3] rather, the change is in perspective. The filial relationship is the
same as in the Old Testament, but in the New it is described *from the
standpoint of the Son,* Jesus. Where *son* appeared in the Old Testament,
in the New we have *Father.* This change, we repeat, has less to do with
matters of culture, or even something more personal or psychological,
and more to do with the appearance of the man Jesus and a change in
perspective: from the Son to YHWH, who is referred to from that filial
point of standing as "heavenly Father."

The second point of relevance is that this expression for God in the
New Testament emerges in the same climate in which circumlocutions
have begun to stand in place of the divine personal name YHWH. Jesus
does not refer to God as Father because of the "aptness of the metaphor," at least not in the first instance. This is a particularly "extramural"
view of this matter, which runs the risk of holding the name *Father* hos-
tage to romantic endorsements (Jeremias) or modern revisions, in which
human fathering or some other argument from nature is the lens through
which the term is refracted and judged satisfactory or lacking.[4] "Father"
as a term of usage by Jesus joins other such terms in the period ("the
Name"; "the Eternal One") and as such it is explicitly linked to Israel's
specific and personally named deity, YHWH. When Jesus refers to "the
Father" he means only YHWH, not a God whose essence is Fatherhood
or Fathering. YHWH, the God of Israel, is addressed by Jesus, the Son, as
Father. Obviously there is a fitness to the term, or else some other neologism would have been proposed. But that fitness exists within a set universe of meaning, whose compass points are determined by Israel's
specific history with its God, the named deity YHWH. To remove the

---

[3]See the essay of Mary Rose D'Angelo ("*Abba* and 'Father': Imperial Theology and the Jesus
Traditions," *JBL* 111 [1992]: 611-20), but also the one to which her essay is addressed, by
Robert Hamerton-Kelly ("God the Father in the Bible," in *God as Father?* ed. Johannes-Bap-
tist Metz and Edward Schillebeeckx [Edinburgh: T & T Clark, 1981], p. 101), who refers to
"the Abba *experience*" (emphasis mine). This experiential emphasis may do more harm than
good, and it has detached the discussion from its Old Testament context.
[4]J. Jeremias, *Abba: Studien zur neutestamentlichen Theologies und Zeitgeschichte* (Gåttingen:
Vandenhoeck & Ruprecht, 1966).

term from its home in Christian Scripture, and especially from its logic within the Old Testament, inadvertently demonstrates how theology that begins with human existence and human categories only leads to political or psychological debates, and impasse.

It is necessary to stay longer with the second point, because there is a peculiarly *Christian* perversion of biblical teaching about God as heavenly Father that must be considered. Jesus refers to God as Father within the context of the Judaism of his day, where the term can only refer to Israel's named deity, YHWH. Modern Christians—with the theoretical exception of Jewish Christians—do not operate from this same perspective. From Jesus' perspective, to use Paul's blunt language in Ephesians, we Gentiles are "strangers to the covenants of promise, having no hope and without God in the world" (Eph 2:12 RSV). Jesus' own more bracing image is of our receiving crumbs, like dogs who wait patiently, from their master's table (Mt 15:26). It is by Christ's death and resurrection that we are adopted into fellowship with Israel's named LORD. Without this we are estranged, without hope, because "without God in the world." Jesus does not introduce a new deity named Father, to be contrasted with the God of the Old Testament—who in the new guise of Father then becomes a matter for late-twentieth-century debate in Western Christianity. To call God "our heavenly Father" is to address God as Jesus did, and only from that christological point of standing does the name refer to The God, Israel's named Lord, YHWH. If "we Gentiles" do not regard this language as a gift, privileging us to speak to God in the first-person plural ("our Father") with Jesus, who is our only point of access to YHWH, then no amount of debate or "revision" will expose why this language is proper and good. Rather, it will only expose our forgetfulness about a gift of incorporation upon which our very lives depend.

Christian Hope and the Name of God

Christian theology does not proceed on the basis of the Old Testament "evolving" into the New, or the New "superseding" the Old, but on the basis of a reflection on God's character as revealed in both, each in its own particular idiom. Here it is significant to note that for Christian theology, what receded in terms of particularity in the divine name YHWH, which is everywhere present in the Old but completely absent in the New, is matched by the emergence of the very specific name Jesus. The same reverence for the Name enjoined in the Old attaches to the name Jesus in the New.

In modern debates about "God language" the Christian starting point remains the name of Jesus. It is only through Jesus that we share in the divine life at all, being at one time strangers to the commonwealth of Israel. The specificity of the personal name YHWH, for Israel, naming its God and the only God, is now matched for Christians by the specific name Jesus. We cannot "get at" the divine life by means of general reflection, for the One God of creation revealed himself in a special and providential way with a particular people Israel, who knew his name and his character, and knew that these two aspects cohered perfectly (Ex 3—14). We are introduced to this special relationship by Israel's own Lord, and in so doing we take our place with those the prophets envisioned, who confess "God is with you only, and there is no other" (Is 45:14 RSV). The God who hides himself (45:15) we outsiders see and know in Jesus. Zechariah speaks of a time when those "from the nations of every tongue shall take hold of the robe of a Jew saying, 'Let us go with you, for we have heard that God is with you'" (Zech 8:23 RSV). That is the confession we outside the household of Israel make, grasping the robe of Jesus.

To call God "Father" proceeds from Jesus' own language and perspective, and without this we have no access to Israel's life with the named God, YHWH. To call God "Son" is to recognize the non-negotiable fact of access through Jesus, in the most elevated sense. To call God "Holy Spirit" is to confess that even how we address God is itself a gift from God, not to be debated or probed but to be received in humility and thanksgiving with the same sense of reverence God's people Israel had for the name YHWH, vocalized now for Christians "Father, Son, and Holy Spirit."

Let me conclude by way of summary. Debating whether "Father" is an appropriate metaphor for God, given modern sensibilities, is a different thing than asking, With what language can God be addressed, such that he will know himself to be called upon, and not another? Language for God is at the most basic level language of prayer, that is, language used "to call upon God" in direct address. In the Old Testament, where we can witness God's people Israel "calling upon God," God is addressed by his name. As this name becomes unutterable, God does not recede or actually lose contact with those who call on his name. Rather, his personal name is glossed by terms that mean to protect his transcendent character without sacrificing his specificity and particularity, as he has revealed himself and made himself known within Israel.

Jesus refers to the God of Israel as Father, and in so doing speaks to that specific God and none other, reversing the direction with which Israel was already familiar: rather than from God to his son, from the Son to God "the Father." When the disciples ask Jesus to teach them to pray, the language of address "Our Father" specifies the God of Israel. The first-person plural "our" means to include us with Jesus, who enables us to address the God of Israel, to call on his name, as had been promised of old for the nations (Is 56:1-8). It is this gracious act of bestowal that the language "Father, Son, Holy Spirit" recalls and bears witness to, while at the same time it names God as he truly is. By invoking the triune name at our baptism, we are ourselves given a name, literally, and a voice to address the One God of Israel, his eternal Son, in the unity of the Holy Spirit.

To call God "mother" or "she" would be to call attention to God as truly gendered, simply by the fact that such language means to serve as a replacement for or improvement on the language biblically grounded. Ironically, the language biblically grounded has the capacity to transcend this framework of discussion, because it emerges as a testimony to God's own name and initiative in revealing it, rather than because it conforms to metaphors whose fitness is determined by human debate or divine defense. To defend God as "Father" by appeal to suitability of metaphor would in fact undo the logic with which the language emerged in the first place, which is riveted to Israel's particular experience of God's revelation, and through the work of Christ its extension at Pentecost to all nations and peoples. "Father, Son, and Holy Spirit" emerges from a particular story.

Our use of this language preserves that particular story and the God who brought it and us into being, making us his people and allowing us to be faithful witnesses who call upon his name, for our own sakes and for the sake of his creation.

2

THE GENDER OF ISRAEL'S GOD

Paul Mankowski

T HE OLD TESTAMENT IS AN ASSEMBLAGE OF WORKS OF HIGHLY DISPAR-
ate genre written by multiple human authors over the span of a thousand
years or more. In the broadest sense it concerns God's self-revelation to
one particular nation through the history of its emergence as Israel—a people set apart. Though it is historically naive in some respects, the Old Testament is conscious of a process of development in the religion of Israel.
The ancestors of the Israelites are understood to have been polytheists and
to have worshiped local gods "beyond the river" in Mesopotamia (Josh
24:1-4). Through a series of trials beginning with the call of Abraham and
culminating in that of Moses, Israel became bound to the worship of one
God to the exclusion of all others, YHWH.[1] The picture provided of
YHWH is entirely consistent in its principal features. YHWH is God without superior, without peer, without parentage or external origin, without a
consort, without offspring. YHWH is also unambiguously "he." The purpose of this essay is to examine the evidence for this claim and its implications for Israel's understanding of God.

The Divine Name and Grammatical Evidence

The name YHWH is used of God some six thousand times in the Old

---

[1]God's name is never fully spelled in the Hebrew text of the Old Testament but rather is indicated by the four letters YHWH, usually seen to represent three true consonants plus a
mater lectionis, used to indicate the presence of a final vowel. Already in Philo Judaeus (fl.
A.D. 35) the writing is called the tetragrammaton.

Testament. The tetragrammaton is understood in Exodus itself[2] and by most scholars today[3] to be a Semitic verb in the imperfect tense. Its meaning is far from certain, although perhaps a majority of scholars assent to the notion that it is a causative verb from a root HWH or HYH, meaning "he causes to be" or "he brings into being."[4] Unlike the case in Indo-European languages, Semitic verbs are inflected for gender as well as for number and person; if the divine name does indeed reflect a verb, that verb must be a third person *masculine* form.[5] When a masculine verb has a unitary determinate subject, that subject is understood to be masculine by rules of grammatical concord.[6] Given the unavoidable assumption that the subject of a verb employed as a name is none other than the bearer of the name,[7] we can infer with confidence that the God YHWH was conceived to be masculine in some sense, without further specifying the content of this masculinity.[8] Indirect corroboration of the masculinity of the referent of the divine name comes from the (relatively late) introduction of ʾădōnāy, meaning "my Lord," as the *qere perpetuum* or substitute pronunciation of the tetragrammaton. The Septuagint's rendering of YHWH as *kyrios*, "Lord," points to the same conclusion.

The masculinity of YHWH is further discernible from the abundant grammatical evidence provided by the verbal system. Though morpho-

---

[2]Ex 3:14. The word-play in Hebrew between *yhwh* (the divine name) and ʾehyeh ʾăšer ʾehyeh ("I am who I am") puts this beyond doubt.

[3]See R. Mayer, "Der Gottesname Jahwe im Lichte der neuesten Forschung," *Biblische Zeitschrift* n.s. 2 (1958).

[4]W. F. Albright, *Yahweh and the Gods of Canaan* (New York: Doubleday, 1968), pp. 168-72. The disparity between the traditional "stative" interpretation (reflected in the first-person formula of Ex 3:14 (ʾehyeh ʾăšer ʾehyeh, "I am who I am") and the "causative" interpretation adopted by Albright et al. has to do with vowels one assigns to the consonants of the Hebrew text. The vocalization *yahweh* reflects the causative *(hiphil)* conjugation of the lexical root, and is a scholarly reconstruction. The tetragrammaton proper is never vocalized in the Hebrew text.

[5]The feminine counterpart would be marked by initial *t-*, *tahweh*, "she causes to be."

[6]The qualifications "unitary" and "determinate" are necessary because the masculine serves as the unmarked inflection in Hebrew. If the subject of a masculine verb is compound it is necessary that only one element be masculine; if indeterminate, its gender is unspecifiable.

[7]Thus, if one names a dog Fido, it is the dog that is to be understood as the subject-referent of "I am loyal."

[8]"Masculine" and "masculinity" are here used in contradistinction to "male" and "maleness" to express a grammatical category as opposed to a sexual or biological reality.

logically it has the form of a verb, the tetragrammaton functions syntactically as a noun. Without exception, the verbs of which YHWH is the
grammatical subject are masculine. This is the case throughout the various levels of documentary strata, from the oldest pre-monarchical po-
ems, though monarchical and exilic texts, down to post-exilic material.
The masculinity of verbs governed by YHWH holds true even in the paradoxical cases where the activity conveyed by the verb is characteristically feminine. As noted, the rules of gender concord oblige us to infer that
the subject of a masculine verb is itself masculine.

The pronominal system is likewise exceptionless in preserving masculine grammatical concord when YHWH is the referent. Although first-person pronouns are not distinguished by gender in Hebrew, the second
and third-person pronouns have distinct masculine and feminine forms,
and it is invariably the masculine form that is used of YHWH. The same
is true of every participle and adjective used attributively or predicatively
of YHWH.

It is important to stress that there is a notable "grammatical asymmetry"
between Hebrew and English gender marking: whereas English grammar
has no masculine-feminine contrast that is without a Hebrew equivalent,
Hebrew has several gender contrasts that have no counterpart in English.
The Hebrew verb is inflected for gender in the third and second persons,
as are the adjective and participle. Hebrew second person pronouns have
distinct masculine and feminine forms as well. Finally, many Hebrew common nouns occur in pairs contrasted for gender where English has a single
unmarked equivalent. The upshot is that the Hebrew reader of the Old
Testament encounters considerably more grammatical reinforcement of
God's masculinity than is possible for the English reader, for there is and
can be no English translation that does not neutralize a great deal of the
gender-marking of the original language.

Examples of this are overwhelmingly abundant. The English rendering
of Psalm 119:137, "Righteous are you, YHWH, and right are your judgments," is completely indifferent as to gender; out of context it is impossible to tell whether the addressee is masculine or feminine. The Hebrew
reader, on the other hand, will hear masculine inflections for "righteous"
(*ṣaddîq*) not feminine (*ṣaddîqāh*), "you" (*'attāh*, not *'attî*), YHWH (not

THWH), and "your" judgments (*mišpāṭêkā*, not *mišpātayk*).[9] The grammatical evidence of the Old Testament is copious, and unanimous, in favor of the masculine gender of YHWH.

Divine Titles and Epithets

The anthropomorphic titles and epithets most often used of YHWH in the Bible—king, prince, lord, shepherd, warrior—have commonly been seen to express what were in Israel conventionally male social roles and thus to corroborate the picture of a masculine deity.[10] Yet in the religions of the surrounding nations we frequently find royal dominion and the status of warrior attributed to goddesses as well as gods, even in those societies where the human counterparts of such offices and activities were reserved to men.[11] Tikva Frymer-Kensky characterizes the Sumerian goddess Inanna (and her Semitic identity Ištar) as the female embodiment of a male function:

> Inanna was the very spirit of battle. Warfare, the "festival of manhood," was "Inanna's dance," a theme that was repeated throughout Mesopotamian history. Iconographically, she is shown with the bow, the classic weapon of war and the standard symbol of manliness. In the words of a first millennium congregational lament, it is in battle that Inanna holds the spindle and the whorl, as she makes the skulls roll.[12]

The fact that occupations understood to be masculine can be attached to deities understood to be feminine—as true of the Greek goddesses Athena and Artemis as of Inanna and Gula[13]—should make us cautious about using the role-language about YHWH as self-standing data con-

---

[9]In the Hebrew of Psalm 119 alone, there are 338 instances in which an explicitly masculine reference to God is necessarily neutralized in the English translation.

[10]For a useful roster of such titles, see D. N. Freedman, "Divine Names and Titles in Early Hebrew Poetry," in *Magnalia Dei: The Mighty Acts of God,* ed. Cross, Lemke, and Miller (New York: Doubleday, 1976), pp. 55-108.

[11]See Tikva Frymer-Kensky, *In the Wake of the Goddesses* (New York: Free Press, 1992), pp. 14-31. Some readers may be inclined to dispute that social roles can be definitively labeled masculine or feminine. This controversy has no bearing on the present argument, for which it is enough to point out that in the life of the societies under discussion specific social functions were assigned according to gender.

[12]Frymer-Kensky, *In the Wake,* p. 66.

[13]Athena was depicted as a warrior, Artemis a huntress, Gula a physician.

cerning gender attribution. The pertinent literature gives no evidence that Inanna's votaries regarded her as less female for her masculine functions; hence it is risky to argue that, because YHWH is said to be a warrior, a shepherd, or a monarch, he is for that reason to be regarded as masculine. Of course, if the masculine iconology of YHWH can be established on other, more solid grounds, the attribution of social roles will give more concrete specification to the picture we are offered of him: his royal sovereignty and warriorship will be imaginatively connected with the male exercise of their human analogs; he will rule as a king and not a queen and fight as a man of war[14] rather than a warrioress. But the decisive evidence must be sought elsewhere.

YHWH as Father

YHWH's fatherhood is the linchpin of his gender identification and marks him as definitively masculine. His fatherhood, however, is entirely distinct from any notion of sexual generation. That fact preserves it from confusion with human begetting on the one hand, and on the other from the pagan religious cultivation of sex, wherein potency and fertility are ritually divinized and the gods are portrayed and worshiped as straightforward sexual beings who lust, mate, conceive, give birth and are accorded the dignities of parenthood.[15] Gerhard von Rad has summarized the data with succinctness:

> For the historian of religion, what is most astonishing is Jahwism's self preservation vis-à-vis the mythicising of sex. In the Canaanite cult, copulation and procreation were mythically regarded as a divine event; consequently, the religious atmosphere was as good as saturated with mythic sexual conceptions. But Israel did not share in the "divinization of sex." YHWH stood

---

[14]For which see Ex 3:15: *yhwh 'iš milḥāmāh*, "YHWH is a man of battle." Cf. Vulgate: *quasi vir pugnator.* W. F. Albright (*Yahweh*, p. 13 n. 34) proposed reading the Hebrew phrase as a verbal clause expressing in itself a divine name, i.e., "he creates the army." Freedman, *Divine Names*, pp. 97, 102 n. 86) regards such an understanding as a secondary historical development.

[15]Frymer-Kensky, *In the Wake*, pp. 45-57; M. Smith, *The Early History of God: Yahweh and the Other Deities in Ancient Israel* (New York: Harper & Row, 1990), pp. 164-66. See also M. J. Lagrange, "La paternité de Dieu dans l'AT," *Revue Biblique* 5 (1908): 481-99; H. Ringgren, "אָב *'ābh*," in *Theological Dictionary of the Old Testament* (Grand Rapids, Mich: Eerdmans, 1974), pp. 1-19.

absolutely beyond the polarity of sex and this meant that Israel could not regard sex as a sacral mystery.[16]

How is it that YHWH can be said to stand "beyond the polarity of sex" and still be accounted masculine? The answer is that YHWH's fatherhood is seen by the Old Testament as a pure and sovereign act of divine will, divorced from any external limitation or constraint, including that of a coexistent female consort into which his seed is implanted. YHWH's becoming a father is not an act of engendering but of decision, of creation. This is already evident in the ancient poem called the Song of Moses (Deut 32):

> Do you thus requite YHWH,
>   you foolish and senseless people?
> Is not he your father,
>   who created you,
>   who made you and established you?
> Remember the days of old,
> consider the years of many generations;
>   ask your father, and he will show you;
>   your elders, and they will tell you.
> When the Most High gave to the nations their inheritance,
>   when he separated the sons of men,
> he fixed the bounds of the peoples
>   according to the number of the sons of God.
> For YHWH's portion is his people,
>   Jacob his allotted heritage.
> He found him in a desert land,
>   and in the howling waste of the wilderness;
> he encircled him, he cared for him,
>   he kept him as the apple of his eye.[17]

Entirely absent here is any implication that "your father who created, made, and established you" engages in procreative activity. It is a people, the nation of Israel, that comes into being through the will of YHWH. The image presented is that of God's decision to become the father of a

---

[16]Gerhard von Rad, *Old Testament Theology*, trans. D. M. G. Stalker (New York: Harper & Row, 1962), p. 27.

[17]Deut 32:6-10. Here and throughout I use the RSV translation, preserving however the tetragrammaton as YHWH.

being that already exists in some sense, but not as his child. It is YHWH's activity of gratuitous concern, his finding and keeping the abandoned Jacob, in virtue of which he is called Father. So striking is this notion of decisive fatherhood that consciously oxymoronic language can be used later in the same poem in the context of rebuke for apostasy: "You were unmindful of the Rock that begot you (*yelādekā*), and you forgot the God who gave you birth (*meḥōlelekā*)" (Deut 32:18). The imagery *is* maternal, but masculine verb forms preclude the possibility that a female deity is to be envisioned. The focus rather is on Israel's ingratitude in the face of a coming-to-be as unsought and unhoped for as a fecund rock.[18]

The principal event in which YHWH's fatherhood is recognized by the Old Testament is that of the exodus, preeminently YHWH's commission to Moses (Ex 4:22-23):

> And you shall say to Pharaoh, "Thus says YHWH, Israel is my first-born son, and I say to you, 'Let my son go that he may serve me'; if you refuse to let him go, behold, I will slay your first-born son."

Here, as in the Song of Moses, the paternity YHWH claims for himself is *supervenient*: it intrudes into the history of an already existent body, yet is inceptive of a profoundly new relationship between superior and subject. YHWH may be said to "create" Israel his son much the way a monarch is said to "create" a peer—that is, strictly in virtue of the superior's sovereign will, conferring a dignity on a being which has a new existence by reason of that dignity. YHWH's activity in the election of Israel is masculine because it is fatherly; it is fatherly because the initiative, the prerogative, and the motive power of creation are his and his alone. The lack of a correlative maternal contribution to YHWH's fatherhood does not make itself felt because there is nothing outside of God's will to be contributed. Much as Athena was imagined to have sprung full grown from the brow of Zeus, so Israel comes to be through the inexplicable choice of YHWH.

The gratuitous nature of YHWH's election of Israel as his first-born provided the prophets with a potent image of national apostasy: the in-

---

[18]A contrary view is presented by Phyllis Trible, *God and the Rhetoric of Sexuality* (Philadelphia: Fortress, 1978), pp. 62-63. See also the discussion in J. W. Miller, "Depatriarchalizing in Biblical Interpretation," *Catholic Biblical Quarterly* 48 (1986): 611. Smith, *Early History*, p. 98.

grate son ignores his father's kindnesses and squanders his inheritance—
in effect, he sins against the fourth commandment. So Malachi 1:6:

> A son honors his father, and a servant his master. If then I am a father,
> where is my honor? and if I am a master, where is my fear?

Malachi extends the burden of divine parentage to include the duty of
reciprocal fidelity and unity among the sons of Jacob:

> Have we not all one father? Has not one God created us? Why then are we
> faithless to one another, profaning the covenant of our fathers? (Mal 2:10)

It is noteworthy that the "one father" and "one God" invoked here is
addressed to Israel only; it is not an appeal to universal brotherhood but
to the brotherhood of election. The same notion of rebuke, tinged with a
more self-conscious sadness, is put forward by Hosea (11:1-3):

> When Israel was a child, I loved him,
>   and out of Egypt I called my son.
> The more I called them,
>   the more they went from me;
> they kept sacrificing to the Baals,
>   and burning incense to idols.
> Yet it was I who taught Ephraim to walk,
>   I took them up in my arms;
> but they did not know that I healed them.

The picture we are given here is of YHWH's coming upon a wounded
slave-boy, lamed perhaps by mistreatment, helping him regain the power
to walk, and then adopting him as a son. This slave turned son is of course
the entire nation of Israel, and the apostasy of the son is the more lamenta-
ble for the father's unowed and unexpected kindness. We see the same re-
monstrance in Isaiah: "Sons have I reared and brought up, but they have
rebelled against me" (1:2); "They are a rebellious people, lying sons, sons
who will not hear the instruction of YHWH" (30:9); and in Jeremiah, "Return, O faithless sons, I will heal your faithlessness" (Jer 3:22).

Prophetic reproach aimed at Israel's dereliction of filial duty finds a natural reversal in the appeal to YHWH to remember his fatherhood and be-
stow paternal graciousness on his children. Such an appeal is implicit in
Jeremiah 3, where YHWH addresses Israel as a daughter turned prostitute:

Have you not just now called to me,
"My father, thou art the friend of my youth—
will he be angry for ever,
will he be indignant to the end?" (Jer 3:4-5)

Much later, the experience of the Babylonian exile frames the appeal made in Isaiah 63:

The yearning of thy heart and thy compassion
    are withheld from me.
For thou art our Father,
    though Abraham does not know us
    and Israel does not acknowledge us;
thou, O YHWH, art our Father
our Redeemer from of old is thy name. (63:15-16)

It is noteworthy that in both passages, pleas for compassion and cessation of anger are framed as appeals to fatherhood, and this in a manner unconscious of paradox or the need for explanation. The sensibility that sees compassion as a typically maternal trait is absent here. Arguments that reason from YHWH's compassion to his femininity involve a *petitio principii*, for they assume that biblical references to compassion are references to a feminine characteristic, and then pretend to deduce divine femininity from the evidence provided by such references. Yet the biblical writers expect fathers to show mercy toward their children simply in virtue of their fatherhood: "As a father pities his children, so YHWH pities those who fear him" (Ps 103:13).

In Isaiah 64 YHWH's fatherhood is once more invoked in appeal; here the image of divine fatherhood is not that of election but of creation or formation:

YHWH, thou are our Father;
we are the clay, and thou are our potter;[19]
we are all the work of thy hand. (Is 64:8)

As does the metaphor of election, the image of creation by forming

---

[19]"Our potter": *yōṣerēnû*, the masculine participle. The word for potter is consistently masculine in the Old Testament.

avoids sexual mythicising of the relation of the Father God to his children. As a potter, YHWH takes the active and intentional (and to that extent paternal) role in the genesis of his people. The clay is not the same stuff as the potter, but outside him and wholly passive to him; similarly, YHWH's people is not split off from YHWH and does not issue from him; his people is the work of his hands, that is, of his intelligent will. The image does not invite curiosity about a mother or feminine contributor to the process of creation; it is complete in itself.

YHWH as Father of the King

The image of divine fatherhood finds further expression in the discourse of YHWH as father of the king. This may be seen as a special instance of the action of divine election; here again the language of fatherhood does not involve procreation. In 2 Samuel 7:11-13, Nathan proclaims to David:

> YHWH declares to you that YHWH will make you a house. When your days are fulfilled and you lie down with your fathers, I will raise up your son after you, who shall come forth from your body, and I will establish his kingdom. He shall build a house for my name, and I will establish the throne of his kingdom for ever. I will be his father, and he shall be my son.

Important in this passage is the qualification "who shall come forth from your [David's] body," a parenthesis that underlines the concern to distance YHWH's paternity from biological or mythological-sexual generation.[20] The language of fatherhood stresses instead the sovereign will of YHWH and his initiative; he is an adoptive father, the king an adoptive son. So Psalm 89:20, 26-27:

---

[20]Perhaps in deliberate contrast to divine pedigree as a commonplace of Near Eastern royal propaganda. In the prologue and epilogue that frame the Code of Hammurapi (c. 1750 B.C.) King Hammurapi refers to himself as "he whom Sin begot," as working with the help of "Dagan his creator" and as invoking "Sin my creator" and "Nintu the mother who bore me." Sin, Dagan and Nintu are all Mesopotamian divinities. In the natural order Hammurapi calls himself the *aplum* (son and heir) of King Sin-muballit. There is no consensus among scholars as to whether the royal claim to divine sonship was simply a way of invoking divine patronage or whether some notion of actual divine generation was intended. It is conceivable that on political grounds the kings in question would want both ideas before the mind of the people. See I. Engnell, *Studies in Divine Kingship* (Uppsala: Almquist & Wiksells, 1943).

I have found David, my servant;
  with my holy oil I have anointed him. . . .
He shall cry to me, "Thou art my Father,
  my God, and the Rock of my salvation."
And I will make him the first-born,
  the highest of the kings of the earth.

Comparable also is Psalm 2:

Yet have I set my King upon my holy hill of Zion.
I will declare the decree: YHWH hath said unto me,
Thou art my Son; this day have I begotten thee.
Ask of me, and I shall give thee the heathen
for thine inheritance, and the uttermost parts
of the earth for thy possession. (Ps 2:6-8 KJV)

The sonship into which YHWH elevates the king establishes a relationship of fidelity, partiality and active concern toward the royal son on
the part of his divine father. As with his people Israel, YHWH's paternity
of the king is supervenient and gratuitous; again, the absence of a maternal contribution is not felt because the sexual paradigm of generation has
been entirely replaced.

Onomastic Evidence for Yahwistic Fatherhood

A valuable source of information about the religion of Israel is its onomasticon, the collection of personal names given to individuals. This is
so because many Israelite names (in common with those of other Semitic
peoples) are short sentences or construct phrases, often expressive of
religious beliefs. Because their meaning would have been intelligible in
most cases to any Hebrew speaker, such names can provide evidence of
the religious practices and attitudes of those who bestowed them on
their children.[21] One type of name that is of particular interest associates

---

[21]Jeffrey Tigay, *You Shall Have No Other Gods: Israelite Religion in the Light of Hebrew
Inscriptions* (Atlanta: Scholars Press, 1986), pp. 5-7. Tigay stresses that the beliefs expressed
by Northwest Semitic personal names are "simple and elemental" and that more theologically ambitious names like *klbyd'l* ("All is in the hand of God") are very rare (p. 6, esp. n.
6). See also Jeffrey Tigay, "Israelite Religion: The Onomastic and Epigraphic Evidence," in
Ancient Israelite Religion: Essays in Honor of Frank Moore Cross, ed. P. D. Miller, P. Hanson
and S. McBride (Philadephia: Fortress, 1987), p. 159.

a deity with a kinship term, expressing a familial relation between the god and the bearer of the name. Again, other Semitic peoples provide abundant specimens of this, such as, for example, Amorite *Šamašabi* ("My father is Šamaš"), and Akkadian *Ummi-Ištar* ("My mother is Ištar"). The Old Testament onomasticon is remarkable for its complete lack of personal names compounded of the divine name YHWH and the words for mother ('*imm*-) or sister ('*āḥôt*). We do find however that there are eight individuals with the name Abijah, meaning "My father is YHWH," and a further three with the name Joab, meaning "YHWH is father." The names of Israelite women are rarely theophorous, but two women bear the name Abijah as well.[22] While names studied in isolation cannot provide precise theological meaning of the fatherhood of YHWH, they add further confirmation that he was understood to be masculine in an elemental way. The personal name Ahijah, "My brother (= kinsman) is YHWH," while it invokes a different image of kinship and partiality, points to the same conclusion.

The Old Testament also provides us with five persons named Eliab and one named Abiel. Their meanings are either "My God is father" and "God is my father" or just possibly "El is my father." El was a deity with the role of a father god in the religions of the Canaanites, and his name also figures as the common noun for "god" in Semitic languages. El and its plural form *elohim* are employed as words for God—specifically, the God of Israel—and as a common noun for god or gods, throughout the Old Testament. It is generally thought that worship of El became assimilated to the worship of YHWH in Israel, although the dates and the progress of this assimilation are much disputed.[23] Frank Moore Cross has argued that there is no instance in the Old Testament where a clear awareness of El as a pagan deity distinct from YHWH is manifest.[24] While it is conceivable that Israelite El-names in the Bible refer to a deity understood to be other than YHWH, it is unlikely; and names with a personal pronoun attached to the El- segment make it probable that

---

[22]The mother of Hezekiah (2 Kings 18:2) and the wife of Hezron (1 Chron 2:24).

[23]Smith, *Early History*, pp. 7-12.

[24]F. M. Cross, *Canaanite Myth and Hebrew Epic* (Cambridge, Mass.: Harvard University Press, 1973), p.43. See also Smith, *Early History*, pp. 8-12.

they can be included as evidence for Yahwistic belief.[25]

The Extrabiblical Onomasticon

Jeffrey Tigay has made a study of 1,200 personal names of pre-exilic Israelites known from epigraphic sources, both Hebrew and non-Hebrew inscriptions. The particular value of inscriptional evidence is that, unlike the biblical text, it almost always represents an autograph and thus conveys the intentions, style and speech of the original writer, unaltered and uncontaminated by later editors or copyists. It therefore provides an objective check on conclusions drawn from the biblical evidence. Tigay shows that the Israelite names from the epigraphic onomasticon are remarkably consistent with those of the biblical onomasticon; he concludes that "the personal names in the Biblical text were not extensively censored."[26] Among the names he catalogs are six persons whose name is "My father is YHWH," nine persons whose name is "My brother is YHWH," five persons with the name "YHWH is father" and another with the name "YHWH is brother."[27] No female kinship terms are found used of YHWH.[28] Further, the grammar of other Yahwistic names comports with that of the Bible, wherein YHWH is exclusively construed as a masculine noun. We can safely conclude that Israel's belief in the fatherhood of YHWH was not a late development in its history tendentiously thrust into the text of the Bible, but represents one element in its religion as old as the cult of YHWH itself.

The Contrary Case Part 1: Evidence for a Female YHWH

In an article titled "On the Nature of God in the OT" published in the supplementary volume to the *Interpreter's Dictionary of the Bible*,[29] Phyl-

---

[25]The same is true to some extent of Baal names, some of which were almost certainly Yahwistic. See Tigay, *No Other Gods*, p. 14.

[26]Ibid., p. 41. It is generally recognized that some censorship did take place with respect to Baal names (p. 8 n. 10), but no alteration of kinship terms has been attested.

[27]Tigay, *No Other Gods: 'byhw* (and variants), p. 47; *yhw'b* (and variants), p. 54.

[28]Because it is difficult to be certain whether bearers of El- names in inscriptions were Yahwists or even Israelites, Tigay simply brackets them in drawing his conclusions. Still, it is interesting that in his catalog listing Israelite proper names with the element *'l-*, there is no name in which *'l-* is compounded with *'b* (pp. 83ff.).

[29]*Interpreter's Dictionary of the Bible*, Supplement (Nashville, Tenn.: Abingdon, 1976), pp. 368-69.

lis Trible advanced what have become the standard arguments for biblical attribution of female characteristics to YHWH. Tending as they do to
conclusions that fly in the face of the massively contrary grammatical evidence, her principal arguments warrant close scrutiny.

A cardinal element in Trible's case is the Old Testament's use of the
lexical root RḤM in its various forms. She writes:

> Designating a place of protection and care, the womb (*reḥem*) is a basic
> metaphor of divine compassion. The metaphor begins with a physical
> organ unique to the female and extends to psychic levels in the plural noun
> רחמים (mercies), in the adjectival form רחום (merciful) and in the uses of
> the verb רחם (to show mercy). It moves from the literal to the figurative,
> from the concrete to the abstract.[30]

A number of complex problems are here given very summary treatment. First, we have no evidence whatever from which to say that the
metaphoric usage of RḤM "begins with a physical organ unique to the
female" and then "extends to psychic levels." In the absence of a well-
documented process of semantic change, it is almost never possible to
judge which usages of a word are primary or primitive and which are
secondary or extended. Even when it can be shown that two words of
the same root shape but different meaning are cognate, it is impossible
(without other evidence) to know whether they are related as siblings or
as mother and daughter; a fortiori it is impossible to say *which* is mother
and *which* daughter. Thus, if one root underlies both *mercy* and *womb*,
there are not one but three possibilities: (1) *womb* is primary and *mercy*
secondary (the Trible Hypothesis); (2) *mercy* is primary and *womb* secondary; (3) *womb* and *mercy* are independent secondary meanings derived from an unknown primary (e.g., *soft, tender*).[31] Those who share
Trible's intuition that the meaning of the "concrete" organ is semantically
prior to the "abstract" meaning do well to consider the Hebrew words for

---

[30]Trible, *Nature of God*, p. 368. The Hebrew words here cited may be transliterated *raḥămîm,*
raḥûm and *rāḥam*, respectively.

[31]Suggested by Theodor Nöldeke, review of W. Robinson Smith, "Kinship and Marriage in
Early Arabia," *Zeitschrift der Deutschen Morganländischen Gesellschaft* 40 (1886): 151 n. 5,
by comparison with Arabic *raxuma*. I cite the meaning "tender" only as a hypothetical fore-
bear; Nöldeke, however, gives some weight to this hypothesis by pointing to the Syriac
cognate *raḥmā* with the meaning "*male* genitalia."

"liver" (*kābēd*) and "heavy" (*kābēd*), where comparison with other Semitic languages makes it all but certain that abstract meaning is primary and the organ meaning derived.[32] In any case, the *assumption* that concrete uses are prior to abstract uses is groundless. Trible says further:

> Distinctive in Mosaic faith is the assertion that YHWH is merciful (רחום) and gracious (Ex 34:6; cf. 33:19). Used only of the deity, רחום is not language for a father who creates by begetting but for a mother who creates by begetting in a womb.

It is not clear what Trible means by the claim that "the assertion that YHWH is merciful" is "distinctive." The attribution of this word to the deity is neither peculiar to the religion of Israel nor restricted by other Semitic peoples to female deities—indeed, the evidence leans in the other direction. In his dictionary of Akkadian, Wolfram von Soden cites twenty-two personal names compounded of the element *rêmu* (RHM) and the name of a god; interestingly, in only two of his citations is the divinity female. Moreover, he cites eleven instances in Akkadian texts in which the verb *rêmu* is used with a (male) god as subject.[33] A. T. Clay lists fifty-two distinct Old Babylonian personal names composed of a divine name plus a form of *rêmu*, including Iri-manni-Marduk, "Marduk had mercy on me." Only five of these name-forms clearly indicate a female deity.[34] The fact that RHM compassion was commonly entreated or predicated of male deities in the ancient Near East centuries before the biblical period weakens the probability that the RHM attributed to YHWH by Israel was a distinctively feminine trait.

Yet uteral language, according to Trible, "functions as a major symbol throughout the history of Israel. In this symbol, divine mercy is analo-

---

[32]The liver is the "heavy" organ; cf. the archaic English "lights" for the lungs. It is also conceivable that reluctance to refer to intimate body parts resulted in a euphemistic name for the uterus as "the compassionate place" (cf. Gk. *aidoia*, Lat. *pudenda*). The point to stress is that the early semantic history of RHM is unknown and that there are rival conjectures that, in the absence of historical evidence, are at least as plausible as Trible's.

[33]Wolfram von Soden, *Akkadisches Handwörterbuch* (Wiesbaden: Otto Harrassowitz, 1972), pp. 970ff.

[34]A. T. Clay, *Personal Names from Cuneiform Inscriptions of the Cassite Period*, Yale Oriental Studies 1 (New Haven, Conn.: Yale University Press, 1912), pp. 194ff.

gous to the mercy of a mother."[35] She argues this way:

> Jeremiah intensifies this [uteral] language in a poem replete with female imagery (31:15-22). Over and against Rachel's lament is the word of Yahweh: "Is Ephraim my dear son? Is he my darling child? For as often as I speak of him, I remember him still. Therefore my inner parts yearn for him; I will have motherly compassion on him (*raḥēm ʾaraḥamennû*) says the Lord" (31:20, author's trans.) As Rachel mourns the loss of the fruit of her womb, so God yearns from her own inner parts.[36]

The Hebrew-less reader with only Trible's translation to hand is at a disadvantage. Rachel does not mourn the loss of "the fruit of her womb" but simply that of "her sons" (*bānêhā*). The artful antithesis suggested to us by Trible is a product of her translation and is not found in the text. Further, the word *mēʿay*, which Trible renders "my inner parts," cannot be used as evidence for the presence of womb-imagery; *mēʿayim* refers to internal organs generally, those of men as well as women. It is used of intestines, of the womb proper, of the digestive tract, and of the belly. Jonah was carried in the *mēʿayim* of the fish (Jon 2:1). It is sometimes used of (male) procreation and refers to offspring (Gen 15:4; 2 Sam 7:12). Trible might justify her reading of *mēʿayim* as womb on other grounds, but to point to the word itself as evidence for such a reading is a paralogism.

Even granting an etymological connection between the noun *womb* and the verb "to be compassionate," we still need grounds on which to argue that womb-imagery is before the mind of the author, or intended to be suggested to the hearer, of this passage. The term *hysterical* is certainly derived from a word meaning uterus (*hystera*), yet it is not likely that a contemporary English sentence employing the word would prompt in many hearers a semantic connection with "a physical organ unique to the female." Further, even a clear and conscious connection between the words for "womb" and "compassion," derived in the manner Trible proposes, would not for that reason entail that the compassion to be understood is a feminine trait. Theodor Nöldeke suggested over a century ago that the semantic relation describes not *motherly* but *broth-*

---

[35]Trible, *Nature of God*, p. 368.
[36]Ibid.

erly love.[37] He compared the RHM words with the semantics of Greek *adelphos*, whose composition points to an original meaning of *frater uterinus*, child of the same womb.[38] Such a connection may have been especially poignant in a society in which concubinage, polygamy or serial marriage due to high female mortality were common.

If we examine how the verbal cognate *rāham* is used elsewhere in the Old Testament, it is still less clear that Trible's reasoning is sound. By her reckoning we should expect the verb to be used primarily of a mother's compassion when employed of a human subject. The actual usage points in the opposite direction. It is used chiefly of males, usually a victorious warrior (so 1 Kings 8:50; Jer 42:12, 6:23, 21:7, 50:42; Is 13:18) and once of a father toward his children (Ps 103:13). In fact, there is only one clear instance where a woman is the subject of the verb *rāham*, Isaiah 49:15:

"Can a woman forget her sucking child,
   that she should have no compassion
on the son of her womb?"
Even these may forget,
   yet I will not forget you.

Here is a mother as the subject of the verb *rāham* and a clearly intentional word-play with *rehem* ("womb"). Yet the point of the image is not a comparison of YHWH's compassion with a mother's but a contrast to it: even a mother's compassion pales beside the fidelity of YHWH.

The blessing of Jacob in Genesis 49 has occasioned considerable comment on the possibility of divine female imagery, especially verse 25:

By the God of your father who will help you,
   by God Almighty *[El Šadday]* who will bless you
   with blessings of heaven above,
blessings of the deep that couches beneath,
   blessings of the breasts and of the womb.

Trible finds in the passage attribution of breast imagery to God—not

---

[37]Nöldeke, review of Robinson Smith, p.151 n. 5.

[38]P. Chantraine says that the etymology of *adelphos* is "composed of copulative ἀ– and a term that signifies the mother's womb . . . thus 'issue of the same womb' " (my translation), and quotes a passage of Hesychius offering the same derivation (*Dictionnaire étymologique de la langue grecque* [Paris: Klincksieck, 1968], pp. 18ff.).

directly to YHWH, in this instance, but to *El Šadday*, one of the names by which God was known to the patriarchs prior to Mosaic Yahwism.[39]

> Genesis 49:25 parallels the God of the Fathers with the God Shaddai. These epithets balance masculine and feminine symbols. Cross holds that Shaddai had the original meaning of female breasts, a meaning that is preserved here through paronomasia. The God of the breasts gives the blessing of the breasts (*shadayim*; cf. Hos 9:14).[40]

What Cross in fact says is "the epithet *šadday* . . . proves to mean 'the mountain one.' "[41] He does not translate *El Šadday* as "the God of the breasts." While he takes *breast* as a primary and *mountain* as a secondary meaning of *šadday*,[42] he stops well short of saying that there is more than a play on words in the passage in question.[43]

Bruce Vawter and David Freedman see in Genesis 49:25 a survival of an earlier cult of a goddess known as "breasts and womb," whom Freedman identifies with "the great Mother Goddess, the consort of El who is the archetypal divine father"—namely, Asherah.[44] The suggestion is intriguing, but is weakened by the lack of evidence that Asherah or any other goddess was known by title or epithet as "breasts and womb." Even if the passage does preserve traces of an early goddess cult, the cultic formula seems to have been completely assimilated into the standard Mosaic framework in which God Almighty is the giver and withholder of human fertility. The "blessings of breasts and womb" are part of his dominion—he bestows them but does not embody them.

---

[39]For the relation between YHWH and *El Šadday*, see Freedman, *Divine Names*, p. 91; Smith, *Early History*, p. 8.

[40]Trible, *Nature of God*, p. 369.

[41]Cross, *Canaanite Myth*, p. 55.

[42]Cross connects Akkadian *šadû/šaddû*, "mountain," and Hebrew *šādayim*, "breasts."

[43]Jo Ann Hackett has argued, partly on the basis of recently discovered inscriptional material, that *šadday* may be the same word as the *šdym* spoken of at Deuteronomy 32:17 and in Psalm 106:37: one of a number of deities obscurely connected with a sacrificial cult in Transjordan. J. Hackett, "Religious Traditions in Israelite Transjordan," in *Ancient Israelite Religion: Essays in Honor of Frank Moore Cross*, ed. P. D. Miller, P. Hanson and S. McBride (Philadephia: Fortress, 1987), p. 133.

[44]B. Vawter, "The Canaanite Background of Genesis 49," *Catholic Biblical Quarterly* 17 (1955): 12; D. N. Freedman, "The Religion of Early Israel," in *Ancient Israelite Religion: Essays in Honor of Frank Moore Cross*, ed. P. D Miller, P. Hanson and S. McBride (Philadephia: Fortress, 1987), p. 324; Smith, *Early History*, pp. 16ff.

The Contrary Case Part 2: Elizabeth Johnson's SHE WHO IS

Because it challenges the conventional understanding of the God of the Old Testament as a preeminently masculine deity, Elizabeth Johnson's book *She Who Is* deserves some notice at this point.[45] The work includes a three-page discussion of the interpretation of the divine name given at Exodus 3:14-15; indeed the title of her book is simply Johnson's re-signification of the tetragrammaton.

After locating the revelation of the divine name in the epiphany at Exodus 3 and correctly glossing the formula *'ehyeh 'ăšer 'ehyeh* as "I am who I am," Johnson says this formula is "safeguarded in the sacred tetragrammaton YHWH." But the name YHWH, as discussed above, if it preserves a verb, indicates a third-person, not a first-person form, and indeed a third-person masculine form. Thus the argument is skewed somewhat from the outset. Johnson goes on to discuss various proposals for the interpretation of the tetragrammaton. However, either because she is herself unaware that YHWH reflects the third-person masculine form, or because she wishes to keep her readers unaware of this fact, she gives translations in the first-person, in which the gender of the referent is not evident: "Thus the name YHWH means 'I bring to pass' or 'I cause to be' or 'I make to be whatever comes to be.' " "YHWH means 'I am who I am' or simply 'I am' in a sense that identifies divine being with mystery itself." But none of these renderings is accurate. The morphology of the Hebrew requires "*he* brings to pass," "*he* is who *he* is," and so forth.

It is important to bear in mind that Johnson's reader does not know (from her exposition) that the Hebrew form of the divine name YHWH is unambiguously third-person and masculine. This makes specious a bit of logical sleight of hand that would otherwise be impossible to carry off. Having briefly expounded the place of the Septuagintal translation of Exodus 3:14-15 in the metaphysical interpretation of the tetragrammaton, Johnson jumps forward more than a millennium to focus on Thomas Aquinas's discussion of whether *qui est*, "he who

---

[45]E. A. Johnson, *She Who Is: The Mystery of God in Feminist Theological Discourse* (New York: Crossroad, 1993). All subsequent citations of Johnson are from pp. 241-43.

is," is the appropriate name of God.[46] She remarks:

> The androcentric character of the standard English translation of the God's
> name as HE WHO IS is piercingly evident. That character is not accidental
> but coheres with the androcentric nature of Aquinas's thought as a whole,
> expressed most infamously in his assessment of women as defective males.

Here Johnson seems to be arguing that the translation of *qui est* as "he
who is" is tendentious (specifically, that it is androcentric) in virtue of the
fact that it contains the masculine pronoun "he." She insinuates that the
English is a mistranslation of the Latin, and then, oddly, shifts her ground
by saying the androcentrism "coheres" with Thomistic thought in general,
which suggests the English rendering accurately preserves androcentrism
present in Aquinas. In this manner the reader has been led to understand
that masculinist bias has wrongly *imported* the pronoun "he" into the
translation of YHWH. This sets up Johnson's next move:

> The original Latin, however, could be rendered differently. It reads, *Ergo hoc
> nomen, "qui est," est maxime proprium nomen Dei.*[47] *Qui est* is a construction
> composed of a singular pronoun and a singular verb. The grammatical gen-
> der of the pronoun *qui* is masculine to agree with its intended referent *Deus*,
> the word for God which is also of the grammatically masculine gender. The
> name could be translated quite literally "who is" or "the one who is," with the
> understanding that the antecedent is grammatically masculine.

But there is no "original Latin" to translate here. It is true that the relative pronoun *qui* can, in a given context, be rendered "who." But
Aquinas is simply taking *qui est* intact from the Vulgate, which in this
case translates the Septuagint, which in turn translates the Hebrew YHWH.
Therefore *qui* is not masculine in order "to agree with its intended referent *Deus*"; it is masculine because YHWH is masculine. The grammatical
gender of *Deus* is irrelevant. Having detached the formula *qui est* from its
biblical context, however, Johnson proceeds to use the English translation "who is" to her own advantage, the English being serviceably decep-

---

[46]Aquinas *Summa Theologica* 1.13 *ad* 11. Though it is not mentioned by Johnson, *qui est* is
the traditional scholastic interpretation of the divine name taken verbatim from the Vulgate
translation of Exodus 3:14, itself literally rendering the Septuagint's *ho ōn*.

[47]"Therefore the name *qui est* is the name of God *par excellence.*"

tive to the extent that it does not preserve the masculine inflection of the Latin or the original Hebrew:

> Naming toward God from the perspective of women's dignity, I suggest a feminist gloss on this highly influential text. In English the "who" of *qui est* is open to inclusive interpretation, and this indicates a way to proceed. If God is not intrinsically male, if women are truly created in the image of God, if being female is an excellence, if what makes women exist as women in all difference is participation in divine being, then there is cogent reason to name toward Sophia-God, "the one who is," with implicit reference to an antecedent of the grammatically and symbolically feminine gender. SHE WHO IS can be spoken as a robust, appropriate name for God.

Non sequitur: the inclusivity of *who* is a historical accident of English grammar and, in and of itself, says nothing whatever about God—nothing, that is, about the God revealed in the Old Testament. The fallacy becomes obvious if we recast Johnson's elenchus in terms of grammatical number instead of grammatical gender:

1. At Psalm 6:2 we read "be gracious to me, YHWH."

2. But in English the words "be gracious" are open to inclusive interpretation and may be used to address not only a single individual but also a multitude of persons.

3. Therefore, there is cogent reason to name a plurality of gods.

Obviously, if one actively seeks out translations, or translations of translations, with the purpose of finding interpretative "openings" decisively excluded by the original text, one has an almost limitless field of innovation at one's disposal.[48] But in such case the rationale for appealing to an authoritative text in the first place is hard to grasp. One can only surmise that the prestige of the sacred text, not its content, provides its principal attraction as the focus of this method of revisionist interpretation. Yet we do well to note that the "highly influential text" to which Johnson applies her feminist gloss comes not from Exodus but the *Summa*. It is unclear, then, to which discourse-community her conclusion is addressed, or even within which discipline (exegesis? linguistics? theology?) it is intended to be a

---

[48]As the orientalist Ephraim Speiser drily comments, "Translations are so much more enjoyable than originals, because they contain many things that the originals leave out" (*Genesis*, Anchor Bible [Garden City, N.Y.: Doubleday, 1964], p. lxiv).

conclusion. This ambiguity vexes Johnson's finale:

> SHE WHO IS: linguistically this is possible; theologically it is legitimate, existentially and religiously it is necessary if speech about God is to shake off the shackles of idolatry and be a blessing for women.

Linguistically, *what* is possible? What is the proposition to which we are invited to assent? Whatever Johnson may mean here, we have shown that it cannot be a valid statement about the language of the Old Testament; there are no linguistic grounds on which YHWH, the God of Israel, can be understood to be "she." To the extent that Johnson's readers draw the contrary conclusion they have been misguided. But more to the point, if *a priori* it is existentially and religiously necessary that God be named SHE WHO IS, the linguistic and theological considerations are, in logical terms, irrelevant. The conclusion has already been determined by imperatives extrinsic to these sciences. That is not to say that Johnson is for this very reason in error, but that she can find in the Bible only what her premises have decreed it necessary to find there. The traditional *exegetical* interpretation of the tetragrammaton is unaffected by her discussion because, on her own terms, that interpretation is never engaged.

Conclusions: The "Monotheist Leap"

The Old Testament presents an account of the history of Israel whereby the polytheism of its early ancestors is displaced by Yahwistic monotheism. There are less obvious but still perceptible indications of an intermediate period of monolatry (recognition of the existence of multiple gods with cult paid solely to one) or henotheism (recognition of the existence of multiple inferior deities and one sole supreme God). The progress of the intermediate stages is extremely difficult to trace, not least because the theoretical theological categories of existence and nonexistence belong to a later, non-Semitic tradition of abstract speculative thought. To ask whether, in eighth-century Yahwism, Asherah was believed not to exist or believed to exist but to be unworthy of worship may be unanswerable. It is clear that certain practices and hymns that were at one time pagan were later incorporated into Yahwism; it is less clear to what extent the deities themselves, and in particular the goddesses, "survive" in the person of YHWH. Tikva Frymer-Kensky, who takes an anthropological approach to the problem, uses the metaphor of "absorption" in accounting for the change she calls "the monotheist leap":

> Until the eighth or seventh century BCE, biblical writers did not categorically deny the existence of other gods. But these deities belonged to other nations: for Israel, there is only YHWH. As we would expect, YHWH, Israel's God, took the supreme position over the pantheon that the young male gods, Ba'al and Marduk, held in polytheism. Moreover, in the monotheist leap, "He," also absorbed all the character and functions of the female goddesses. As a result, the dynamic interactions between the polytheist gods disappeared into the unity of the One.[49]

Mark Smith, writing as a historian of religion, views the transition in terms of the kinds of discourse used of YHWH:

> In sum, the picture of Yahweh, the male god without a consort, dominated religious discourse about the divine in ancient Israel, at least as far as the sources indicate and assuming these sources correspond with historical reality to a reasonable degree. At the same time, male language for Yahweh stood in tension both with less anthropomorphic descriptions for the deity and with metaphors occasionally including female imagery or combining it with male imagery. This state of affairs resembles neither a Greek philosophical notion of Deity as nonsexual Being nor some type of divine bisexuality. Rather, Israelite society perceived Yahweh primarily as a god, although Yahweh was viewed also as embodying traits or values expressed by various gendered metaphors and as transcending such particular renderings.[50]

Frymer-Kensky and Smith express the principal conclusions to be drawn about the gender of Israel's God, conclusions to which biblical grammar, iconology, narrative and onomasticon all point, and which are corroborated by the extrabiblical data: YHWH is unarguably known to Israel as a god and not a goddess. YHWH is invariably "he," even though utterly divorced from the anthropomorphism of sex.[51] Because YHWH is supreme, his sovereignty extends over the whole of the created order, including aspects of that order that are feminine or maternal. But neither

---

[49]Frymer-Kensky, *In the Wake*, p. 86.

[50]Smith, *Early History*, p. 103.

[51]Thus Trible's gloss on Jeremiah 31:20, "God yearns from *her* own inner parts," cannot responsibly be used of YHWH.

Frymer-Kensky nor Smith attempt to account for the truly unique aspect of Yahwistic gender iconology: that YHWH is revealed as the sole creator, without reference to the feminine principle that is almost a conceptual necessity. As argued above, it is through the notion of creation as fatherhood that this is accomplished. This is a theological innovation, and it is the premier achievement of the religious genius of Israel. YHWH becomes a father not by approaching a woman but by electing a son, an election that in virtue of itself creates the son.

The fatherhood of YHWH is thus also a means of creation that shatters and completely replaces the sexual creation metaphor. "Thus says YHWH, Israel is my first-born son." Later, when Israel broadened its attention from its own history and began to speculate about cosmogony, the beginning of the world was pictured not as the sowing of seed or the bursting of a ripe womb, but as election, the deliberate and benevolent creation of order out of chaos. The universe comes into being as Israel comes into being: not by chance, but by choice; not by lust, but by unexpected and inexplicable love. The conceptual and imaginative power of this innovation helps to explain why neither the Old Testament nor the New engages in polemics against goddess worship or against feminizing God. The Bible insists God is merciful, tender, compassionate, and so forth, and yet these attributes do not threaten his sovereign masculinity, precisely because that masculinity utterly and finally transcends maleness in the image of elective fatherhood.

Excursus: The Language of Isaiah

Much of the language proposed by contemporary scholars as evidence of female imagery for YHWH is found in the postexilic chapters of Isaiah.[52] In these passages the anguish of YHWH for his people is forthrightly associated with the travails of childbirth and the feeling of mothers for their children. When such passages are isolated from their rhetorical context they appear at odds with the cumulative picture of YHWH:

> For a long time I have held my peace,
>> I have kept still and restrained myself;

---

[52]Smith, *Early History*, p. 99, lists Isaiah 42:14; 46:3; 49:15 and compares Isaiah 45:10-11 and 66:9, 13.

now I will cry out like a woman in travail,
  I will gasp and pant. (Is 42:14)

Hearken to me, O house of Jacob,
  all the remnant of the house of Israel,
who have been borne by me from your birth,
  carried from the womb. (Is 46:3)

Shall I bring to the birth and not cause to bring forth?
  says YHWH;
shall I, who cause to bring forth, shut the womb?
  says your God. (Is 66:9)

As one whom his mother comforts,
  so I will comfort you;
You shall be comforted in Jerusalem. (Is 66:13)

The vivid language of obstetrics that serves as a leitmotif in these chapters is indeed meant to attribute a notion of motherhood to YHWH; however, the motherhood presented to us functions as a narrowly rhetorical and deliberately paradoxical conceit. In fact, the particular beneficence of YHWH that is accomplished by his "motherhood" is very nearly the opposite of the symbology of the maternal as conventionally understood. Consider Isaiah 42:14 together with the preceding and following verses:

YHWH goes forth like a mighty man,
  like a man of war he stirs up his fury;
he cries out, he shouts aloud,
  he shows himself mighty against his foes.
For a long time I have held my peace,
I have kept still and restrained myself;
  now I will cry out like a woman in travail,
  I will gasp and pant.
I will lay waste mountains and hills,
  and dry up all their herbage;
I will turn the rivers into islands,
  and dry up the pools.

YHWH is a warrior, the *man* of war (*îš milḥāmāh, vir pugnator*) recalling Exodus 15:3; he comes to the rescue of Israel in a frenzy of destruction, and his fury comes over him with a suddenness and thrill of dementia that recalls the onset of labor. His "gasping and panting" accompanies the nearly insane impatience of the warrior lusting for the slaughter to begin. The language of childbirth is overly vivid, and intentionally so, for the prophet's relish in the vindication to come finds its expression in exaggerated paradox. The conceit is carried further in Isaiah 66:8-15:

> Who has heard such a thing? Who has seen such things?
> Shall a land be born in one day? Shall a nation be brought forth in one
>   moment?
> For as soon as Zion was in labor she brought forth her sons.
> Shall I bring to the birth and not cause to bring forth? says YHWH;
> shall I, who cause to bring forth, shut the womb? says your God.
> Rejoice with Jerusalem, and be glad for her, all you who love her;
> rejoice with her in joy, all you who mourn over her;
> that you may suck and be satisfied with her consoling breasts;
> that you may drink deeply with delight from the abundance of her glory.
> For thus says YHWH: "Behold, I will extend prosperity to her like a river,
> and the wealth of the nations like an overflowing stream;
> and you shall suck, you shall be carried upon her hip,
>   and dandled upon her knees.
> As one whom his mother comforts, so I will comfort you;
> you shall be comforted in Jerusalem.
> You shall see, and your heart shall rejoice;
>   your bones shall flourish like the grass;
> and it shall be known that the hand of YHWH is with his servants,
>   and his indignation is against his enemies.
> For behold, YHWH will come in fire, and his chariots like the stormwind,
> to render his anger in fury, and his rebuke with flames of fire.
> For by fire will YHWH execute judgment,
>   and by his sword, upon all flesh;
> and those slain by YHWH shall be many.

The "rhetorical questions" that begin the passage are used precisely as rhetorical markers, indicating that we are now to be told something utterly contrary to our experience and expectation, something unknown and unseen before now, and therefore outside the economy of domesticity and family. Jerusalem/Zion is to give birth to sons "in one moment," that is, she will be populated instantly and unexpectedly by those who love her, thanks to the apocalyptic action of YHWH. On that day those who love Mother Zion will be invited to indulge themselves in the caresses of infancy (notice again the too-vivid language)—nursing at her breasts, being dandled on her hip, and so forth. As a mother comforts her babes, so YHWH will comfort Israel in Jerusalem. But what will this "comfort in Jerusalem," this motherly love, consist in? Slaughter carried out once more in fury and indignation, by means of chariots, flame and the sword. In this grisly metaphor Zion gives birth to sons not by their return from exile but in the act of butchery whereby YHWH slays her captors. The mincing phrases of nursery endearment only serve to adumbrate more strikingly the horrors to come. The hearer is not seriously invited to picture YHWH as a comforting mother here, for the discourse is too violently paradoxical to permit it. Motherhood is used as a literary/rhetorical device to shock the hearer with the apprehension of a glorious reversal of circumstances beyond his hope or expectation.

Less violent is the imagery of Isaiah 46:1-4, although the context of sudden catastrophe is the same:

> Bel bows down, Nebo stoops, their idols are on beasts and cattle;
> these things you carry are loaded as burdens on weary beasts.
> They stoop, they bow down together, they cannot save the burden,
>   but themselves go into captivity.
> Hearken to me, O house of Jacob, all the remnant of the house of Israel,
> who have been borne by me from your birth, carried from the womb;
> even to your old age I am He, and to gray hairs I will carry you.
> I have made, and I will bear; I will carry and will save.

The pagan gods, which the prophet reviles as identical with their manufactured cult images, are carried away in flight by Israel's captors, to no avail. But YHWH is not to be carried on a pack animal; rather, he has "carried" the house of Israel from its very beginnings. The Hebrew does not make clear whether the carrying in question is carrying *in utero* or cradling in arms *post partum*; the imagery of the oxen transporting the pagan idols seems to favor the latter. Whatever the correct reading, it is the dramatic reversal of the commonplace that the image is meant to serve, and there is nothing here that invites the imagination to consider YHWH as a divine mother or satisfies it in the attempt to do so. The grammatical masculinity of YHWH is preserved intact throughout Isaiah as in the rest of the Old Testament, a fact which further sharpens the paradoxical conceit of bloodthirsty yet tender maternity.

3

THE PRONOUNS OF DEITY

A Theolinguistic Critique
of Feminist Proposals

_____

Donald D. Hook &
Alvin F. Kimel Jr.

A REMARKABLE EFFORT AT REFORM IS NOW OCCURRING IN ENGLISH-speaking Christian discourse. This effort is the ongoing proposal of feminist theologians that the exclusive use of masculine third-person pronouns to refer to God be eliminated. The traditional usage is rejected on the ground that it identifies the Godhead as *male*. Several alternatives to this usage have been suggested, and some of them are now being tested in various quarters of the church. In this essay we disclose theolinguistic implications of the use of pronouns in reference to divinity and offer a critique of current reformist proposals.

The Problem of Pronouns

In her influential essay "De Divinis Nominibus: The Gender of God"[1] Gail Ramshaw presents what has become the now classic argument against using the masculine pronoun for the deity. She argues that because of the disappearance of grammatical gender in English, "nouns no longer are arbitrarily assigned to categories called gender which

_____

[1]Gail Ramshaw-Schmidt, "De Divinis Nominibus: The Gender of God," *Worship* 56 (1982): 117-31. This essay has been reprinted in Gail Ramshaw, *Searching for Language* (Washington, D.C.: Pastoral Press, 1988), pp. 189-204. All citations will be from this latter work.

influence pronoun selection and verb endings *[sic]* through rules of agreement." Rather, grammatical gender has been largely replaced by natural gender, which corresponds to actual sexual distinction: a female being is assigned a feminine pronoun, a male being a masculine pronoun, and nearly everything else a neuter pronoun.[2] Consequently, the continued use of the masculine pronoun for God communicates emphatically the sexual identification of the deity as male. "It is time," Ramshaw concludes, "to break the model of God-he. The abandonment of grammatical gender in modern American English forces religious language to alter its terminology—a move to which the church remains lamentably resistant. If increasingly in American English 'he' denotes male sexuality, it becomes a simple matter of idolatry to refer to God as 'he.' "[3]

Ramshaw's solution to this perceived theolinguistic problem is to refrain altogether from the expository use of third-person pronouns when referring to the deity. She recommends the simple repetition of *God,* the reflexive use of *Godself* and the use of *divine* in possessive constructions.[4] Her recommendation has made strong headway among theological writers, composers of liturgies and hymns, and the clergy and bureaucrats of the American mainline Protestant churches.

Not all reformists have followed suit. Elizabeth Johnson, for instance, has forcefully argued that because humankind, male and female, is made in the image of God, both male and female images for God should be equally used.[5] Paul K. Jewett has applied this reasoning to the use of pronouns. Because the Christian God is profoundly personal, Jewett argues, the avoidance of personal pronouns is not only linguistically difficult but theologically distorting. Consequently, while acknowledging its potential

---

[2]Ramshaw, *Searching for Language,* pp. 198-99.

[3]Ibid., p. 200. Nancy A. Hardesty writes: "Using the male pronoun exclusively for God is theologically limiting and makes God into a gendered [i.e., sexed] object" (*Inclusive Language in the Church* [Atlanta: John Knox Press, 1987], pp. 101-2). I ask Ramshaw and Hardesty, Is the Christian God perceived to be less "male" in genderless languages such as Finnish or Hungarian?

[4]Ramshaw, *Searching for Language,* p. 202.

[5]Elizabeth Johnson, "The Incomprehensibility of God and the Image of God Male and Female," *Theological Studies* 45 (1984): 441-65.

for confusion, he chooses to alternate between the masculine and feminine pronouns (except when referring to the incarnate Christ).[6] This dual usage has the advantage of emphasizing the inclusion of masculine and feminine attributes or principles within the Godhead, as well as iconoclastically breaking all sexual images of God.

A third solution may also be mentioned, more for its uniqueness than for its plausibility. Essayist and fiction religious writer Madeleine L'Engle has adopted the practice of using *El*, or *el*, the ancient Hebrew name for God, as a substitute for pronouns. In possessive constructions we would then have *el's*, in reflexive constructions *elself*. "I find it helpful," L'Engle explains, "wherever and whenever possible, to call God El, or el, rather than using the masculine or feminine pronoun, because the name *el* lifts the Creator beyond all our sexisms and chauvinisms and anthropomorphisms."[7]

The most radical solution we have seen to date is the substitution of the feminine personal pronouns for the masculine pronouns. Some advance this solution as an expression of Goddess or God/ess religion, where feminine language for divinity is seen to be appropriate and necessary. The feminine pronoun is simply the natural pronoun for this deity.[8] We will not consider this proposal in this essay, because it belongs more to pagan or post-Christian spirituality rather than to a reform of orthodox belief and practice. Others, however, propose the consistent use of the feminine pronoun as a sex-neutral pronoun. We will consider this option below.

Gender and Pronouns

An evaluation of these linguistic proposals depends on a grasp of some linguistic fundamentals.

---

[6]Paul K. Jewett, *God, Creation & Revelation: A Neo-evangelical Theology* (Grand Rapids, Mich.: Eerdmans, 1991), pp. 44-48.

[7]Madeleine L'Engle, *And It Was Good* (Wheaton, Ill.: Harold Shaw, 1983), p. 25. In justice to L'Engle, I must state that as far as we know she has not proposed this convention to the wider church.

[8]See, e.g., Carol Christ, "Why Women Need the Goddess: Phenomenological, Psychological, and Political Reflections," in *Womanspirit Rising: A Feminist Reader in Religion* (New York: Harper & Row, 1979), pp. 273-87. Christ is herself critical of sex-neutral language for God because it does not force people to confront their sexism. See her "Symbols of Goddess and God in Feminist Theology," in *The Book of the Goddess: Past and Present*, ed. Carl Olson (New York: Crossroad, 1983), p. 241.

In grammatical classification, gender refers to two or more subcategories within a grammatical form class (e.g., noun, pronoun, adjective) of a given language. It is thus to be clearly distinguished from the sexual categories of male and female, a distinction we will maintain throughout this essay. The number of gender classes varies from language to language.: Hebrew, Spanish, and French, for example, have two (masculine and feminine); Greek, Latin, and German have three (masculine, feminine, and neuter); Swahili six (not any of which correspond to the categories of male or female); Hungarian and Turkish none. Although occasionally arbitrary, gender is often based on such distinguishing characteristics as word shape, animateness or inanimateness, and sex; and these in turn establish agreement with and selection of other grammatical forms (feminine adjectives modify feminine nouns; neuter nouns take neuter pronouns, et cetera).

Most of the Indo-European and Semitic languages possess what is called grammatical gender: the formal gender classification of a word, once established in common usage, determines obligatory grammatical concord with other words, regardless of the leading characteristics of the referent. Gender markers—no matter what their formal titles—are little more than classification tags for which the designation A, B, C or X, Y, Z or 1, 2, 3 would be just as appropriate. Particularly in reference to inanimate objects and abstract concepts, there is little or no correlation between gender and sex. To illustrate: the German word for table, *der Tisch,* is masculine; the French word for table, *la table,* is feminine; and Italian often utilizes two words for table, one feminine and one masculine—*la tavola* (fem.) and *il tavolo* (masc.). Such seeming illogicalities abound in gendered languages.

It is important to note, however, that in reference to human beings, words referring to males usually receive masculine gender and words referring to females usually receive feminine gender—unless, say, the shape of a suffix causes the gender of the base noun to change. In German, for example, the word for man is *der Mann* and is masculine gender; but when a diminutive is created from it, *das Männlein* ("little man," as a mother might address her young son), the word is neuter gender and the pronouns referring to that word are also neuter. Moreover, a clash between grammatical and natural gender can be felt even in fully gendered languages, resolution often being sought in syntax or choice of pronouns. For example, how does one say in French "The new professor is beautiful" when the referent is female? The noun for "professor," *le professeur,* is masculine; and gender concord requires that adjectives occurring in the predicate also be masculine. But the sentence *"Le nouveau professeur est beau"* necessarily refers to a male professor, while the sentence *"Le nouveau professeur est belle"* is ungrammatical. The conflict is resolved by constructing the sentence along these lines: *"Elle est belle, le nouveau professeur"* ("She is beautiful, the new professor").[9] In German today there is the distinct tendency, especially in speech, to use the feminine pronoun (in all of its declined forms) to refer to such obviously female persons as *das Fräulein* ("young woman," "miss") and *das Mädchen* ("girl"), instead of the grammatically correct neuter. Similarly, in the Greek text of John 16:13, the Holy Spirit (neuter) is assigned a masculine pronoun, possibly to emphasize the personal reality of the Spirit or the identification of the Spirit with the Paraclete.

Modern English, in contrast to grammatically gendered languages, enjoys natural, or more accurately, notional gender: nouns and pronouns, but not adjectives or verbs, are classified according to semantic, meaning-related distinctions—and in particular, sexual distinctions.[10] With some exceptions, there is generally total correspondence between the gender of an English word (masculine, feminine, or neuter) and the sex, or lack of sex, of its referent. In the sentence "The American athlete won a silver medal in the 100

---

[9]See John Lyons, *Introduction to Theoretical Linguistics* (London: Cambridge University Press, 1968), pp. 283-88.

[10]On notional gender, see Randolph Quirk, Sidney Greenbaum, Geoffrey Leech and Jan Svartik, *A Comprehensive Grammar of the English Language* (New York: Longman, 1985), pp. 314ff. The significant differences between grammatical and notional gender should not lead one to conclude that English nouns do not possess gender, nor should it lead one completely to reduce English gender to sex-reference (contra Ramshaw, *Searching for Language,* p. 204). Gender is not sex. Gender as grammatical classification must also be clearly distinguished from gender as cultural-sociological identification of the learned behaviors of men and women. Ruth C. Duck improperly conflates the two: *Gender and the Name of God: The Trinitarian Baptismal Formula* (New York: Pilgrim, 1991), pp. 32-40. For a thorough discussion of gender, see Greville Corbett, *Gender* (New York: Cambridge University Press, 1991).

meter race," the gender of the noun *athlete* is either masculine or feminine, depending on the sex of the individual denoted. Gender in English may be described as covert in nominals but overt in the third-person singular pronouns. An important exception is paired personal masculine/feminine nouns (such as *steward, stewardess; host, hostess; bride, bridegroom; widow, widower,* and precisely to our purposes, *God, Goddess*), whose gender is morphologically marked and thus explicitly indicated.[11] Since gender implications are more prevalent in the pronouns of the third person than anywhere else, we need to take a close look at personal pronouns.

The common definition of a pronoun as "a word that stands for a noun," although accurate to a degree, is incomplete. A pronoun is a word belonging to the form class of the same name that is used as a substitute for a noun (or noun phrase). It refers to that which is named, requested, or understood in the context. A noun and a pronoun are therefore related as a consequence of their respective content: the noun has a meaning sphere, a semantic component (what Karl Bühler called the *Zeigfunktion*).[12] First- and second-person pronouns, though, may be more accurately described as deictic nouns: they point to elements within the immediate situation or utterance and thus supply their own meanings. (For example, in the sentence "I want you to go to the store," *you* refers directly to the individual addressed by the speaker.)[13] By contrast, third-person pronouns—formally termed anaphoric pronouns—allow syntactical cross-reference and have no meaning except their syntactical relationships. They merely point to their noun-antecedents. For example, in the sentence "John caught the fly ball at the warning track, but he was unable to throw the ball to the catcher in time to stop the tying run," the pronoun *he* has no content of its own. It directs us, rather, to the personal name *John,* for which it serves as substitute or anaphora. An anaphoric pronoun functions in the coreferential way, even though its antecedent may possess characteristics not immediately associated with a pronoun of that gender. (See the examples below

---

[11]Quirk et al., *Comprehensive Grammar,* pp. 314-15.

[12]Jerzy Kurylowicz, *The Inflectional Categories of Indo-European* (Heidelberg: Carl Winter, Universitätsverlag, 1964), p. 244.

[13]See, e.g., Leonhard R. Palmer, *Descriptive and Comparative Linguistics: A Critical Introduction* (London: Faber & Faber, 1972), p. 112.

of exceptional uses of the anaphoric pronoun.).

Pronouns (like prepositions, determiners, conjunctions, and linking verbs) belong to the category of function or structure words and form a closed class, additions to which are only rarely made. The items of the various closed classes in the English language are limited in number, totaling less than a couple of hundred. In contradistinction, nouns, adjectives, full verbs, and adverbs—known as content or lexical words—form open classes and are definitely extendable. It takes relatively little effort to list all the pronouns, but no speaker of English can begin to name the hundreds of thousands of words found in the lexicon.[14] Yet lexical words may be invented with relative ease—consider the multitude of new words that have been added to our vocabulary over the past twenty years just from the computer and scientific fields—in comparison to the extreme difficulty of creating a new pronoun. A new pronoun has not been added to the English language for over a thousand years.

The exclusivity and fewness of function words are explained by their integral role within the syntactic structure of linguistic communication. Function words are the binding of complex utterance, linking content words into meaningful speech. Their meaning is essentially tied to the construction of which they are a part. By dint of their functional nature, as well as their smaller number, they necessarily appear more frequently. The project by Quirk and others gives us a semantic corollary of this: "Closed-class members are mutually exclusive and mutually defining in meaning: it is less easy to state the meaning of an individual item than to define it in relation to the rest of the class."[15] So basic are function words to the grammar of discourse that even over long stretches of time they remain stubbornly intransigent to change or addition. Thus they establish the possibility and continuity of transgenerational communication. The open classes of lexical words, on the other hand, are precisely that— open, open to change and open to new members. It is this freedom and flexibility that is the power of language. Adaptable to reality in all of its complexity and variety, the increasing and ever-changing words of the

---

[14]For the purposes of this essay, "lexicon" will signify the totality of open-class items.
[15]Quirk et al., *Comprehensive Grammar,* pp. 67, 71-72.

lexicon bring the world to articulate speech.

In the first and second person, and throughout the plural for all persons, English personal pronouns are unmarked as to gender. It is only in the third-person singular that masculine, feminine, and neuter gender are marked for the nominative, possessive, and objective cases; and this marking, as already discussed, is mainly based on sexual distinctions. But there are exceptions to this status. Despite the claim to the contrary, the generic, or unmarked, use of the masculine pronoun has not yet disappeared from the spoken and written language.[16] Ships and other vehicles, Mother Earth, church, and nations are often referred to by feminine pronouns. And compare the common use of masculine pronouns to refer initially to dogs and feminine pronouns to refer initially to cats. Language is never as simple and clear-cut as we would sometimes like.

The grammatical rule is that the gender of the pronoun must correspond to the gender of its antecedent. Break this rule and linguistic confusion is the likely result.

An interesting problem arises when one attempts to translate a fully gendered language into modern English with its notional gender. What considerations must the translator take into account? In fully gendered languages inanimate objects and abstract concepts may enjoy masculine or feminine gender, but with no suggestion of sexuality. Thus, for example, both the Hebrew and Greek words for "wisdom," *hokmâh* and *sophia,* possess feminine gender; however, when translated into English as *wisdom,* neuter pronouns are ascribed to it.[17] The key considerations are animateness and personhood. If the object lacks both, it is generally assigned neuter pronouns. If it possesses both, then the personal pro-

---

[16]Evidence on both sides of the question is largely anecdotal. It seems to be true that the "consciousness" of Americans has been "raised" to a greater extent than that of peoples elsewhere in the English-speaking world. It follows from this assumption that Americans should be wary of extrapolating too much from their own experience. On recent movement toward an epicene pronoun see Donald D. Hook, "Gender and Number in American English Pronouns," *IRAL* 27 (February 1989): 64-66; and Donald D. Hook, "Toward an English Epicene Pronoun," *IRAL* 29 (November 1991): 331-39.

[17]English translations of the Bible assign feminine pronouns to wisdom in the book of Proverbs and the Wisdom of Solomon. The deciding factor here, though, is not the grammatical gender of *hokmâh* and *sophia* but the personification of wisdom as a woman.

nouns are assigned, at which point the sex of the object becomes determinative. If it possesses only animateness, the assigned pronouns may or may not be neuter (as with higher animals).

The Gendered God

Throughout the Old and New Testaments masculine pronouns are consistently assigned to the deity because their antecedents are grammatically masculine. This fact in itself does not guarantee a male identification, for the Hebrew and Greek languages possess grammatical gender. When translators, though, have rendered the Hebrew and Greek text into modern English, they have universally attributed masculine personal pronouns to God, a practice that is continued in the New Revised Standard Version and the Revised English Bible. (The NCC inclusive language lectionary is an exception, but its motive was propaganda rather than translation.) How do we explain this? Simply to reject this convention as patriarchal or sexist is ideological dismissal rather than linguistic analysis; nor is it sufficient to explain it as an artifact from an earlier time when English was fully gendered[18]—by the time of the sixteenth and seventeenth centuries, when the first great English translations of the Bible were composed, the language had already moved into notional gender.

In the literary and narrative portrayal of divinity presented in the Scriptures, the gender of the God of Israel is unquestionably and unashamedly masculine.[19] While it is true that grammatical gender does

---

[18]Contra Ramshaw, *Searching for Language,* p. 198.

[19]On the masculine gender of the biblical God see Tikva Frymer-Kensky, *In the Wake of the Goddesses: Women, Culture, and the Biblical Transformation of Pagan Myth* (New York: Free Press, 1992), pp. 162-67, 187-89; Mark S. Smith, *The Early History of God* (San Francisco: Harper & Row, 1990), pp. 7-21, 97-104; Mary Hayter, *The New Eve in Christ* (Grand Rapids, Mich.: Eerdmans, 1987), pp. 7-44, 83-94; Elizabeth Achtemeier, "Exchanging God for 'No Gods': A Discussion of Female Language for God," in *Speaking the Christian God: The Holy Trinity and the Challenge of Feminism,* ed. Alvin F. Kimel Jr. (Grand Rapids, Mich.: Eerdmans, 1992), pp. 1-16; Roland M. Frye, "Language for God and Feminist Language: Problems and Principles," in *Speaking the Christian God,* pp. 17-43; Paul Mankowski, "Old Testament Iconology and the Nature of God," in *The Politics of Prayer: Feminist Language and the Worship of God,* ed. Helen Hitchcock (San Francisco: Ignatius, 1992), pp. 151-76; Patrick Arnold, *Wildmen, Warriors, and Kings: Masculine Spirituality and the Bible* (New York: Crossroad, 1991), pp. 200-215.

not necessarily indicate sexual identity, the correspondence in fully gendered languages between gender classification and the sex of personal beings is, we recall, broad, general and usual. More significantly, the principal titles, names and metaphors used to portray this God are also masculine. God is Father, King, Shepherd, Judge, Husband, Master. Titular, metaphorical and pronominal identification thus cohere into a unified narrative and anthropomorphic depiction that is structural and foundational of the biblical witness. Feminine images for God are subordinated to this primary characterization. Given the masculine rendering of deity—and given the fact that the only pronouns available in English to denote personal beings are the masculine and feminine pronouns—the decision of both past and present English translators to designate the God of the Bible as grammatically masculine would appear to be both appropriate and necessary.[20]

We must remember that although the graphic and phonological shape of the word for God can mark the word as to gender, this is not the only factor at work. In many languages *God* carries the semantic quality of maleness or masculinity, and in more languages there is a pairing of god/goddess (though, significantly, not in Hebrew) that necessitates gender distinction. Within the history of the English language, the word *God* has been profoundly informed by its use to designate the Judeo-Christian deity, and as a result has been assigned masculine gender. This is true even etymologically: the Old English *god* (masc. in sg.; pl. *godu, godo* neut., *godas* masc.) is parallel to the Old Norse *god, guð* (neut. and masc.; pl. *god, guð* neut.) and the Gothic *guð* (masc. in sg.; pl. *guða, guða* neut.). The Gothic and Old Norse words always follow the neuter declension, but when used to refer to the Christian deity, they are syntactically

---

[20]To speak of God as possessing masculine gender assumes the normative status of the Holy Scriptures and its grammatical-narrative identification of the deity. In fidelity to the gospel, the church may not abstract from the biblical narrative to speak of a genderless, nonhistorical, nonanthropomorphic deity of whom no story may be told. Thus we are compelled to speak of the storied God who is assigned masculine gender yet who transcends the sexual and cultural categories of male and female. See Garrett Green, "The Gender of God and the Theology of Metaphor," in *Speaking the Christian God,* pp. 44-64.

masculine.[21] Linguists believe that the Old English *god* can be traced back to the neuter proto-Germanic *gud*. They conjecture that the adoption of masculine gender is due to Christian usage and assimilation to the masculine rendering of deity in the Scriptures and the Latin *deus* (masc.) of the Vulgate.[22]

If the modern English *God* is masculine gender—and it is, when one considers there is a feminine counterpart, namely, *goddess* or *Goddess*—then the corresponding pronouns must also be masculine.[23] Conversely, if the masculine pronouns are consistently and conventionally employed to refer to the deity—as is the case throughout the English-speaking tradition, up to the present—then we may rightly infer that *God* has been given masculine gender.

This understanding of the gender of God—specifically, the God who comes to speech in the biblical narrative—does not question the theological assertion that the creator utterly transcends the biological categories of male and female. Gender cannot be reduced to sex. The Scriptures themselves radically qualify the "maleness" of the deity by insisting on the second commandment prohibition of imaging YHWH in worship, by insisting that as Creator he is to be qualitatively differentiated from the fertility gods and goddesses of Canaanite religion, as well as from nature, and by insisting on the asexuality of the divine nature—YHWH has no

---

[21] *Oxford English Dictionary* (Oxford: Clarendon Press, 1978), 4:267. Note the following translated statement from a famous Gothic grammar: "The word *gud*, which according to its form is neuter, is used for the Christian God with masculine gender" (Wilhelm Braune and Karl Helm, *Gotische Grammatik*, 13th ed. [Halle/Saale: Max Niemeyer Verlag, 1952], §94, anm. 3). But note especially this listing in the glossary of Samuel Moore's and Thomas A. Knott's respected Old English grammar, *The Elements of Old English*, 9th ed. (Ann Arbor, Mich.: George Wahr, 1942), p. 310: "[OE] God, masc., God [i.e., Christian God] [OE] god, neuter., masc. (heathen god)."

[22] *Oxford English Dictionary*, 4:267.

[23] Ramshaw writes, "Since God is not a male being, there is no need for the word goddess" (*Searching for Grammar*, p. 199). This statement is an example of theory triumphing over linguistic reality. If *goddess* were an unnecessary word, it would simply cease to be used. Given the burgeoning market for books on goddesses and the rediscovery of the Goddess by feminist, ecological, and New Age religionists, this obviously is not the case. Duck concedes that the word *goddess* "may give credence to the idea that [the word] 'God' is masculine," but she is willing to accept this for the larger goal of iconoclasm and the breaking of false images (*Gender and the Name*, pp. 36-37).

female consort. In his linguistic presentation God may possess masculine gender, but he is not male. Nor does this understanding of divine gender contest the claim that the biblical deity has what we might traditionally call masculine and feminine dimensions or attributes.[24] Holy Scripture authorizes the use of both masculine and feminine images to construe God's relationship with and ministry to his people.[25]

Our point is the simple but important one that despite the different way gender functions in the biblical languages and in English, this difference does not create any real problems either for the purposes of translation or comprehension. The claim that the notional gender of modern English masculinizes the deity beyond that of the original biblical languages is unsupported by the linguistic realities. At least as far as the grammar is concerned, the original hearers and readers of the Scriptures would have understood their God as no more and no less male than we English speakers do today when we read contemporary translations of the Scriptures or hear God spoken of as "he" from the pulpit.

The explanation of anaphoric pronouns given above is apposite here: pronouns do not *mean* in and of themselves; they point beyond themselves to their antecedents. This is as true for pronouns in natural gendered languages as pronouns in fully gendered languages. The anaphoric pronouns must not be artificially divorced from their referents

---

[24]See, e.g., Phyllis Trible, "God, Nature of, in the OT," in *Interpreter's Dictionary of the Bible,* supplement (Nashville: Abingdon, 1976), pp. 368-69; Phyllis Trible, *God and the Rhetoric of Sexuality* (Philadelphia: Fortress, 1978); but cf. John W. Miller, "Depatriarchalizing God in Biblical Interpretation: A Critique," in *Biblical Faith and Fathering* (New York: Paulist, 1989), pp. 55-65.

[25]It is important, however, to distinguish descriptive metaphors and similes from vocative titles (such as "Father," "Lord, "Master,"): the latter have unique reference and function as identifying titles of address. The notional gender of modern English (unlike more formal gendered systems) requires that the overt or covert gender of vocative titles agree with the gender of their referent. If the gender of the biblical God is masculine, then all vocative titles for God must also be masculine. ("Father" and "Lord," e.g., are overtly marked for the masculine gender; "Savior" and "Redeemer" only covertly so.) It is quite permissible to speak by way of metaphor or simile of (the grammatically masculine) God in feminine and maternal terms—under biblical and theological constraints, of course. It is grammatically impermissible to address God as "Mother," which is a term explicitly marked for the feminine gender. To do so is to disrupt gender concord and thus confuse the hearer. (As we might expect, there are exceptions: one might address, with perhaps ironic intent, one's mother or female friend as 'Dad' when she is acting in paternal fashion.)

nor from the overall semantic context nor from the public communicatory intent of the speaker. To detach and isolate the pronoun from the context of a speaking event, and then analyze it in respect to its semantic content, effectively nominalizes it and converts it into something that it is not. Such nominalization of pronouns would result, for example, in the absurd conclusion that because everyone refers to her as "she," an ocean liner is an animate being possessing female genitalia. *He, his, himself,* therefore, connote maleness only to the extent that their antecedents are apprehended or conceptualized as male. If it is taught and believed that the Christian deity transcends biological sexuality, then the use in English of the masculine pronouns will in no way compromise this conceptualization. Intent and recognition of intent are requisite to successful communication, and together they effectively make possible the sex-neutral function of masculine terms.[26] To argue that the use of masculine pronouns promotes the masculinization of the deity is to put the cart before the horse; anaphoric pronouns must be subjected to their noun-referents, or to put it slightly differently, nouns are semantically prior to pronouns. As Roger Scruton observes, "That [a pronoun] should bear a gender of its own is a grammatical fact of no semantic consequence. For semantically, its gender is the gender of the noun for which it stands proxy."[27]

It is interesting to note that the much criticized traditional default-masculinity of the English language—the convention that masculine nouns can refer generically to both sexes (e.g., actor, poet, lion, priest)—actually confers a freedom to English-speakers to "whitewash" the more sex-specific traits from our concept of God. Linguist Aryeh Faltz states, "[T]he default-masculinity of English usage makes it easier to apply a masculine word like Father to God *without* transferring male characteristics than it is to apply a feminine word like Mother without transferring feminine characteristics."[28] English-speakers simply are used to making

---

[26]See Jane Duran, "Gender-Neutral Terms," in *Sexist Language: A Modern Philosophical Analysis,* ed. Mary Vetterling-Braggin (Totowa, N.J.: Rowman & Littlefield, 1981), pp. 147-54.

[27]Roger Scruton, "Ideologically Speaking," in *The State of the Language,* ed. Christopher Ricks and Leonard Michaels (Berkeley: University of California Press, 1990), p. 121.

[28]Aryeh Faltz, "Comments on the Supplementary Liturgical Texts," *Prayer Book Studies* 30 (1990): 16.

these unconscious, tacit adjustments. The irony is that to the degree the contemporary critique of generic usage is accepted by the population, the word *God* will become more sex-specific in meaning in secular consciousness, thus requiring more explanation on the part of Christian evangelists, catechists and teachers.

Perhaps at this point a word about the Holy Spirit is in order. Recognizing that the masculine personal pronouns are the proper pronouns for God the Father and Jesus the Son, some reformists have proposed that the feminine pronoun be assigned to the Holy Spirit, the third person of the Holy Trinity. They argue that the Hebrew, Aramaic and Syriac words for "spirit" are feminine gender and that this provides a foundation for the assignment of feminine gender to the Spirit in modern English. Yet as we have seen above, the assignment of grammatical gender to inanimate and abstract nouns is arbitrary and communicates nothing materially about the object denoted. Thus the Greek *pneuma* is neuter, while the Latin *spiritus,* Old English *gāst* (from which *ghost* derives), and German *Geist* are masculine. In the specific case of the Holy Spirit (or Holy Ghost), the recognition of grammatical gender is irrelevant to the question of translation into modern English.[29]

The English word *spirit* normally receives neutral gender, since it usually denotes an inanimate or nonpersonal reality (e.g., "team spirit," "the right spirit," "the spirit of the party," or "a person is composed of body, mind, and spirit"). An evil spirit normally receives neuter gender (with the exception of Satan, Lilith and a few others who exhibit distinct personality). Even in the case of a spirit as ghost, the neuter pronoun is often chosen, unless the sex of the dead individual is clearly known

The Holy Spirit, however, poses a unique problem. If the Spirit is construed as the power, life, love, activity of God, the neuter pronoun might seem most appropriate. Thus the AV assigns the neuter gender to the Spirit in Romans 8:16, 26 (but cf. RSV), as does the RSV in Acts 8:16 (but cf. AV). But does not this choice of neuter gender necessarily suggest the contextual impersonality of the Spirit?

If, following the dogmatic tradition, the Holy Spirit is construed as in

---

[29]Contra Hardesty, *Inclusive Language,* p. 53.

some sense a person or subject distinct from both the Father and the Son, then a personal (masculine or feminine) pronoun must be assigned. The neuter gender is inappropriate, for it removes from the Spirit the essential elements of individuality, particularity, and personal identity that we associate with the third person of the Holy Trinity. Thus the AV assigns the masculine gender to the Spirit in Acts 8:16 and John 14 and John 16, the latter texts most clearly identifying the Spirit as personal agent. But why is the masculine gender to be preferred over the feminine? Contemporary translations of the New Testament (RSV, NEB, NIV, JB, NJB, TEV) have assigned the masculine pronoun to the Holy Spirit, and there are no examples of the feminine pronoun referring directly to the Spirit in any of them.[30] Even the recent NRSV and CEV use the masculine pronoun for the Spirit in the Gospel of John, despite constructing sentences elsewhere in the New Testament so as to avoid pronouns altogether. How do we justify this practice?

Perhaps the strongest linguistic argument is a negative one: the use of the feminine pronouns for the Holy Spirit, while continuing to use the masculine pronouns for the Father and the Son, will inevitably introduce sexuality into the Godhead. Competent speakers of English will most likely hear this language as referring either to a bisexual deity or to three separate gods, two males and one female. Within the context of discourse ruled by the creedal grammar, the consistent use of the masculine gender when referring both to the specific persons of the Holy Trinity and to the Godhead considered as one being actually allows the hearer to dissociate the deity decisively from all sexuality, thereby enabling the conceptual distinction between God as grammatically masculine and God as sexually male, female or some hermaphroditic combination of the two.[31] This neutrality-by-sameness, produced by the exclusive use of

---

[30]In a survey of an English hymnal, Brian Wren observes that of the forty-one pronominal references to the Holy Spirit, forty are masculine and one is neuter. He also notes that masculine titles are also assigned to the Spirit (e.g., "Lord," "Father of the poor"). See Brian Wren, *What Language Shall I Borrow? God-Talk in Worship: A Male Response to Feminist Theology* (New York: Crossroad, 1989), pp. 118-19.

[31]This argument actually applies to the use of any single gender, though the biblical narrative disallows the assignment of the neuter or feminine gender to all three persons of the Trinity or to the one God.

the masculine gender, is interrupted by the insertion of the feminine into the immanent life of the Trinity; the masculine-feminine duality compels the hearer to compare and contrast. The attribution of sexual and fertility roles to the hypostases of the Godhead thus becomes inescapable. Linguistic analogy permits us to assimilate the word *Spirit* to the masculine gender of the one God and therefore avoid the sexualization of deity. Despite the well-intentioned theological motivations for employing the feminine pronoun for the Holy Spirit, the linguistic factors will generate confusion and distortion.

As a positive argument in support of the traditional pronominal identification of the Spirit, it seems intuitively proper that the Holy Spirit, who is the third person of the Godhead and possesses totally the divine being, should also be specified by that pronoun used to specify the *one* triune God.

> And the Catholic Faith is this: That we worship one God in Trinity, and Trinity in unity, neither confounding the Persons, nor dividing the Substance. For there is one Person of the Father, another of the Son, and another of the Holy Ghost. But the Godhead of the Father, of the Son, and of the Holy Ghost, is all one, the Glory equal, the Majesty co-eternal. Such as the Father is, such is the Son, and such is the Holy Ghost. . . . So the Father is God, the Son is God, and the Holy Ghost is God. And yet they are not three Gods, but one God. *(Quicunque Vult)*

The Holy Spirit is the one transcendent and holy Creator. If an argument could be established demonstrating the symbolic affinity of masculine imagery with divine transcendence,[32] then we would be well on our way to positively justifying the intuitive assignment of the masculine gender to God the Paraclete. In any case, short of a compelling theological argument for the unique symbolization or embodiment of a divine feminine principle in the hypostasis of the Holy Spirit—a possibility we cannot rule out by theolinguistic considerations alone—the pronominal

---

[32]See, e.g., Walter J. Ong, *Fighting for Life: Contest, Sexuality, and Consciousness* (Ithaca, N.Y.: Cornell University Press, 1981), pp. 167-83; Achtemeier, "Exchanging God," pp. 1-16; Manfred Hauke, *Women in the Priesthood? A Systematic Analysis in the Light of the Order of Creation and Redemption,* trans. David Kipp (San Francisco, Ignatius, 1986), pp. 121-94; Donald G. Bloesch, *Battle for the Trinity* (Ann Arbor, Mich.: Servant, 1985), pp. 29-41.

identification of the Spirit as masculine is proper and fitting. Within English-Christian discourse, the Holy Spirit is grammatically masculine, for he is the third person of the one God who is grammatically masculine.

Critique of Reformist Proposals

The avoidance of anaphoric pronouns in reference to the deity is the most popular of the reformist proposals, but will this practice in itself disrupt or alter the masculine identification of God? We very much doubt that it will. In English *God* traditionally enjoys masculine gender. The counterpart of God is *goddess* or *Goddess,* the *-ess* suffix morphologically marking *Goddess* as feminine gender, and is always assigned feminine pronouns; conversely, the word *God* receives masculine pronouns. Even if speakers should self-consciously choose not to use the masculine pronouns for *God,* the fact remains they are self-consciously choosing *not* to use them; they are *intentionally deciding* to go against internalized grammatical convention and the deep, unconscious habits of the society. The assignment of linguistic gender is complex, nonreflective, sometimes dialectal, but above all societal, cultural, historical, and beyond the control of the individual. As long as the *God/Goddess* pairing exists within viable English vocabulary, the gender of *God* will be masculine and as such will be internalized by English-speakers. Thus the practice of avoiding the masculine pronoun when talking about God will never become habitual and routine; such practice must and will remain at the level of self-aware rebellion. Furthermore, to the extent that American society is influenced and shaped by the biblical stories of the God of Israel and the Father of Jesus Christ—and that influence has been pervasive—the popular conception of God will in fact be formed by these stories. As we have seen, these stories portray divinity as a grammatically masculine (though not sexually male) being. The deliberate avoidance of masculine pronouns will not, in and of itself, change this semantic reference nor alter the public consciousness.

One can argue with some degree of plausibility that by stigmatizing, and thus politicizing, the use of the masculine pronouns for God, one will advance a project of "consciousness-raising." The proscription of a conventional, internalized speech-act creates guilt and discomfort within the speaker, presumably leading, according to theory, to new linguistic practice and the transformation of awareness and attitude. The experiences of post-revolutionary France and Russia, though, are not encouraging in this respect. As philosopher Michael Levin notes: "The failure of [the terms] 'comrade' and 'citizen' to induce political equality suggest that language does not and cannot shape thought in the manner or to the extent supposed by egalitarian reformers. Attempts to alter putatively biased thinking by altering the language which expresses this thinking reverse cause and effect.[33] Furthermore, the process of consciousness-raising only lasts until the new language usage becomes the *un*conscious norm, after which point the unacceptable attitudes and prejudices remain unchallenged, thus necessitating an endless cycle of linguistic revolutions.[34]

The reformist, of course, can respond to this argument by asserting that the proposed linguistic convention must be accompanied by teaching and instruction; but this option is also available to the traditionalist who wishes to insist on the nonsexual identity of the grammatically masculine Christian God.

Reformist avoidance of third-person pronouns for God, using *Godself* in reflexive situations, is objectionable for three other reasons. First, in English such a practice is vulnerable to serious misunderstanding. Out of context, for example, the sentence "Joan sent Joan's son" is ambiguous.[35] It does not necessarily communicate that the son who was sent is the son of the first cited Joan. On the contrary, the sentence appears to indicate just the opposite, for many females may bear the proper name *Joan*. "Where the initial instance of a proper name," Robert Jenson explains,

---

[33]Michael Levin, *Feminism and Freedom* (New Brunswick: Transaction, 1987), p. 252. The thesis that language determines thought is known in linguistic circles as the Sapir-Whorf hypothesis. In its strong form it has received extensive critique. For an introductory discussion see Michael Devitt and Kim Sterelny, *Language and Reality: An Introduction to the Philosophy of Language* (Cambridge, Mass.: MIT Press, 1987), pp. 172-84, 201-6.

[34]Levin, *Feminism and Freedom,* p. 259. For a critique of the ideologization of language and grammar see Scruton, "Ideologically Speaking," pp. 123-29.

[35]I owe this point and example to Robert W. Jenson, "The Father, He," in *Speaking the Christian God,* pp. 98-99. Also see Dwight Bolinger, *Language: The Loaded Weapon* (New York: Longman, 1980), p. 95.

"has in the semantic context effected a successful identification, its later repetition in place of a pronoun positively suggests that two different persons are referred to."[36] Similarly, it can be argued that within common discourse *God* functions not as a concept but as a proper name; consequently, in the sentence "God sent God's son' the repetition of the possessive *God's* linguistically marks or implies two different Gods. We can, of course, stipulate that there is only one God (that is, the specific God we are talking about); but the fact remains that in the two sentences just cited—and in all others like them—the natural tendency and unconscious habit is to substitute a possessive pronoun for *Joan's* or *God's*. Anything else goes against the grammatical grain. Hence it is unlikely that this practice of avoiding pronouns will ever enter into the habitual linguistic habits of the society; it does not facilitate good communication; on the contrary, it impedes it.

This is not to say that by political and social pressure this practice cannot be successfully enjoined for a time—only that it will cease when the pressure ceases to be consciously and effectively applied. An example of an earlier attempt to enforce a grammatical convention is cited by sociologists Brigitte Berger and Peter Berger.[37] Like many other Indo-European languages, Italian has forms of address distinguishing between familiar and formal relationships: *tu* is the singular second-person familiar pronoun, and *voi* its plural; *Lei* and *Loro* are, respectively, singular and plural third-person pronouns used for centuries as the formal pronouns for "you" (cf. Sp. *Usted, Ustedes;* and Ger. *Sie,* singular and plural in meaning but plural in form). In the 1930s Mussolini castigated the normal and ordinary use of *Lei* as an effete mode of speech. The virile Fascist did not use *Lei* but rather *voi* as his preferred polite form (cf. Fr. *vous)*. This practice became the mark of the Italian whose consciousness had been properly raised, the verbal equivalent of the Fascist salute. Today we would call it politically correct speech. This convention lasted until the collapse of the Fascist movement, after which Italian-speakers quickly returned to

---

[36]Jenson, "Father, He," p. 99.
[37]Brigitte Berger and Peter L. Berger, *The War over the Family* (Garden City, N.Y.: Anchor, 1984), pp. 48-49.

the old standard. The syntax, function words, and deep structures of language are intractable to individual manipulation and ideological enforcement.

Second, the proposed neologism *Godself* as a reflexive pronoun is impracticable. In English the reflexive pronouns are made by adding the suffix *-self* (pl. *-selves)* to the determinative possessive forms of the first and second person and to the objective form of the third person. The very shape of the word *Godself* precludes the word from ever being accepted as a reflexive pronoun. Nouns do not become pronouns.[38] Furthermore, the attachment of the morpheme *self* to nouns is as a prefix, not a suffix (e.g., self-promoter, self-help, self-denial). Nor do all nouns accept *self* (e.g., self-dog, self-table, self-air, self-god). Apparently the noun must have some active aspect to it or be derived from a transitive verb. *Godself* is, therefore, doubly unacceptable, as would be *Maryself* or *Johnself* or *Jesusself.*

But can't we simply make up a word—or specialize current vocabulary for specific meaning—and prescriptively insist on its use? We've seen this happen before, we say, the most evident example in the United States being the movement from *colored* to *negro* to *Negro* to *black* to *Black* to *Afro-American* to *African-American* as nouns to refer to members of a specific ethnic group. But the situations are not analogous. *Negro, black, and African-American,* etc., are all lexical terms; and such terms, as noted above, can be made up at will and with enough popular support established in common usage (i.e., open class). Pronouns are grammatical terms, however, and must be associated with a noun somewhere in a sentence, whether stated or implied. Such terms are exceptionally resistant to change and as a class are relatively inhospitable to newcomers (i.e., closed class). As linguist Joseph Beaver observes:

> The forces of *grammar* are not as malleable as are items such as nouns used to describe things of clear and specific referential content. . . . It is a simple matter to devise a new referential lexical noun—it happens all the time. It is

---

[38]This argument also applies to the use of *Godself* as an intensive pronoun. The sentence "God Godself is active in the life of God's church" is gibberish.

not easy, perhaps it is impossible, to invent a preposition or pronoun. . . .
[T]hough you can coin and substitute real lexical items, you cannot blithely
alter the glacial-like grammatical functionaries.[39]

Not only is the problem one of structural morphemes (here, pronouns) versus lexemes (here, nouns), it is also one of frequency of use.
Those items of language of constant and agreed-upon use (e.g., sense
markers, pronouns, demonstratives and articles, inflectional and deriva-
tional morphemes) are of such high frequency that they resist change
tooth and nail. Witness the persistence of such forms as the vowel-
changing preterits and past participles of strong and anomalous verbs
(e.g., *speak, spoke, spoken; go, went, gone*).

Godself most naturally reads as a noun denoting some sort of divine
substance. In the sentence "God gives Godself to humanity in Jesus
Christ," the immediate sense is that God gives something to us which is
not identical to his person. *Godself* will not be heard—indeed, cannot be
heard—as reflexively referring to the antecedent *God*. Theologians and
others can pretend that it functions as a pronoun—and they can keep
this up for as long as they have the energy and desire to do so—but *Godself* will never become a pronoun within the English language or even
within the smaller community of the Christian church, no matter who attempts by fiat to legislate the practice.

Third, we fear that the practice of avoiding third-person pronouns will
lead to the depersonalization of the deity. Roland Mushat Frye advances
the following argument:

> In English speech and writing . . . personhood and personality are conveyed
> by a choice of pronouns, and in our syntax and lexicon there is simply no
> means to convey this affirmation of person apart from choosing between the
> singular masculine and feminine pronouns. The elimination of pronouns

---

[39]Joseph C. Beaver, "Inclusive Language Re-examined," *Dialog* 27 (Autumn 1988): 302-3. Also
see Dennis Baron's account of the many unsuccessful attempts in the past two centuries to
create and establish an epicene pronoun (*Grammar and Gender* [New Haven, Conn.: Yale
University Press, 1986], pp. 190-216). Baron concludes: "We cannot legislate new words
into existence, and no unified mechanism of prescriptive grammar exists to enforce a rule,
should we manage to agree on one. Furthermore, it is not likely that a new pronoun with
ideal characteristics can be devised in the same way we create wonder drugs or market pet
food" (p. 215).

would subvert the Christian belief in a personal God.[40]

Here Frye has identified a crucial point. What will happen to the church's understanding of God if the personal pronouns are excised from our discourse about God? Will our apprehension of the Christian God be as vital and personal if we consistently avoid those pronouns that signify personality?[41] In our readings of theological writings and liturgies that follow this practice, we have often been struck by the flatness, hollowness, and abstractness of the deity portrayed or discussed. Does not the intentional avoidance of personal pronouns when speaking of God positively suggest his/her/its *impersonality* or *nonpersonality?* The consequences of this practice for Christian faith and personal religion may be immense. Emil Brunner warned many years ago that the rejection of anthropomorphism in our religious speech is nothing less than the rejection of the personal God of the Scriptures.[42] And as another scholar suggests, when we eradicate gender from our conception of God, our "religiosity becomes a transaction imbued with as much warmth as two computers interfacing."[43]

Rather than avoiding pronouns, some reformists advocate the practice of alternating between masculine and feminine pronouns. This usage sunders the agreement between noun and pronoun, a grammatical law of English usage. In clear communication masculine and feminine pronouns ought not to be used to refer to the same noun; the notional gender of modern English precludes such arrangement. The grammatical categories of masculine and feminine are mutually exclusive. (And how could one ever use the feminine pronoun to refer to God the Father or Christ the Son?) This convention, if ever widely practiced within the

---

[40]Frye, "Language for God," p. 25. Cf. Jewett, *Ordination of Women,* pp. 44-47, 123-29.

[41]For some reformists the depersonalization of deity is itself part of the project. See, e.g., Rebecca Oxford-Carpenter, "Gender and the Trinity," *Theology Today* 41 (April 1984): 7-25.

[42]Emil Brunner, *Dogmatics,* vol. 1, *The Christian Doctrine of God,* trans. Olive Wyon (Philadelphia: Westminster Press, 1950), pp. 124-25. A discussion of the significance of anthropomorphism in Christian discourse is beyond the scope of this essay, but it does seem to us that it is at this point the theological issue must ultimately be joined. Post-Christian feminist Daphne Hampson agrees. See her *Theology and Feminism* (Cambridge, Mass.: Basil Blackwell, 1990).

[43]Arnold, *Wildmen, Warriors, and Kings,* p. 200.

church, can only have one of two consequences. Either the church will come to believe that its deity is a hermaphrodite, combining within him-and-herself both masculine and feminine principles (perhaps along the lines of some of the Gnostic deities of the second century or the androgynous God of Carl Jung), or semantic confusion will reign, as hearers keep wondering which God everyone is talking about.

Then there is the practice of Madeleine L'Engle, who substitutes *el, el's* and *elself* for the masculine pronouns. The impossibility of this proposal has been well demonstrated. Such convention belongs more to the private language of the poet than to the public discourse of a community. Pronouns cannot be so fabricated.

Finally, we must consider the proposal to substitute the feminine pronouns for masculine pronouns when referring to the deity, intending them sex-neutrally. There is no precedent in English, however, for the sex-neutral use of the feminine pronoun in referring to persons. (To experience the odd sensation of such an attempt, try reading Harold Bloom's recent book *The American Religion.*) Since the arrival of notional gender within the English language, during the Middle English period (c.1100-1500), *she, her, hers, herself* have always referred to female beings or to personified inanimate objects. These pronouns are linguistically marked for the feminine gender, and this marking cannot be undone by an act of individual or organizational will. All such attempts to institute the feminine pronouns as the singular common-gender pronouns for modern English have failed miserably. English-speakers simply hear these words—and cannot help but hear these words—as referring to female persons.

Of course, those who employ feminine pronouns in reference to the deity are free to explain that while their deity is grammatically feminine, she transcends all sexual categories. This rejoinder, however, simply positions them with the traditionalists, who are themselves busy with their own similar explanations. Instead of having to contend with a masculine God, with theological qualification, we now have a feminine God, with theological qualification. The most obvious consequence of such a practice would be a community-wide alienation from the biblical narrative and the catholic tradition.

A general observation needs to be made about all proposals to alter the traditional pronominal identification of God. Synthetic languages (such as Greek, Latin and German) are those languages in which syntactic relationships and distinctions are indicated by varying the forms of words. In some of these highly inflected languages, for instance, the subject pronoun of a sentence is often part of the verb morphology (e.g., It. *canto* "I sing, I am singing"; *canta* "he, she, it, you sing[s]"; Cz. *Dávám* "I am giving," *dává* "he, she, it is giving"). This synthetic typology contrasts with the analytic typology of modern English or Chinese. Analytic languages are characterized by the regular use of function words, auxiliary verbs, and changes in word order to indicate syntactic relationships and distinctions. It is a normal requirement of English that the subject of a sentence be explicitly stated. While there are occasions in conversation when the subject of a verb might be omitted—because it is clearly understood by the speech partners—this is the exception.

Given the syntactic requirement of explicitly stating the subject of a sentence, anaphoric pronouns are a necessity in modern English and not a luxury. They provide a service that is indispensable and essential. Anaphoric pronouns enable us to speak clearly without having to repeat common or proper nouns. Such repetition creates grammatical and semiotic redundancy, for it necessarily *emphasizes* the noun[44]—precisely what is avoided by the use of pronouns. This is because lexical words in English always receive linguistically-assigned stress; function words seldom do.[45] Consequently, the unnatural repetition of a common or proper noun is invariably awkward and inherently confounding, for it violates the English-hearer's internalized grammar. In the sentence "When I saw Mary, Mary was getting Mary's self ready to go visit Mary's cousin, and I

---

[44]It is important to distinguish linguistically assigned stress, which is the phonological component of an individual's internalized grammar, from performance stress, which is the vocalized stress given to syllables and words by the speaker for a special purpose. In a given utterance the two may or may not be identical. I am grateful to Joseph Beaver for calling my attention to this point.

[45]Responding to the complaint of redundancy, Hardesty comments, "How strange that we never felt that way about using *he* three or four times in the same sentence" (*Inclusive Language,* p. 57). But this is precisely the point! The repetition of a noun linguistically stresses in a way that the repetition of a pronoun does not.

asked to go along with Mary," who is who and who's doing what? Pronouns add needed simplicity, clarity, and specificity: "When I saw Mary, she was getting herself ready to go visit her cousin, and I asked to go along with her." The pronouns here confer no information; they are empty words, helpfully pointing away from themselves to their antecedents.[46] Anaphoric pronouns, in other words, properly do not draw attention to themselves. They like to hide offstage and allow the spotlight to shine brightly on those terms with true semantic significance.

All of the current pronoun proposals transgress the cardinal rule of the anaphoric pronoun: they draw excessive attention either to the pronoun (or pronoun substitute) or to the proper noun, often with undesirable syntactic and semantic consequences. In the words of linguist Dwight Bolinger, they refuse "to take the back seat that all languages reserve for pure anaphora."[47]

Conclusion

Can the perceived theolinguistic problem of divine maleness be solved by grammatical innovation? We think not. The problem—to the extent there is a problem—arises neither from the grammar nor the syntax of the English language. If the God of the Gospel is conceived in some circles as sexually or culturally male, it is not simply because he is spoken of as "he" in the discourse of the church. Other factors must also be at work. Gail Ramshaw's condemnation of the traditional pronominal identification of the deity as being idolatrous must therefore be rejected.

The prospects for genuine ecclesial and societal acceptance of the above-discussed proposals for pronoun reform are virtually nil. The proposals all crash upon the adamantine rock of unconscious grammatical habits internalized by English-speakers in early childhood (between the ages of eighteen months and six years). Such habits are changed only with great, perhaps insuperable, difficulty; and since the reformist proposals will actually create serious syntactical and semantic problems, we

---

[46]See Bolinger, *Language,* pp. 95-96.
[47]Ibid., p. 96. Bolinger was speaking specifically about the "clumsiness" of the double "he or she" pronoun in secular discourse.

may expect definitive rejection by the linguistic body. Grammar, after all, exists to serve communication, not to obstruct or frustrate it.

But what if the improbable becomes reality? What if the reformist proposals are indeed embraced by the English-speaking church, fully and completely? In our opinion, the consequences to the church's life and mission would be serious. They would most likely include an increasing alienation from the surrounding linguistic society, as well as from our own Scriptures and doctrinal tradition, and the crippling of our ability to proclaim the biblical story with dramatic and lively particularity. Moreover, if the reformists are correct in their analysis of the problem—namely, that as long as masculine pronouns are exclusively used to speak of the deity, we will conceive God as a super male—then their program cannot and must not stop with pronoun reform. The church must expunge from its speech to and about God all masculine terms of address, such as "Father," "Lord," "King," or at the very least must alternate them in iconoclastic fashion with feminine titles. The logic of this position would finally commit the church to a thorough rewriting of Scripture, hymnody and liturgy. Otherwise, there will be dissonance between our discourse and the sources and authorities of our faith, and such dissonance will assure the defeat of all attempts to transform consciousness.

What is at stake in this issue of pronouns for the deity? Nothing ultimately less than the faith, identity and mission of the church of Jesus Christ.

4

THE CHRISTOLOGICAL PHALLICY
IN THE GOSPELS

Thomas E. Schmidt

HERE IS NOW GENERAL AGREEMENT THAT THE VEIL TO WHICH THE
Evangelists refer as torn at the moment of Jesus' death was the outer veil of
the temple, that between the porch (אולם) and the sanctuary proper.[1] This
conclusion relies primarily on Josephus's account of this veil as embroi-
dered to represent "the panorama of the heavens."[2] The veil-rending, or
symbolic sky-rending, thus represents not a new way into God's presence
as in Hebrews 6:19 and 10:20[3] but rather the passage of God's Spirit
through the barrier of the heavens.[4] This view finds strong support by reference to Mark 1:10, where the veil of the sky is "torn apart" (σχίζω, only

---

[1]D. Ulansey, "The Heavenly Veil Torn: Mark's Cosmic *Inclusio*," *JBL* 110 (1991): 123-25. For
an extended discussion of the passage and bibliography, see H. M. Jackson, "The Death of
Jesus in Mark and the Miracle from the Cross," *NTS* 33 (1987): 16-37; also M. de Jonge, "Two
Interesting Interpretations of the Rending of the Temple-veil in the Testaments of the
Twelve Patriarchs," in *Jewish Eschatology . . . , Collected Essays,* Supp1NT 63 (Leiden: E. J.
Brill, 1991), pp. 220-32, and bibliography, pp. 314-26 n. 31, 32, 78. For a description of the
Temple see B. Narkiss, "Temple," *Encyclopedia Judaica* (Jerusalem: n.p., 1972), 15:942-48.
The outer veil could be seen through the 40 x 20 cubit opening in the אולם from a vantage
point outside and above the Temple mount (i.e. the Mount of Olives), but probably not
from within—due to the height of the walls around the Temple courts. The Gospels are
vaguely suggestive that the rending of the veil was seen from the place of crucifixion (see
Mk 15:39 [especially the ambiguous ἐξ ἐναντίας αὐτοῦ: is the centurion observing the Temple or Jesus?]; Mt 27:54; Lk 23:47).
[2]Josephus *J.W.* 5:212-214; cf. Josephus *Ant.* 3:184.
[3]W. Lane, *The Gospel According to Mark* (Grand Rapids, Mich.: Eerdmans, 1974), p. 575 n. 79.
[4]For a discussion of the nature and significance of Jesus' spirit-exhalation see R. H. Gundry,
Mark: A Commentary on His Apology for the Cross (Grand Rapids, Mich.: Eerdmans, 1993),
pp. 947-50, 970-71; and T. E. Schmidt, "Cry of Dereliction or Cry of Judgment? Mark 15:34 in
Context," *Bulletin of Biblical Research* 4 (1994): 145-53.

here and at Mk 15:38) at Jesus' baptism immediately before the descent of
the Spirit and the heavenly voice. The two incidents, apparently intentionally recounted by Mark, quite consciously for the Second Evangelist, mark
out the parameters of Jesus' public ministry in suitably apocalyptic terms.
Close scrutiny reveals that the incidents have several common features in
addition to the veil imagery of the sky, and that similar or analogous features appear in key christological narratives in the other three Gospels. I
will show how this "divine penetration" theme is drawn on by all four
Evangelists—consciously, to a varying degree—and offers some clues
about the structure of the respective narratives. In a postscript I will introduce some implications for theological response.

The Sky God in Antiquity

Scholars searching for background material on the baptism of Jesus have
been content to find parallels in Semitic apocalyptic literature, but for our
purposes it is instructive to go further back and to cast the net more
widely. We are indebted to Mircea Eliade's *Patterns in Comparative Religion* for a wealth of information about the relation between deities and
the sky in primitive and ancient religion.[5]

Virtually every religion begins with a supreme sky deity. This god is
generally distant, passive and abstract. Eventually he is supplanted by a
creator-god who is more in touch with the earth. Eliade documents this
development in Mesopotamia, India, Greece, and other Indo-Aryan cultures, maintaining that the

> meaning is in each case . . . a movement away from the transcendence and
> passivity of sky beings towards more dynamic, active and easily accessible
> forms. One might say that we are observing a "progressive descent of the
> sacred into the concrete."[6]

This development is particularly interesting in the case of Greece.
Eliade draws attention to Hesiod's *Theogony* (c. 600 B.C.).[7] Here, instead of Zeus and Hera in the beginning as we might expect, we find

---

[5]M. Eliade, *Patterns in Comparative Religion* (New York: Meridian, 1963).
[6]Ibid., p. 52; see part two—"The Sky and Sky Gods"—pp. 38-123.
[7]Ibid., pp. 75-77.

Οὐρανός the sky god as the central player in the drama, the progenitor and "the ever-sure abiding place" for the other gods.[8] Implicit in this phrase is his inevitable abstraction from a god to the place name for sky or heaven.

It is more difficult to trace the development of the sky god theme in Hebrew religion, but the concept of Jahweh as spatially "up" hardly requires documentation. He is "Most High" (over thirty times; e.g., Gen 14:18-22; Ps 18:9-17; Is 14:14); he rides the clouds (Ps 68:4, 33; 104:3; cf. Ps 113:5); he is approached on mountains (Ex 3:1; 24:12-18; Ps 27:5; Is 40:9; Ezek 40:2).[9]

It is natural that a culture developing from nomadic people who contemplated the star-strewn night sky would describe heaven as a garment or tent.[10] According to Psalm 102:25-26, "the heavens are the work of thy hands. They will perish, but thou dost endure; they will all wear out like a garment. Thou changest them like raiment, and they pass away." Psalm 104:1-2 reads, "Thou art clothed with honor and majesty, who coverest thyself with light as with a garment, who hast stretched out the heavens like a tent." And Isaiah 40:22, similarly, affirms that it is Yahweh "who stretches out the heavens like a curtain, and spreads them like a tent to dwell in."[11]

Tents were made of skins. This simple fact may help to explain a number of seemingly divergent metaphors which in fact all derive from the same material. The sky may be rent or unstitched (Is 64:1; LXX Job 14:12; *Jos. Asen.* 14:2), or it may be rolled as a scroll (*Sib. Or.* 3:82; 8:233;

---

[8]Hesiod *Theog.* 126-28: "And earth first bare starry Heaven, equal to herself, to cover her on every side, and to be an ever-sure abiding place for the blessed gods." Compare 176-77: "And heaven came, bringing on night and longing for love, and he lay about earth spreading himself full upon her."

[9]The eventual condemnation of "high places" (e.g., 2 Kings 23:8; Ezek 6:1-4) does not contradict this: Jahweh refuses to be supplanted after the fashion of other sky gods. Instead, he is enlarged by the absorption of new metaphors and abstractions.

[10]Eliade, *Patterns in Comparative Religion,* p. 48. See also R. Eisler, *Weltenmantel und Himmelselt* (München, 1910), pp. 87-90.

[11]We should include here numerous other references to God "stretching out the heavens" without an explicit reference to fabric: Job 9:8; Is 42:5; 45:12; 48:13; 51:16; Jer 10:12; 51:15; Zech 12:1. Compare Hag 2:6, 21: "I will shake the heavens." LXX Job 14:12 contains this interesting expression: "Until the heavens are no longer stitched together (ὁ οὐρανὸς οὐ μὴ συρραφῇ) men will not rise from their sleep."

8:413). It may exhibit windows.[12] Most simply, of course, heaven simply "opens" (Ezek 1:1; 3 Mac 6:17-18, *T. Levi* 2:6; 18:6-7; *T. Jud.* 24;2; *T. Abr. A* 7:3; *2 Apoc. Bar.* 22:1).[13] The Jews retained this "skin" imagery even as their cosmology developed to the point of a seven-layered heaven. The lowest level, seen from below as the vault of the sky and separating man from the waters above—and ultimately God, high above (*T. Levi* 2:6-9)— was called וילון, from the Latin *velum.*[14]

The preceding description clarifies the placement of a sky image between the porch (אולם, 1 Kings 6:3; Ezek 40:7-40) and the sanctuary. To move horizontally into God's house was to pass in a symbolic sense vertically into the upper heavens. The porch itself was a staging place for the activity within the temple (2 Chron 29:17; *m. Menaḥ* 11:7) and was linked to the altar in its holiness.[15] The vertical correspondence, suggested physically by the twelve steps to the porch (*m. Mid.* 3:6), may also be seen in the statement of R. Jacob (A.D. 150) that "this world is like a vestibule before the world to come; prepare thyself in the vestibule that thou mayest enter into the banqueting hall."[16] Ezekiel's vision (Ezek 43) takes place in the inner court[17] of the temple where he is transported by the spirit. There he observes the glory of the Lord and hears the voice of the Lord himself (not an angel as in the preceding vision), who announces that he will henceforth "dwell in the midst of the people of Israel for

---

[12]Gen 7:11; 8:2; 2 Kings 7:2, 19; Is 24:18; Mal 3:10.

[13]For classical examples of the phenomenon see Ovid *Fast.* 3:347-48, 367-73; Cicero *Div.* 1.43.97; Virgil *Aen.* 9:19-21; Orpheus *frag.* 19:16. In the NT see Acts 7:55-56; 10:11; Rev 4:1; 11:19; 19:11; cf. *Shepherd of Hermas* 1.1.4. As a later development, beyond windows we encounter gates or doors, but there is no question by this time of their being *tent* doors: Ps 78:23; *1 Enoch* 11:1; 14:8-18; *T. Levi* 5:1; *3 Apoc. Bar.* 2:2; 6:13; 11:2-5. The point does not *hinge* on these texts; nevertheless, the imagery is arguably derivative of the earlier notions.

[14]On the cosmic veil in general, see Eisler, *Weltenmantel,* pp. 87-90; in the Talmud, see *b. Yoma* 77a, *b. Ḥag.* 12b, 15a, 16a, *b. B. Mes.* 59a, *b. Sanh.* 89b, *b. Bek.* 18b.

[15]2 Chron 8:12; Joel 2:17; *m. 'Erub.* 10:15; *m. Kelim* 1:8-9; cf. Lev 4:4-6.

[16]*m. 'Abot* 4:16. *Vestibule* = פרוזדור from πρόθυρον. אולם is used primarily of the temple porch (cf. Ezek 40-46), and פרוזדור never is. It would be convenient to find a word play between "world" (עולם) and "porch" (אולם), but to my knowledge this does not occur in rabbinic literature.

[17]The word *vestibule* (אולם) is used repeatedly in chaps. 40—46, but only in 40:48-49, 41:15, and 41:25-26 for the entrance to the sanctuary (cf. 8:16). Elsewhere it refers to the entrance to the outer court (40:7-27; 44:3) or the entrance to the inner court (40:28-47; 46:2, 8). For an attempted reconstruction, see W. Eichrodt, *Ezekiel* (Philadelphia: Fortress, 1970), p. 537.

ever" (v. 7). All of this follows God's entry into the temple through the gate (v. 4, cf. 44:1-2). It is also noteworthy that this "horizontal" theophany corresponds to the beginning of the previous vision, where the prophet is taken up to the top of "a very high mountain" (40:2). These details are interesting in themselves, but they take on added significance when we observe the explicit connection made to the initial vision in 1:1-4,[18] which is often viewed as the pattern for the Gospel baptismal narratives.

Divine Penetration in Gospel Narratives

In all four accounts of Jesus' baptism (Mk 1:10-11; Mt 3:16-17; Lk 3:21-22; Jn 1:31-34) the Spirit descends upon Jesus from heaven as a dove and the phenomenon is followed immediately by the voice of God proclaiming Jesus as Son.[19] The Synoptic Gospels report a preceding phenomenon in the sky: Mark has the more graphic "rending" (σχιζομένους) of the heavens, while the others report that the heaven(s) "were opened" (ἠνεῴχθησαν, Mt 3:16) or "opened" (ἀνεῳχθῆναι, Lk 3:21). The difference may be accounted for by the association on the part of Matthew and Luke of sky-rending with judgment, as in Isaiah 64:1, "O that thou wouldst rend the heavens and come down." Sky-opening, on the other hand, was associated with revelation (Ezek 1:1; *T. Levi* 2:6; *T. Abr. A* 7:3 *2 Apoc. Bar.* 22:1).[20] But Isaiah 64:1 employs ἀνοίγω in the LXX and could hardly be understood to lie behind Mark 1:10.[21] Sky-opening, moreover, occurs in several judgment passages (Is 24:18; 3 Macc 6:17—18; *Sib. Or.*

---

[18]Not only are many parallels present—wind, light, vision, voice—but for the first time since the opening chapters the author draws an explicit connection: this vision is "like the vision which I had seen by the river Chebar" (3:3). See W. Zimmerli, *Ezekiel* (Philadelphia: Fortress, 1983), 2:412.

[19]The texts differ as to witnesses of the phenomena. In the Fourth Gospel, John is the only stated witness. Luke makes no explicit reference to witnesses, perhaps in order to objectify the phenomena. Mark specifies that "he" saw the sky open and the Spirit descend, and the referent technically could be Jesus or John, but Jesus is far more likely. Matthew moves εἶδεν to the other side of the sky opening and changes the proclamation to the third person, implying a public event. See W. D. Davies and D. C. Allison, *The Gospel According to Matthew* (Edinburgh: T & T Clark, 1988), 1:330; M. Michaelis, "ὁράω, κτλ." *TDNT* 5:353.

[20]Davies and Allison, *Gospel According to Matthew*, 1:329.

[21]F. Lentzen-Deis, *Die Taufe Jesus nach den Synoptikern: Literarkritische und gattungsgeschichtliche Untersuchungen* (Frankfurt am Main, 1970), pp. 101-2.

8:413); sky-rending, conversely, occurs in a key revelation passage, *Jos. Asen.* 14:2(3), where the proselyte heroine's angelic visitation follows immediately after "the heaven was torn apart (ἐσχίσθη) and great and unutterable light appeared." The simplest explanation of the Synoptic differences is that Matthew and Luke, missing the connection to the rending of the temple veil in Mark 15:38, altered his graphic account with a more familiar expression. "Open" (ἀνοίγω) is employed in LXX Ezek 1:1, which has been demonstrated to be the pattern-text for the baptismal narratives.[22] The riverside setting, the sky-opening, the presence of the Spirit ("a stormy wind," Ezek 1:4, cf. 2:2), and a voice immediately following the visual phenomena are all notable parallels.

The announcement to Nathanael in John 1:51 culminates the disciples' call narratives following the baptism in the fourth Gospel. Jesus demonstrates supernatural vision, to which Nathanael responds by confessing him to be the Son of God and king of Israel. Jesus then says:

> "Because I said to you, I saw you under the fig tree, do you believe? You shall see greater things than these." And he said to him, "Truly, truly, I say to you, you will see heaven opened [ἀνεῳγότα], and the angels of God ascending and descending upon the Son of man." (vv. 50-51)

H. Odeberg cites *Gen. Rab.* 68.18 on Genesis 28:12 to suggest that John operates with the understanding of the rabbis that angels ascended and descended on Jacob rather than the ladder.[23] The disciples will come to understand Jesus, the new Israel/Jacob, the Son of Man, as the meeting point of heavenly glory and earthly appearance.[24] Odeberg argues further that this passage and 10:9, which describes Jesus as "the door," refer to the same spiritual reality, in other words, enlight-

---

[22]Ibid., pp. 107-8; note especially the parallel to Mt 3:16. Ezek 1:1: ἠνοίχθησαν οἱ οὐρανοί, καὶ εἶδον; Mt 3:16: ἠνεῴχθησαν οἱ οὐρανοί, καὶ εἶδεν.

[23]H. Odeberg, *The Fourth Gospel Interpreted in Its Relation to Contemporaneous Religious Currents in Palestine and the Hellenistic-Oriental World* (Uppsala-Stockholm, 1929; reprint Amsterdam, 1968), pp. 33-35.

[24]Ibid., p. 36. As R. H. Strachan puts it, "the wide open heaven, and the ascending and descending angels symbolize the whole power and love of God, now available for men, in the Son of Man" (*The Fourth Gospel: Its Significance and Environment,* 3rd ed. [London: SCM Press, 1941], p. 6). See also J. G. Gammie, "Spatial and Ethical Dualism in Jewish Wisdom and Apocalyptic Literature," *JBL* 93 (1974): 360-72.

enment concerning the significance of Jesus.[25]

Apart from the reference to sky-opening and the revelatory function of the logion, there is an interesting parallel structure between this passage and the Thomas narrative in John 20:24-29 which may suggest a correspondence to the seemingly conscious intentional boundary function of Mark's baptism and crucifixion narratives. Belief in Jesus, John's explicit theme, occurs in narrative for the first time in the question in 1:50, for the last time in the question in 20:29. Each narrative begins with a doubting disciple who observes the extraordinary power of Jesus[26] and then offers a high christological confession. In each narrative Jesus (the "heavenly voice") challenges the disciple's basis of belief and follows with an affirmation of *spiritual* comprehension. Significantly, it is at 20:30-31, and not at the end of chapter 21, that John summarizes, "these (things) are written that you may believe that Jesus is the Christ, the Son of God." Neither the connection to the narrative culmination in 20:24-29 nor the connection of that narrative to 1:43-51 have been noted by commentators in efforts to explain the structure of the book.[27]

Although there is no explicit reference to the penetration of a physical barrier, the transfiguration narratives (Mk 9:2-8; Mt 17:1-8; Lk 9:28-36) include enough related features to warrant their inclusion among the relevant passages. The narrative begins with a movement "up a high mountain" (Mk 9:2, cf. Ezek 40:2). Elijah and Moses appear, and they presumably must have come "down."[28] The extraordinary phenomena

---

[25]Odeberg, *Fourth Gospel*, pp. 323-26.

[26]See below for a discussion of the penetration theme in 20:24-27.

[27]It might be asked, Why not move 20:24-29 to the end of chapter 21? It would disrupt the flow of chapter 20 to insert the material, say, between 20:18 and 20:19. The stories in chapter 21 have more to do with discipleship or leadership than with conversion/evangelism, and in any case they would destroy the consistent placement in Jerusalem of the events in chapter 20. The difficulty of accounting for the awkwardness of the extant text is described by R. E. Brown, *The Gospel According to John* (Garden City, N.J.: Doubleday, 1966), 2:1055-61, 1077-85; and by R. Schnackenburg, *The Gospel According to St. John* (New York: Herder & Herder, 1968), 3:336-51.

[28]Elijah, of course, was last seen going "up by a whirlwind into heaven" (2 Kings 2:11). Moses is dead and buried in the biblical tradition (Deut 34:5-6), but the (lost) apocryphal Assumption of Moses (perhaps the incomplete Testament of Moses) suggests by its title that there was a tradition of Moses as "up." See J. Priest, "Testament of Moses," in *The Old Testament Pseudepigrapha*, ed. J. H. Charlesworth (Garden City, N.J. Doubleday, 1983), 1:924-25.

culminate in a heavenly voice that affirms Jesus as the Son of God. It might be argued that the mountaintop setting obviates a sky-opening, and so God speaks from a cloud.

The element of bright light (here ascribed to garments and in Mt 17:5 to the cloud) is new in the sequence of passages as we consider them here but not in the tradition. The wind of Ezekiel 1:4 is followed by "a great cloud, with brightness round about it, and fire flashing forth continually" (cf. 43:2,5: Ps 18:12; *1 Enoch* 14:9-13; *T. Abr. A* 7:3; *Jos. Asen.* 14:2 [3]).[29] This physical indication of the glory of God will appear in several subsequent passages.

I made reference earlier to the link between Mark's baptismal narrative and the "sky"-rending of the temple veil in Mark 15:38. The formal pattern is evident here when we note that the very next sentence is the remark of the centurion. In a subtly ironic manner, *he* becomes the "heavenly voice" who affirms Jesus as Son of God.[30] Another element of balance with the baptismal narrative is the role of the Spirit. The last word in verse 37 (repeated in v. 39) is ἐξέπνευσεν, and the καί which begins verse 38 may be understood as ecbatic. Thus the exhalation of Jesus constitutes an act of power, a Spirit-wind which rends the veil and impresses the centurion.[31] In this view, the scene does not involve God moving *down*, as in the traditional view of his symbolic entrance into the Holy of Holies. Rather, in a spatial reversal of the baptismal narrative, the Spirit moves *up* from Jesus through heaven (*i.e.* the veil) to God. The veil is much more than a convenient sky-symbol which did not happen to be

---

[29]See also Cicero *Div.* 1.43.97; Virgil *Aen.* 9.19; Acts 9:3; Rev 1:13-14; 11:19. Two Old Latin manuscripts (a, fourth century; g[1], seventh[?] century) at Matthew 3:15 add that when Jesus "was baptized, a tremendous light flashed forth from the water, so that all who were present feared." *The Gospel of the Ebionites* 4 (possibly early second century) similarly states that after the heavenly voice, "immediately a great light shone around the place."

[30]The parallel of the rending-proclamation sequences in 1:10-11 and 15:38-39 is noted by W. Lane, *Gospel According to Mark*, p. 576; and J. Gnilka remarks that "Markus habe ein Inthronisationmodell mit Adoption (1,11), Präsentation (9,7) und Inthronisation (15,39) im Rahmen seiner Gottesohn-Christologie benutzt" (*Das Evangelium nach Markus* [Zürich, 1979], 2:325). See Ph. Vielhauer, "Erwägungen zur Christologie des Markusevangeliums," in *Zeit und Geschichte, Fs. R. Bultmann,* ed. E. Dinkler (Tübingen, 1964), pp. 155-69.

[31]Jackson, "Death of Jesus," pp. 27-32 n. 1.

close at hand at the baptism. Its rending may foreshadow God's judgment on the temple;[32] but, at a deeper level, it signifies the departure of God's Spirit from the Jews. It is more than coincidental that a "prophetic" *gentile* is the next speaker in the narrative.[33]

In Matthew there are additional portents. These words intervene between the rending of the veil and the remark of the centurion (and other observers):

> And the earth shook, and the rocks were split; the tombs also were opened, and many bodies of the saints who had fallen asleep were raised, and coming out of the tombs after his resurrection they went into the holy city and appeared to many. (Mt 27:51-52)

The most suggestive—and rarely noted[34]—Old Testament text lying behind Matthew 27:51 begins with a sky-opening: "the windows of heaven are opened, and the foundations of the earth tremble. The earth is ut-

---

[32]Ibid., pp. 28-32. An interesting passage in the Talmud, *b. Yoma* 39a, may refer to the veil rending: "Our rabbis taught: during the last forty years before the destruction of the Temple . . . the doors of the sanctuary would open by themselves, until R. Johanan b. Zakkai rebuked them, saying: Sanctuary, Sanctuary, why wilt thou be the alarmer thyself? I know that thou wilt be destroyed." Cf. *y. Yoma* vi 43c; *J.W.* 6:293-94 (following portents of the destruction of the Temple): "The eastern gate of the inner court . . . opened of its own accord." There are two references to the rending of the temple veil as a sign of judgment in *T. 12 Patr.*, *T. Levi* 10:3 and *T. Benj.* 9:4; both are probably later Christian interpolations. See notes by H. C. Kee in *The Old Testament Pseudepigrapha* 1:792, 827; R. Pesch, *Das Markusevangelium* (Freiburg, 1977) 2:498-99; and cf. M. De Jonge, as referred to in n. 1.

[33]It is worth considering in this regard that the quotation of Psalm 22 in v. 34 may be a cry of dereliction of the Jews rather than a cry of the dereliction (or triumph) of Jesus. The blindness revealed in the subsequent comment ("Behold, he calls Elijah") stands in obvious contrast to the insight of the centurion.

[34]Only a few scholars have made reference to Isaiah 24:18: Gaechter, *Das Matthäus Evangelium* (Innsbruck, 1962), p. 932 n. 81; E. Huhn, *Die messianischen Weissagungen des israelitisch-jüdischen Volkes,* vol. 2, *Die alttestamentlichen Citate und Reminiscenzen im Neuen Testamente* (Tübingen, 1900), p. 38; and W. Dittmar, *Vetus Testamentum in Novo* (Göttingen, 1903), p. 70. E. Lohmeyer (*Das Evangelium des Matthäus* [Göttingen, 1956], p. 396) and E. Schweizer (*The Good News According to Matthew* [Atlanta: John Knox Press, 1975], p. 515) cite 1 Kings 19:11. R. H. Gundry argues against the relevance of 1 Kings 19:11 because a wind is the operative force in the text (*Matthew* [Grand Rapids, Mich.: Eerdmans, 1982], p. 577). This is not inconsistent, however, with the rending of the veil and Ezekiel 1:4. A better reason to discount 1 Kings 19:11 is that the context is dissimilar. It is unlikely that the reference foreshadows the resurrection, as Gundry maintains, because the key phrase to signal that event is the *opening* of the tomb (28:2), which is supplied here in v. 53a.

terly broken, the earth is rent asunder, the earth is violently shaken" (Is 24:18-19).[35] Similarly, Isaiah 64:1 reads, "O that thou wouldst rend (LXX ἀνοίξῃς) the heavens and come down, that the mountains might quake at thy presence."[36] In verse 53 tombs are opened, a feature reminiscent of Ezekiel 37:13: "And you shall know that I am the LORD, when I open your graves, and raise you from your graves, O my people."

These visible signs, then, supplement the underlying tradition in the composition of Matthew's death account.[37] The simple parallelism of Mark is lost, and along with it the focus on the departure of the Spirit, but the "voice" of verse 54 is rendered more weighty by the richly varied series of events from which its proclamation is deduced.

The birth and death narratives involve angels or the risen Jesus coming "down" or returning "up" to heaven, but explicit reference to sky-openings *per se* is lacking. The purpose of this section is to explore the linguistic and literary links between the barriers represented in the previous section by the sky and temple veil and those represented here by the virgin womb of Mary and the stone-sealed tomb of Jesus. It would be fanciful to suggest that the Evangelists themselves were aware of these links; rather, the point is to show the underlying connections that allow for a consistent mode of christological expression and the theological balance of the narrative. The connections also begin to touch more directly upon theological gender issues.

Consider first the annunciation to Mary and the dream of Joseph (Lk 1:26-38; Mt 1:18-21). There is a long history of association between fe-

---

[35]This reference is also noteworthy for its closing line: "Then the moon will be confounded, and the sun ashamed" (24:23; cf. Mt 27:45).

[36]The only use of σχίζω in a related passage is *T. Levi* 4:1: "Know, then, that the Lord will effect judgment on the sons of men. For even when stones are split (σχιζομένων), when the sun is extinguished, the waters dried up . . ." For classical texts describing earthquakes, ghosts, and other portents at the deaths of important figures, see Lucian *Peregr.* 39; Pausanias *Ach.* 25.3; Ovid *Met.* 7.200-206; Virgil *Georg.* 1.475; Dio Cassius 51.17.4-5. It is curious that Matthew would report phenomena after the pagan style. Could this, like the visit of the magi, be a subtle message about the inclusion of gentiles?

[37]On the soteriological import of the passage, See D. P. Senior, *The Passion Narrative According to Matthew* (Leuven, 1975), pp. 307-11. On Luke's apparently weaker account ("Certainly this man was innocent," 23:47), see J. A. Fitzmyer, *The Gospel According to Luke* (Garden City, N.J.: Doubleday, 1958), 2:1520.

male genitalia, virginity, and architectural chambers and barriers. To enter a woman's tent was a common euphemism in the Old Testament for intercourse,[38] and Jahweh himself opens the wombs of Leah and Rachel in Genesis 29:31, 30:22. To the rabbis, an "open door" was a euphemism for lack of virginity (*b. Ketub.* 9a-b), and in one place the open sky and (plowed) open earth are likened to "the female that opens for the male" (*y. Ta'an.* I 64b, ref. Is 45:8). *M.Nid.* 2:5 reveals that the rabbis referred to female genitalia in architectural terms, with the vagina, significantly, termed the "vestibule."[39] In several rabbinic texts, the vagina is referred to as the "*house* of love."[40] The Song of Solomon contains numerous double entendres, including "a garden locked is my sister" (4:12), "I would lead you and bring you . . . into the chamber of her that conceived me" (8:2), and "if she is a wall . . . but if she is a door" (8:9).[41] 5:2-8 is the most (metaphorically) explicit: the maiden hears her lover cry "open to me," she is undressed, he puts his "hand" through her "door," and she "opens" to her beloved.[42]

Joseph and Asenath is most significant in this regard. The heroine is a virgin, and the author spares us no detail in describing her abode high in an impregnable tower surrounded by a gated and walled garden filled with fruit trees (2:1-12). She sees the hero Joseph from her window (5:2, 7), her mother brings her down to present her to him (8:1), but he rejects her as an idolater (8:5-7). Impressed by his charm, she retreats to her chamber, fills her window veil (10:2(4), καταπέτασμα, used almost exclusively for the temple veil) with ashes, and begins a long repentance (10:3-13:15). At this point the virgin heroine looks out the window to see the sky rent (14:2[3]), and an angel ("the chief of the house of the Lord,"

---

[38]Gen 6:4; 16:4; 19:31; 30:3; 38:8-9; 39:14; Deut 22:13; 25:5; Judg 15:1; 16:1; 2 Sam 12:24; 16:21; 20:3; Prov 2:19; 6:29; Ezek 23:44; *y. Yebam.* II, 3ᶜ, *y. Ker.* II, 3; *Cant. Rab.* to 4:12. J. B. White documents the ANE notion of entering a tent or hall as a euphemism for sexual consummation (*A Study of the Language of Love in the Song of Songs and Ancient Egyptian Poetry,* SBLDiss 38 [Missoula, Mont.: Scholars Press, 1978], pp. 93, 96, 152).

[39]"Vestibule" (פרוזדור) is used exclusively in this sense in the Talmud: *b. Sabb.* 86b, *b. Yebam.* 71b; *b. B.Bat.* 24a, *b. Hul.* 68a, 72a; *b. Bek.* 46b; *b. Nid.* 17b, 18a, 42b.

[40]*b. Sabb.* 64a; *b. Hul.* 51a 70a (3x): *b. B. Bat.* 16b; *b. Nid.* 3a, 25b.

[41]M. H. Pope, *Song of Songs* (Garden City, N.J.: Doubleday, 1977), p. 680.

[42]Ibid., pp. 517-19.

14:8) enters her chamber "from heaven" (14:3-5; cf. 17:9). The angel tells her not to be afraid (14:11), commends her righteousness (15:2-6; cf. 15:13, "I have found favor in your sight") and promises her numerous blessings, including Joseph (14:6-7, 16:16).

Luke's account of the annunciation presents some obvious parallels. Gabriel, the angel visitor, is "sent from God" and "enters in to her" (εἰσελθὼν πρὸς αὐτήν, Lk 1:28). Her virginity is stressed not by imagery but by repetition in v. 27. Favor is announced, fear is assuaged, and, immediately, blessing is promised. But in this case, the proclamation focuses on the identity and role of Jesus: the first statement begins (v. 31a) and the second ends (v. 35) with an affirmation of his divine sonship. Another new element here with connections to other penetration passages is the key role of the Holy Spirit (v. 35, cf. Ezek 1:4, 43:5; Mk 1:10 par.).

Matthew's announcement is to Joseph in a dream,[43] but several of the same elements are in place. Immediately following the information in the narrative that Mary is pregnant and Joseph is distraught, an angel informs him that the child will be the savior of Israel, Emmanuel.

The similarity of these narratives resides in the pattern observed in other passages. A physical barrier—in this case, Mary's virgin womb—is "penetrated" by God. Immediately in the narrative a heavenly message reveals the significance of Jesus. In this case, there can be no question of a conscious attempt to construct the passage according to a pattern. But it is nonetheless intriguing to observe, along with other features typical of revelatory narratives at key points in the career of Jesus, an underlying linguistic connection to the theme of barrier penetration.

The story of the announcement to the shepherds (Lk 2:8-15) contains several patterned elements and so warrants inclusion among the relevant passages.[44] There is no explicit sky-opening, but it may be inferred from

---

[43]For the purposes of this investigation I do not regard as qualitative the distinction between a dream, a vision and a historical occurrence. Most of the narratives present some ambiguities, and we might even speak of an objectivity continuum, perhaps beginning with Joseph's dream and ending with the resurrection. See the related discussions in Gaechter, *Matthäus,* p. 102 (baptism); Michaelis, ὁράω, p. 356 n. 18.

[44]I choose to include the story here rather than with the-sky-opening passages with which it is properly classed because of its similarity to 1:26-38. It is best to group it temporarily under the rubric "birth narratives" and to make further distinctions in the conclusion.

the closing reference, "the angels went away from them into heaven" (εἰς τὸν οὐρανόν, v. 15). The shepherds are reassured by an angel after witnessing "the glory of the Lord" (δόξα κυρίου, v. 9; cf. Ezek 43:5; Mk 16:5 par.; Acts 7:55). The heavenly voice immediately reveals that the infant Jesus is the Savior (vv. 10-12; reiterated in chorus, vv. 13-14).

In the announcement of the resurrection (Mk 16:4-7; Mt 28:2-7; Lk 24:2-9; Jn 20:1-18), the object of our interest is the sealing-stone at the tomb. The symbolic value of burial stones stretches back to earlier civilizations. Eliade explains that the stone protected against death by "containing" the soul of the deceased.[45] The sealing-stone of a tomb retained something of this significance for the Jews. Mourning rites commenced "from the closing of the grave with the sealing-stone" (*b. Sanh.* 47b). "The dead man knows all that is said in his presence until the sealing-stone closes the grave" (*b. Sabb.* 152b).[46] Contact with this stone, not only with the dead, brought about uncleanness (*m. Nazir* 7:3, *m. Ohol.* 2:4; *b. Hul.* 72a, cf. Num 19:16). This uncleanness even extended to the plane extending above and below the stone (*b. Nazir* 54a).[47] The sequence of Ezek 37:12-13 ("I will open your graves, and raise you," cf. *Odes Sol.* 42:15-17; 17:9), repeated in the resurrection accounts, is significant: as the stone seal signifies death, so the rolled stone signifies resurrection.

In Mark 16:4 the women witness the penetrated barrier. It is significant that they must enter the tomb in order to encounter the heavenly messenger: they must view the event from the "earth" side of the barrier. For the message of triumph which immediately follows is that the barrier

---

[45]Eliade, *Patterns*, pp. 216-19. He comments on the Jacob passage that the patriarch sets up a stone, the one he had slept on, after the ladder vision and calls the stone the "house of God": "both a name for God and one of the words used for a sacred stone or bethel. Jacob went to sleep on a stone, at the place where heaven and earth opened up to each other; it was a 'centre' like the 'gate of heaven.' " He recounts that locals later worshiped the stone itself as a deity or manifestation of deity. It is noteworthy that later Jewish tombs were patterned after houses to the extent that there was a *vestibule* inside the door: *b.* Sota 44a; *b. Bat.* 101a.

[46]Precisely what rites are in view at this point is not certain, since at least some "official" grieving appears to have begun earlier (e.g., Mt 9:39; Mk 5:38). The point is that the sealing stone was a significant mark of closure, both literally and figuratively.

[47]The seal of a tomb, even if it was not stone, could not be made of an animate object (*m. 'Erub.* 1:7; *b. Sukk.* 23a). This was apparently not due to its perishability so much as to its *life;* to associate a departed soul with a living object would be to mix kinds.

penetration is now reversed: whereas all previous movements were *down*, this one is *up*—"He has risen" (v. 6). By leaving the tomb through its sealing-stone, Jesus moves through the "sky" to heaven. From this point on, the appearances of Jesus, including the ascension, are appearances of the risen Lord from heaven.[48]

A similar pattern is evident in the other three Gospels. Although differing in detail, all four make a point of the sealing-stone being rolled away. All immediately follow the discovery of the empty tomb with an angelic (or in John, dominical) announcement of triumph. Luke (24:4) and John (20:12) follow Mark in placing the angels inside the tomb; while Matthew places a single angel atop the stone (perhaps a symbol of triumph), and he adds the details that the angel "descended from heaven" following an earthquake to alight there (28:2). All four make reference to the bright clothing of the angels (Mt 28:3; Mk 16:5; Lk 24:4; Jn 20:12). The most common details fit the pattern observed in previous texts: the barrier is penetrated and a heavenly messenger speaks words of triumph concerning Jesus.

The appearance of Jesus in a room with closed doors (John 20:19, 26) is all the more interesting for the apparent development of the story from Luke 24:36-43, where Jesus merely appears suddenly among the disciples. In the first instance, John 20:19, the doors are shut "for fear of the Jews." The reason is not given when the shut doors are mentioned in 20:26. This is not simply because the disciples are less fearful,[49] but because the Evangelist wants to stress the "impenetrability" of the room in

---

[48]Michaelis, ὁράω, p. 356; see below on the ascension. This view appears to be in conflict with the narrative statements of John 20:17 and perhaps Mark 16:7, which seem to imply that Christ has not yet gone "up." On the other hand, several enthronement texts (e.g., Acts 2:33; Eph 1:20; Heb 1:3; 10:12) appear to suggest that Christ is exalted at the point of the resurrection. Neither group of texts, however, constitutes definitive evidence. The post-resurrection narratives concerning Christ describe *appearances* (Lk 24:34, John 21:1, 14; Acts 1:3; 1 Cor 15:5-8) and do not account for his location between appearances. On the other hand, the enthronement texts may be "telescoping." We must allow for a measure of ambiguity regarding his post-resurrection, pre-ascension existence. But whether or not Michaelis's view is correct, it is legitimate to speak of Jesus as a *heavenly being* from the point of the resurrection; and so, for the purposes of this article, to understand his post-resurrection appearances as in some sense "down."

[49]C. K. Barrett, *The Gospel According to John,* 2nd ed. (London: SPCK, 1978), p. 572.

order to heighten the impression to be made on the skeptical Thomas.[50] Coupled with the teaching of Jesus (v. 27, cf. Lk 24:39), it shows that the Lord is heavenly, not ghostly. Thus the closed doors signify a movement from *above*. The pattern is once again evident: Jesus enters from heaven through the barrier of a closed door, and Thomas functions ironically as the messenger, proclaiming "My Lord and my God!" (v. 28).[51]

The location of the ascension (Acts 1:6-11) is like that of the transfiguration, on a mountaintop (v. 12).[52] Again, the glory of God is indicated by a cloud, which in this case takes Jesus "up . . . into heaven" (vv. 9, 11). Angels appear and pronounce the phenomenon a symbol of the Parousia. This is important, because if the ascension were to be understood as a symbol of his movement from earth to heaven, it would create confusion with both the resurrection and transfiguration narratives. Therefore, we should understand the initial appearance here (v. 6) as a descent from heaven and his taking up as the phenomenon calling for the angelic pronouncement.

Post-Ascension Penetration Texts: Stephen and Saul

In Acts 7:55-56, Stephen, "full of the Holy Spirit, gazed into heaven and saw the glory of God, and Jesus standing at the right hand of God; and he said, 'Behold, I see the heavens opened (διηνοιγμένους), and the Son of man standing at the right hand of God.' " This incident involves opening without penetration, but otherwise it contains the basic elements encountered in other texts: open sky, extraordinary phenomena, and immediate revelatory comment, in this case by the saint and soon-to-be martyr who is thus tantamount to a heavenly messenger. Acts 9:3-7, Saul's conversion, also fits the pattern in significant respects. Saul is

---

[50]Schnackenburg, *John,* 3:331. See Asenath's response to her angel visitant in JosAsen 14:5 (cf. 10:3): "Who is he that calls me, because the door of my chamber is closed, and the tower is high, and how then did he come into my chamber?"

[51]We might observe, alternately, that Jesus acts as messenger by announcing, "Peace be with you" and by showing his wounds as a gesture of triumph, in which case the statement of Thomas functions as an "audience response" à la Lk 2:20; Mt 1:23; 28:8; Jn 20:18; Lk 24:52-53.

[52]See chapter two (pp. 35-61) above for the significance of the mountain vis à vis sky-opening.

blinded by a bright light which comes "from heaven" (ἐκ τοῦ οὐρανοῦ, v. 3). The voice follows immediately, and its mere identification is all the revelation necessary for Saul.[53]

Conclusion

The search through primary sources for evidence of a pattern has turned up several noteworthy items which that should be noted independently of the pattern. Among these are the relation of Ezekiel 43 to the baptism and temple veil stories, the boundary function of John's Nathanael and Thomas narratives, the parallels between *Jos. Asen.* and Luke 1:26-38, and the significance of the sealing stone in the resurrection narratives.

What of the pattern itself? To the extent that it is proper to speak of a pattern or theme, it is doubtful that the Evangelists (except Mark in the baptism-crucifixion parallel) are drawing consciously on the notion of barrier penetration as a signifier of divine self-disclosure. A review of the findings with respect to each Gospel indicates something of the limitations and possibilities of the notion of a connecting theme.

In Mark the three vocal christological statements, the explicit "rendings" and the lack of details about the birth and resurrection result in an apparently deliberate boundary function for the Christ event. The Transfiguration is in the middle either as an anticipation of the resurrection (or Parousia) or as a "presentation" prior to the "enthronement" of the cross. In Matthew, the addition of birth narratives and details concerning the resurrection result in a widening of the boundaries. But while his editorial details add interest to several of the narratives, there is no appearance of conscious structuring apart from the possibility that he understands the Transfiguration as a sort of central fulcrum—the mountain location is convenient—after which Jesus moves toward Jerusalem (Mt 16:21; cf. Mk 10:1). Luke offers numerous additional details at both ends and appears

---

[53]I choose not to include the vision of Peter in Acts 10:9-16, which includes sky-opening and a heavenly voice, not because the passage is visionary (cf. n. 43 above) but because its subject matter falls too far afield of the focus on the career of Jesus. Revelation 4:1-2; 11:19; 19:11—the other NT sky-opening references—are passed over for the same reason.

to make the terminal spatial movement more explicit by means of the ascension story. The fulcrum function of the transfiguration is even more clear than in Matthew (see Lk 9:51). In other respects, as in Matthew, the boundaries do not appear to be part of an organizational scheme. John, on the other hand, expresses his theme of belief in two clearly parallel narratives which employ elements of the form. Here, perhaps most clearly among the Evangelists, we encounter christological affirmations that are calculated as narrative boundaries.

Whatever the degree of conscious planning on the part of the Evangelists, the patterned elements in the various narratives suggest that the barrier penetration texts serve as spatial boundaries of the key events of the gospel story, as indicated in figure 1.

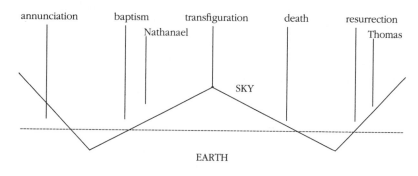

Figure 1. Spatial and chronological movement in penetration texts

It is likely that the Evangelists operated on the assumption that pronouncements from heavenly messengers immediately followed key events, and the balanced placement of these in the respective narrative structures of the Gospels may be, with the exception of the transfiguration account, inevitable. It might also be argued that the connection between these narratives is to be sought in anthropological or psychological terms. Indeed, it does not require a Jung to suggest that deeper forces than literary dependence may be at work here. We should expect that such cataclysmic events as those described in the gospel will find expression in the fundamental terminology of birth and rebirth.[54] The sky, the womb and the tomb represent the basic tensions which must be resolved, the fundamental mysteries which must be explained, the barriers which must be penetrated. And so people lend order to these mysteries by describing them as houses with porches and doors, and they build temples to embody their explanations. The ultimate explainer sends messengers, signs and voices to help the process of resolution. Such an explanation accounts for both the deep, barely intentional nature of the language and interconnected imagery on the one hand, and the occasional explicit pronouncements on the other hand.

Postscript: Divine Penetration and Goddess Alternative

One implication of this research is that the "patriarchalism" of the Gospel narrative is deeper than accommodation to first century expectations of male messiahs. The story employs typological imagery commonly (perhaps universally) embedded in human religion and language, especially in Judaism. Recognition of this imagery may only deepen the divide between traditionalists and feminists, both of whom will respond to these findings with an energetic "I told you so!"

The response of some feminists builds on the supposition that the biblical story of redemption cannot be redeemed from such deep-seated phallocentrism. In their view, such imagery necessarily creates and justifies a male-dominant society.[55] The alternative is a kind of emasculation of the cosmos and a substitution of new religious symbols and language.[56] The sky god, the Father, must go, leaving the earth goddess, the

---

[54]Fourth Ezra 4:41-42 (late first century) is an interesting example of overlapping imagery: "In Hades the chambers of the souls are like the womb . . . these places hasten to give back those things that were committed to them." The Jews and other people buried bodies in the fetal position. Aeschylus *frag.* 44 reads, "The holy sky is drunk with penetrating the earth." See also Zimmerli, *Ezekiel*, 2:441-42 for early Christians on the closed temple of Ezekiel 43 as a type of Mary (only God can enter and exit).

[55]M. Daly, *Beyond God the Father* (Boston: Beacon, 1974), p. 13.

[56]C. P. Christ, "Why Women Need the Goddess: Phenomenological, Psychological, and Political Reflections," in *Womanspirit Rising: A Feminist Reader in Religion* (San Francisco: Harper & Row, 1979), pp. 273-86. See also E. E. Culpepper, "Contemporary Goddess Theology: A Sympathetic Critique," in *Shaping New Vision: Gender and Values in American Culture*, ed. C. W. Atkinson, C. H. Buchanan and M. R. Miles, Harvard Women's Studies in Religion 5 (Ann Arbor, Mich.: UMI Research Press, 1987), pp. 51-71.

Mother, as the foundation of theology and the only appropriate object of worship. Goddess and the female self are closely identified. In one writer's words, "the simplest and most basic meaning of the symbol of Goddess is the legitimacy of female power as a beneficent and independent power."[57] Spirituality is reconstituted around issues of empowerment, community, and care for the environment. A modified, feminized Christ (Christa) and the New Testament message of liberation may be useful to mediate or to signal movement away from the patriarchal law toward egalitarian grace, but ultimately Jesus and New Testament writers are likely to be viewed as vestiges, or at best pioneers. The settlers in the promised land, the children of the kingdom, look for strength not to the hills and the sky beyond; rather, they look within to the female Self and its earth-like cycles.

While this approach is still too radical for most feminists, it has strengths that may increase its influence. It appears coherent, logically consistent, and responsive to important contemporary concerns about human justice and the welfare of the planet. It explores rich symbolic connections between cycles of nature and those of the female body. It borrows from religious traditions of long standing while it stresses the normativity of emerging experience.

One place where the Earth Mother or Goddess theology may be open to challenge is at the point where image and norm meet to influence theology and ethics. The seemingly inescapable conclusion that biblical salvation history is phallocentric—even and especially at the critical juncture of the story of Jesus—does not require or justify patriarchalism in theology and ethics. It is possible to mark out and evaluate the *function* of the male dominant imagery of Scripture, including elements of ongoing relevance, while at the same time finding an egalitarian *application,* the seeds for which are sown in Scripture itself.

A trinitarian deity, a being-in-fellowship, creates humanity in that image: a subcreator who begins as two complementary beings in cooperation to fulfill a purpose. Thus community is born, and community is maintained in part by justice. The Fall is an enormous setback, but the in-

---

[57]Christ, "Why Women Need the Goddess," p. 277.

carnation and resurrection accelerate movement forward. Early indications of this renewed direction include the important place of women in the Gospels and the theological egalitarianism of Galatians 3:28. Even New Testament views of divorce and marriage, while not radical by our standards, point the way toward egalitarian gender roles. While traditionalists may dismiss these texts as few and undeveloped, they are rooted in the creation story and watered by the Lord himself. And all of these texts find their perfection in the image of the kingdom, the perfected community where justice is complete and believers are all feminine as the bride of Christ.

The church must explore such biblical images in the meeting place between sky and earth, where we are called to live as male and female in fellowship and in hope, or many will move toward one or another gender-based belief system. This division will produce neither community nor justice, only at best a balance of power. The call for those suspended between opposing imageries is not to prevail but to strive, theologically and ethically, for a *new* heaven and a *new* earth.

5

FEMINIST HERMENEUTICS
Some Epistemological Reflections

Francis Martin

FEMINIST HERMENEUTICS IS A PARTICULAR INSTANCE OF SOCIOCRITICAL and sociopragmatic interpretation whose critical stance derives from linguistic and philosophical positions established primarily in the twentieth century. An essay of the proportions adequate to the goals of this volume can hardly attempt to assess adequately the whole of feminist hermeneutics nor the critical analysis that forms its basis. I will rather offer a few reflections from a philosophical, primarily epistemological, perspective on feminist hermeneutics as an instance of critical and pragmatic critique.

There will be two parts. I will first look at the theories of language that currently are being used in various forms of social and pragmatic critique.[1] Then, I will try to offer an evaluation of some trends in feminist hermeneutics. In so doing I will also consider feminism as a mode of revisioning the hermeneutic enterprise itself.

KNOWLEDGE, LANGUAGE AND SOCIETY

There are two areas of linguistic philosophy that bear on our question. The first concerns defining the relation between the knower and what is

----

[1]The distinction between sociocritical and sociopragmatic critiques will be discussed more at length below. For a useful treatment see Anthony C. Thiselton, *New Horizons in Hermeneutics: The Theory and Practice of Transforming Biblical Reading* (Grand Rapids, Mich.: Zondervan, 1992), especially chaps. 11, 12.

known, and the second considers the relation between what the knower knows and how language communicates or fails to communicate what is known.

☐ *The knower and what is known.* The modern dilemma in regard to this difficult question is the result of the turn to subject and the turn to language. We will consider each briefly.

☐ *Attention to the subject.* The initial stages of the turn to the subject, whose roots go back to the search for certitude in William of Ockham and the Soncinians, are found, as is commonly acknowledged, in René Descartes.[2] Instructive in this regard is his famous statement:

> I realized that it was necessary, once in the course of my life, to demolish every-thing completely and start again right from the foundations if I wanted to establish anything at all in the sciences that was stable and likely to last.[3]

Descartes finally found these "foundations" in his own self-conscious-ness. It was but a short step from seeking the foundations for knowledge within the self-consciousness of the thinking subject, to searching within the subject for the conditions which would make knowledge possible. This was all the more necessary in that, since Ockham, the world of nature was considered to be an alienated quasi-mechanistic system that was only ren-dered intelligible by the subject's naming of it. Freedom was opposed to the necessity of nature, whose fearsome anonymity was brought into the sphere of humanity by the domesticating force of the mind.[4] Here the fa-mous passage from Kant's *Critique of Pure Reason* comes to mind.

> We have now not merely explored the territory of pure understanding, and care-fully surveyed every part of it, but have also measured its extent, and assigned to everything in it its rightful place. This domain is an island, enclosed by nature

---

[2] I have treated this more at length in Francis Martin, *The Feminist Question: Feminist Theol-ogy in the Light of Christian Tradition* (Grand Rapids, Mich.: Eerdmans, 1994), especially chap. 6.

[3] René Descartes, *Meditations on First Philosophy* 1, in *The Philosophical Writings of Des-cartes*, trans. John Cottingham, Robert Stoothoff and Dugald Murdoch (Cambridge: Cam-bridge University Press, 1985), 2:12. See also the appeal to mathematics as having "firm and solid foundations," *Discourse on Method* 1, trans. Cottingham, 1:114.

[4] For an important study of the modern trajectory in this regard see Louis Dupré, *Passage to Modernity: An Essay in the Hermeneutics of Nature and Culture* (New Haven, Conn.: Yale University Press, 1993).

itself with unalterable limits. It is the land of truth—enchanting name!—surrounded by a wide and stormy ocean, the native home of illusion, where many a
fog bank and many a swiftly melting iceberg give the deceptive appearance of
farther shores, deluding the adventurous seafarer ever anew with empty hopes,
and engaging him in enterprises which he can never abandon and yet is unable
to carry to completion.[5]

The shift from Descartes to Kant, while it accomplished the turn to the
subject, was not homogeneous from every point of view. Descartes
seems to have thought that sense impressions were made directly on the
brain and that consciousness somehow received these impressions and
registered and organized them. Kant, on the other hand, attributed a decisive role to the categorization of sense impressions according to the
pre-existing structure of the thinking subject. In Lonergan's terms,
thought moved from a consideration of the "really out there" to the conviction that all that was actually known was the "really in here."[6] One
oversimplified understanding gave way to another.

A position of critical realism acknowledges the "Copernican revolution" effected by Kant's appreciation of the decisive role of the thinking
subject. But this position insists that by its intentional orientation and
through its receptive capacity the mind—that is, really, the person by using the mind—"imitates" reality by receiving it and transposing it to another level of being.[7] Imitation is not "representation" or "reproduction."
If, when asked to imitate a beautiful table I produce its replica, I do not
imitate, I reproduce. To imitate the table I must transpose it to another
level of being by painting it, photographing it, writing a poem about it
and so forth. In a much more intimate manner, through my mind I imitate reality and can further communicate this original imitation by trans-

---

[5]Immanuel Kant, *Critique of Pure Reason,* trans. Norman Kemp Smith (New York: St. Martin's, 1929), p. 257.

[6]For a helpful study of this point and its relation to feminism see Paulette Kidder, "Woman
of Reason: Lonergan and Feminist Epistemology," in *Lonergan and Feminism*, ed. Cynthia
S. W. Crysdale (Toronto: University of Toronto Press, 1994), pp. 33-48. Also useful and in the
Lonerganian school is Michael H. McCarthy, *The Crisis of Philosophy*, ed. Robert Cimmings
Neville, SUNY Series in Philosophy (Albany: State University of New York Press, 1990).

[7]For another account of this process see Bernard Lonergan, "The Subject," in *A Second Collection: Essays by Bernard Lonergan, S.J.*, ed. B. Tyrell and W. Ryan (Philadelphia: Westminster Press, 1974), pp. 69-86.

posing to yet another level, that of language, what I have conceived.

Because there is what Maritain calls "the basic generosity of existence,"[8] the mind is able—because of its energy, usually called its "light"—to receive what exists and effect an "original concord between thing and intellect," in the "resonant symmetry of knower and known."[9] Truth is not primarily in the proposition but rather in the symmetry, the imitation, of what exists. This view of knowledge lies midway between naive objectivism and the excessive subjectivism, each in his own way, of Descartes and Kant. But while it is midway, it is also on another plane, much like the top of a pyramid is the integrating point of its contrasting sides.

This brief metaphysical description of the act of knowledge is, obviously, quite schematic and leaves room for many different ways of providing a more extensive account. The point of presenting the schema here is to avoid the necessity of repeating it at every turn. Most theories of language and of the interpretation of linguistic artifacts usually begin from an assumed position regarding the metaphysics of knowledge, one that, in a Kantian manner, contents itself with an analysis of the thinking subject that regards it as enclosed, if not entrapped, with a framework of categories and of language. It is to this latter aspect that we now turn.

Language and Communication

In order to understand what language is, it is important to distinguish, along with Kenneth Schmitz, "noetic" and "epistemic" discourse. The first level of discourse, noetic, "is an original, spontaneous, yet receptive discourse under the influence of the concrete situation. . . . It has its own integrity and can find expression in various ways."[10] The second mode of discourse is called by Schmitz "epistemic."

> It is a secondary modification of the discursive character of language, a modification which arises out of the methodical preoccupation with the conditions of truth and the systematic possibilities of cognition. . . . Epistemic discourse is methodically

---

[8]Jacques Maritain, *Existence and the Existent* (New York: Doubleday, 1957), p. 90.
[9]Kenneth Schmitz, "Neither with nor Without Foundations," *Review of Metaphysics* 42 (1988): 15.
[10]Ibid., p. 18.

assertive language about some referent, however vague and elusive that referent may be.[11]

The problem of the relationship between thought and language is somewhat different depending upon whether we are considering noetic or epistemic discourse. Noetic discourse is a more spontaneous actualization of language, though by no means need it be devoid of artistry and creativity. To employ the terminology forged by Ferdinand de Saussure, and to which we will return, the preexisting system of language (*langue*) is less reflectively actualized in a concrete instance of speech or writing (*parole*). Because the language preexists both the communicator and the recipient and is held in common by them, the actualization of language "says something about something";[12] there is a communicative event.

The other level of language, epistemic discourse, is attentive to the manner in which truth is mediated according to preestablished norms of speech communication. At this level certain cognitive values are selected as presuppositions and they operate as the general hermeneutical framework of the discourse. While this level of language allows for greater precision according to predetermined norms, it can have a deforming effect on thought, resulting in an artificially established canon by which all truth claims are measured. As Schmitz observes, this set of interests and norms actually makes a foundation for the form of thought in question. Rather than noetic discourse being the basis for epistemic discourse, the foundations

> are rather the implicit preferences or explicit epistemological decisions taken in favor of a project ordered towards methodically justified truth—a truth justified insofar as the method, horizon, canons and relevant evidence permit.[13]

The irony of this type of closure can be, as we will see, that the most

---

[11]Ibid., p. 19.

[12]This phrase is found in the study by Paul Ricoeur, "Structure, Word, Event," in *The Philosophy of Paul Ricoeur: An Anthology of His Work*, ed. Charles E. Reagan and David Stewart (Boston: Beacon Press, 1978), pp. 109-19.

[13]Schmitz, "Neither with nor Without Foundations," p. 23. Louis Dupré makes a telling observation regarding this type of foundational deformation when speaking of religious truth: "Religion has been allotted a specific field of consciousness ruled by methods of its own, but the final judgment on truth has been withdrawn from its jurisdiction and removed to the general domain of epistemic criteriology." ("Notes on the Idea of Religious Truth in the Christian Tradition," *The Thomist* 52 [1988]: 509.

strident critique of the supposed hegemony of masculinized discourse—one that often accuses the social use of language of being an exercise of power—is itself, especially in the form of a sociopragmatic critique, the most thoroughgoing imposition of an arbitrary set of principles on human discourse that can be imagined.

The story of how, for many, language itself must be considered a means of domination is a narrative that begins with Charles S. Pierce and Ferdinand de Saussure, leads through the misunderstanding of Saussure by Maurice Merleau-Ponty and Roland Barthes, and proceeds in such different directions as Jacques Derrida on the one hand and the Frankfurt School, itself quite diversified, on the other.[14]

Since Saussure's influence was predominant we will restrict ourselves here to an account of his thinking. The most basic principle of linguistics, according to Saussure, is that of the distinction between *langue*, the language system as such, and *parole,* the actuation of the language system in a speech act. In regard to the first of these, *langue,* we should note the following. First, that it is an arbitrary series of signs: there is no intrinsic reason why the term *chair* or *sedilla* should designate something to sit on. Second, *langue* is a closed and finite reality that can become the object of an empirical science. Third, words are only significant in contrast: they have meaning only in their difference from other words. Thus the famous phrase "in a language there are only differences." Fourth and finally, *langue* may be considered as a static system, as a synchronic state or as being in process, a diachronic state; the second state, however, is always to be subordinated to the first.

This last observation has been the reason why Saussure's influence can be felt in the various schools of thought mentioned above and why it has drawn the criticism of such philosophers as Paul Ricoeur. If the language act (*parole*) is totally subordinate to the system, then language can have no history, no real development; it cannot be the vehicle for the freshness and newness of genuine knowledge, especially that of discovery. The second observation, namely that language is a closed system, has been expanded to mean that it is impossible to establish any tran-

---

[14]For a good account of this narrative see Thiselton, *New Horizons,* chap.3.

scendent norms by which language can be judged: this is the position of Derrida on the one hand and much sociopragmatic criticism on the other. However, before moving on to criticize the positions just outlined it will be useful to look at the position of Saussure itself.

Regarding the first point, there is really nothing to say. It has been recognized for a long time that sound images are conventional. Whether there was a time when their sounds were imitative of what they signified is impossible to tell, though it is of some interest to note the onomatopoeic quality of some English words (such as splash, buzz, hum, swish, etc.). The second observation, namely that language, as a system, is closed, has been frequently challenged, very ably, for instance, by Paul Ricoeur.[15] Usage, that is speech (*parole*), *expands* the very system it activates and thus develops it, making it a different system as time goes on: *langue* has a history. The third observation, which is almost a presupposition, is also in need of correction.[16] It is simply not true that the value of a term results solely from the presence of other terms within which it serves to indicate difference. The correlatives "signifier" and " signified" (roughly "word" and "concept") are transposed by their use in a sentence. The whole function of a sentence is to press the various terms into service in order to refer outside itself:

> If we take the sentence as the unit of discourse, then the *intended* of discourse ceases to be the signified correlative to each signifier within the immanence of a system of signs. With the sentence, language is oriented beyond itself. It says something *about* something.[17]

The last point, that *langue* is a static entity, is seen to be false the moment it is understood that in the sentence the word is no longer a lexical phenomenon but part of an utterance whose totality, the sentence or the text, is "saying something about something." Thus, every actualization of

---

[15]In the essay already referred to, "Structure, Word, Event."

[16]Note, for instance, this remark of Saussure, one that could be multiplied many times: "Puisque la langue est un système dont tous les termes sont solidaires et où la valeur de l'un ne résulte que de la présence simultanée des autres." Ferdinand de Saussure, *Cours de Linguistique Général*, 3rd ed., *Études et Documents Payot* (Paris: Payot, 1969), p. 159.

[17]Paul Ricoeur, *Time and Narrative*, trans. Kathleen McLaughlin and David Pellauer (Chicago: University of Chicago Press, 1984), 1:77-78, italics in original.

langue by speech changes the linguistic system itself. The word, having achieved a new actualization, returns to the system with new possibilities, and the system is no longer the same. This is, of course, especially true when the word is pressed into service by a creative genius. In such a case we see an intense paradigm of all linguistic usage. The limited nature of the preexisting code is, on the one hand, a restriction, but it is also the limited context necessary for the exercise of *freedom*, and the creation of a communicative instance. Saussure seems to acknowledge this in some way with his notion of the diachronic dimension of *langue*. However, in the last analysis system absorbs change but is not really changed.

The critiques just made of Saussure's linguistic theories will be important in an assessment of the application of these insights to larger contexts where they have more serious consequences. These latter consequences play a significant role in much of feminist hermeneutics.

From Linguistics to Philosophy

One of the most striking characteristics of the modern linguistic turn is the fact that speculation unavoidably moves from reflections on language to reflections on hermeneutics and then to metaphysics, or at least to a denial of metaphysics. The starting point is the distinction between a given code context and its actualization. The basic distinction between a system of signifiers-signifieds making up a concatenation of necessary conventions and an actualization of the system, while highly developed in Saussure, was by no means unique to him. Roman Jakobsen spoke of "code" and "message" and Charles Pierce used the terms *type* and *token* to refer to much the same phenomenon.[18] Saussure's understanding of the distinction and its function in verbal communication formed the basis for further development when it was extended to include all the forms of communication that constitute a culture. In tracing this development we will restrict ourselves to the principal protagonists who have had the most influence on feminist hermeneutics.

Roland Barthes was one of the first to apply the thinking of Saussure

---

[18]See Thiselton, *New Horizons*, p. 86.

to the social and anthropological dimensions of semiotics. Combining the "hermeneutics of suspicion" of Freud and Marx with the anthropological uses of Saussure initiated by Claude Lévi-Strauss and the idiosyncratic understanding of Saussure by Maurice Merleau-Ponty, Barthes concluded that linguistic codes already embodied not only a language system but also a value system. It is the role of semiotics to unmask the latent operation of this system which for Barthes, in his earlier studies, is the bourgeois power interest. Later in life Barthes went further and considered every semiotic interpretive system to be itself subject to an ulterior analysis, and finally concluded that the process could be endless. In this process the prior analytical language system forms the basis for a metalanguage which then becomes the basis for a further metalanguage and so forth. The net result is that language becomes concerned with language and human interaction is caught up in a web of power-laden language systems where meaning is determinable only in terms of the system itself and its effect on social positioning.

That the study of humanity, its history, language, culture, and customs, etc., is a study of reality as refracted through human activity is a commonplace. Wilhelm Dilthey had already said as much in his understanding of *objectiver Geist:* "Everything on which man has impressed his stamp forms the object of the human studies."[19] Though Dilthey establishes a large gap between the "explaining" of natural phenomena and the "understanding" of human constructs, he does not consider that these latter are so divorced from nature as to constitute a self sufficient world of their own.[20] The difference now is that this world of life expressions has become for Barthes a closed world similar to the closed system or code of Saussure's *langue.* It can be transcended only by constructing a "metaworld" which interprets the first world: we have only the tissue of

---

[19]Wilhelm Dilthey, *Der Aufbau der Geschichtlichen Welt in den Geisteswissenschaften, Gesammelte Schrifte,* vol. 7 (1927; reprint, Berlin: Teubner, 1962), p. 148; cited in Rudolf Makkreel, *Dilthey: Philosopher of the Human Studies* (Princeton: Princeton University Press, 1975), pp. 306-7.

[20]For an example of the complexity and subtlety of Dilthey's thought in this regard see "The Understanding of Other Persons and Their Life-Expressions," in *The Hermeneutics Reader: Texts of the German Tradition from the Enlightenment to the Present,* ed. Kurt Mueller-Vollmer (New York: Continuum, 1988), pp. 152-64.

language. Latent in this view is a distorted view of the relation between knower and known and the subsequent ability of the knower to communicate, not his thoughts only, but *what is known*, the reality itself as it has been transposed by no matter how many successive acts of knowing.

Once the act of communication is restricted to language and the *what* of the communication is not attended to, the world of human creation becomes an arbitrary system hanging in the air, having no meaning and no relation to anything else. Study of Dilthey's *objectiver Geist* degenerates into an effort, "not to discover how consciousness forms a system of being and meaning, but how system forms the being and meaning of consciousness."[21] The only way for those involved in linguistics and hermeneutics to maintain contact not only with the rest of the human race but with their own linguistic practices is to acknowledge, in some form or other, the unity of knower and known in the realm of noetic discourse, and to understand that epistemic discourse arises not only from noetic discourse but also from the *realities* mediated by noetic discourse. There is really no point in discussing those forms of feminist hermeneutics which, consciously or unconsciously, derive from the position that language is only about language. Such a discussion must return to the more basic point: that of the relation between knower and known.[22]

The other philosopher whose influence is widely felt in hermeneutics, and whose ideas find a place in some feminist hermeneutics is Jacques Derrida. The two principal aspects of Derrida's thought that most impinge on hermeneutics are what can be called "diversity" and "pluralism." By diversity I mean the insistence that there can be no such thing as "unity," and by pluralism I mean the notion that there can be no such thing as "uniqueness." I will consider each briefly.

Derrida's basic argument against unity is that the very origins of the concept lie in the ancient metaphysical illusion created by the experience of

---

[21]Robert Detweiler, *Story, Sign and Self: Phenomenology and Structuralism as Literary-Critical Methods* (Philadelphia: Fortress; and Missoula, Mont.: Scholars Press, 1978), p. 17; cited in Thiselton, *New Horizons*, p. 97.

[22]Such a necessity is more easily recognized by feminist philosophers than feminist biblical interpreters. An example can be found in the article by Paulette Kidder, "Woman of Reason."

self-identity: "the experience of the simultaneous self-presence of the speaker to his own speaking."[23] In order to destroy this illusion Derrida sets out to destabilize, decenter and defer the understanding of traditional Western texts. He is engaged in what Jean-François Lyotard has called "the war on totality."[24] Ironically, the war is waged by creating the totality of language as a prior and all-embracing reality, not only in the sense that outside of language there is nothing at all but also in the sense that language itself refers to nothing but itself.[25] Within this totality there is only *diférence/différance.* The Saussurian understanding that words only signify by differing from each other is expanded to include the whole of utterance. Saussure, Derrida maintains, was still too much under the influence of Platonic and Aristotelian metaphysics to understand that difference is more than opposition. Opposition implies a certain unified standpoint from which the opposites, binary or otherwise, can be understood: presence-absence; full-empty; small, medium, large, and so forth. *Différance,* on the other hand, means only that nothing is prior to or explicative of the contrasts in language; they are simply *there*, and their significance is deferred by the endless possibility of new combinations of words creating new *différances.* Diversity, not unity, is the basic category, but it is not a category, nor is it an opposite. Unmoored in a sea of language, the linguistic subject has no stable reality: the subject is destroyed and there is only language. Such is Derridean diversity.

The problem is that such a diversity becomes, despite all protestations to the contrary, a unity, a principle, a totality that encloses all. Betrayed by the very nature of being and the mind, Jacques Derrida the non-subject, free of the illusion of self-identity, has established his subjectivity and identity in the totalizing assertion that these do not exist.

The revolt of Derrida, Barthes and others against the subject-oriented

---

[23]Kenneth Schmitz, "Postmodern or Modern-plus?" *Communio* 17, no. 2 (1990): 157.

[24]Jean-François Lyotard, *The Post-Modern Explained: Correspondence 1982-1985*, trans. D. Barry (Minneapolis: University of Minnesota Press, 1984), p. 16.

[25]For an analysis of the ways in which Heidegger's understanding of Being and language both resemble and differ from Derrida's, see Jarava Lal Mehta, *Martin Heidegger: The Way and the Vision* (Honolulu: University of Hawaii Press, 1967). Briefly, Heidegger sought to dismantle (*Destruktion*) logocentricity in order to arrive at Being no matter how long the wait must be for Being to make itself known. Derrida, on the other hand, wished to deconstruct logocentricity in order to arrive at nothing.

preoccupations of existentialism, itself a derivative of Cartesian and Kantian subjectivity, lead them to a myopic reading of all premodern philosophical texts. These were understood to be nothing more than subtle assertions of the self and its identity rather than what they purported to be, namely attempts to account for reality and our knowledge of it. At the same time, the all-pervasive influence of a Kantian view that language is an opaque creation of the thinking subject led them, as it did Heidegger, to look for a way to penetrate the wall of language—either to discover Being (Heidegger) or to discover the nothing behind language (Derrida). The misguided revolt against Cartesian and Kantian epistemology lies as well at the base of the second important dimension of Derrida's thought, that of pluralism and its close correlate, intertextuality. If there is no unity, there can be no one understanding of a given utterance, particularly a given text. A text is not a unity: "It is no longer a finished corpus of writing, some context enclosed in a book or its margins, but a differential network, a fabric of traces referring endlessly to something other than itself, to other differential traces."[26]

Here, once again, the Saussurian *différance* serves not only to restrict meaning to contrast but also to postpone meaning indefinitely through *différance* or deferral. In such a view, any interpretation is a narrowly restricted photograph of a moving train. Not only are other angles possible but the whole is on the move toward an indeterminate goal which makes any "reading" as good as another. A text is merely an instance of "discourse," it refers to nothing and is merely another instance of the temporary agglutination of the whole cultural and linguistic code with no identity and an indefinitely deferred "meaning." Texts are not instances of intersubjective communication, they are inter-related language phenomena without a subject. Interpretation, in such a view, is but another moment of "intertextuality": the use of a prior text to produce another text whose relation to the former text is but one more "discourse." There can be no interpretation that is more correct or faithful to the "original" text than any other. The irony is that once again, the effort to destroy all identity-centered reliance on

---

[26]Jacques Derrida, *Of Grammatology*, trans. Gayatri Chakravorty Spivak (Baltimore: Johns Hopkins University Press, 1974), p. 41.

"principles" ends by making language the all-inclusive reality that precedes, follows and determines discourse. Language, even in its indeterminacy, has become the principle, that is, the foundation.

While few interpreters are willing to draw such radical conclusions, it is a characteristic of feminist hermeneutics either to speak of "subverting" or "deconstructing" a power-laden discourse or to insist on "multiple competent readings" or other forms of reader-determined interpretations. It is, however, not easy to connect their practice with the philosophies and hermeneutical theories that have, distantly or proximately, initiated them. We will discuss this more at length in a moment.

From Linguistic Philosophy to Social Criticism

Though the movement from linguistics to linguistic philosophy to social criticism occurred often in one and the same thinker, it is not amiss to distinguish the three moments for the sake of clarity. This is particularly important since feminist hermeneutics took its origin as a type of social criticism linked to liberation theology and has in some quarters moved back to a more general hermeneutical stance. There are, therefore, two categories of feminist hermeneutics to be considered: (1) a critique directed mainly to the interpretation of the biblical text and which appeals to the biblical text, or parts of it, as a transcendent source of judgment; (2) a critique which accuses the biblical text itself of being dominated by patriarchy and in need of correction, looking either to praxis or to a prior principle as the ruling criterion. The first of these orientations searches for a "canon" within the canon, while the second looks for a "canon" outside the canon. I have treated of these two approaches at length elsewhere.[27] Here, I want to offer some philosophical reflections particularly on the latter of these two approaches.

> *Sociocritical hermeneutics* may be defined as an approach to texts (or to traditions and institutions) which seeks to penetrate beneath their surface-function *to expose their role as instruments of power, domination, or social manipulation.*[28]

---

[27]Martin, *Feminist Question,* chap. 7.

[28]Thiselton, *New Horizons,* p. 379, italics in original. I am indebted to this part of Thiselton's study for some of the basic orientations of my own treatment of social criticism.

As is evident from the above description by Thiselton, sociocritical hermeneutics accepts the basic notions of Saussure as developed by others—that language and culture are codes that both enable and restrict the extent and nature of their actualization. A critique of these codes can show them to be not only means of communication but also "masks" for "ideologies," that is, socially determined justifications for certain "interests." It is clear that the basic inspiration of this approach is Marxism; the basic model is provided by Freud. Marx highlighted the fact of socially sanctioned forces of alienation while Freud contributed the notion that many of these forces are unconscious and operate like energies in nature. The goal of critical hermeneutics is "emancipation," that is, a bringing to consciousness of the alienating forces that deprive people of genuine self-appropriated activity. With consciousness comes the capacity to change.[29] The manner in which this analysis is carried out determines what kind of critique will be offered. As I mentioned at the beginning of this essay we may, with Thiselton, distinguish between socio*critical* hermeneutics and socio-*pragmatic* hermeneutics. The former seeks for a transcendent norm by which to judge the societal situation. This norm, which in the nature of things must be metacritical and metasystemic, is established in various ways by philosophers such as Habermas, Gadamer and Apel. The latter approach denies that exit from the system is possible and either abandons the search for any extracontextual norm or seeks it in a consensus of the more enlightened or "successful." Thinkers such as Horkheimer, Adorno, Rorty and Fish, though they differ among themselves, are representatives of this view. The application of critical

---

[29]Emancipation is thus defined by Joseph Bleicher: "that process of reflection through which individual and social processes are rendered transparent to the actors involved, enabling them to pursue their [the actors'] further development with consciousness and will—rather than remaining the end-product of a causal chain operative behind their backs" (*Contemporary Hermeneutics: Hermeneutics as Method, Philosophy and Critique* [Boston: Routlege & Kegan Paul, 1980], p. 148). For further analysis of this concept see Alberto Bondolfi, "'Emancipation': Notes de lexicographie et de réception théologique," in *Autonomie: Dimensions éthiques de la liberté*, ed. Carlos-Josaphat Pinto de Oliveira, Etudes d'Ethique Chrétienne 4 (Paris: Cerf, 1978), pp. 161-75. For a basically Christian application of this insight see Paulo Freire, *Pedagogy of the Oppressed*, trans. Myra Bergman Ramos (New York: Herder & Herder, 1970).

hermeneutics effected in feminism can be of either type. Rather than prolong this essay unduly, I will proceed immediately to a discussion of various forms of feminist hermeneutics and point out their affinity to, or dependence upon, the linguistic, philosophical and critical view just outlined.

FEMINIST HERMENEUTICS AS A CRITICAL HERMENEUTIC

We are now in a position to utilize the previous discussion in an analysis of feminist hermeneutics. This will be done in two sections. First, we will look at feminist hermeneutics as a critical procedure and then we will consider valid and invalid ways of using "feminine experience" as a heuristic category.

Feminist Critical Hermeneutics and the Scriptures

The basic question we will ask in this section is that of the relationship between the heuristic framework utilized by various feminist writers and some extracontextual critical norm. There are several possibilities.

1. The text itself can be taken as authoritative. In this case feminists can seek to recover or retrieve overlooked aspects of the text and use them to critique the way the text has been employed to legitimate attitudes and practices that, in fact, are not biblical. It is also possible to seek a deeper and more ample understanding of the biblical text by a better reconstruction of the historical milieu in which it was written. There are several examples of this procedure, which seeks to establish a new and productive perspective.[30]

2. The text itself can be considered to be partially or totally the product of an irremediable patriarchal orientation. In this case the text must be corrected or subverted or destabilized. The question here is that of establishing the norm according to which the deficiencies of the text are to be judged and neutralized. Various answers are given which, if allowance is made for several forms of approach, can be reduced to two. For the first answer, the critical norm is women's experience; for

---

[30]I have treated this point at greater length in Martin, *Feminist Question*, chap. 3.

the second, to use the term of the Frankfurt School, it is "emancipation"—that is, whatever brings about greater clarity concerning oppression and the need for its overthrow is a valid interpretation of the Bible. This second approach is no longer a perspective on the text but a stance in regard to the text which judges its "truth" in terms of its capacity to be used in the *praxis* of liberation.[31] The problem with the first critical norm is that there is no recourse to any norm outside the system that can be brought to bear in judging the resulting interpretation. If the text itself, or the traditional interpretation of it, is the product of a totaling and power-laden form of discourse, where is the norm by which this new understanding can prove itself to be free from the same kind of power-discourse? May it not be a means by which a new elite, through the use of power, imposes itself on the rest of humanity, even in the name of liberation?[32]

3. The text is understood to be no text at all, but merely, in the Derridean fashion, another instance of discourse with no center and no stable "meaning." In this case, the text can say whatever anyone wants it to say, provided of course that this "saying" is only one more moment in an endless series of deferrals or, in a less extreme form, one among the many possible readings.

I wish to give some examples of the second and the third approaches: namely, a critique of the text in the light of an overriding intracontextual norm, and also a treatment of the text that considers the reader to be the effective principle of its meaning. It will be noted that these two understandings of the text are often used conjointly.

Examples of these approaches. One can find a good collection of feminist interpretive writings in the book edited by Elisabeth Schüssler Fiorenza, *Searching the Scriptures*, the first volume of which is concerned with introductory matters and the second volume contains commentary on forty different ancient texts, including those which make up

---

[31]The term *praxis* is being used here in the derived Marxist sense of theoretical considerations that facilitate and direct practice.

[32]An essay which is sensitive to the danger of totalizing even as it makes a strong point regarding womanist theology is Katie G. Cannon, "Womanist Perspectival Discourse and Canon Formation," *Journal of Feminist Studies in Religion* 9, nos. 1-2 (1993): 29-38.

the canon of the Christian New Testament.[33] The choice not to privilege
the texts of the traditional canon is explicit since no text is considered to
have any authority other than as a witness to antiquity and a source of
feminist understanding.[34] In another work Fiorenza states that her interest
in critiquing the Bible stems from the belief "that feminists must develop
a critical interpretation for liberation not in order to keep women in biblical religions, but because biblical texts affect all women in Western society."[35]

In the second volume of *Searching the Scriptures* there is a twofold
movement in many of the commentaries: first, to identify and denounce
texts which are "non-liberating," and second, to perform the same functions in regard to androcentric interpretations of the texts. Sometimes the
commentary does this more from what was defined above as a "perspective," but more often it is done from what was described as a "stance."
Thus, Carolyn Osiek's commentary on Philippians, while it highlights
"everything in the Letter to the Philippians that can contribute to a feminist liberation interpretation or that poses special problems for such an
interpretation,"[36] proceeds in basically an evenhanded fashion. In regard
to the hymn in Philippians 2:5-11 Osiek points out that, in addition to the
traditional interpretation which understands the text to be speaking of
preexistence, divinity, humility, and so on, there is another interpretation
that considers the hymn to be drawing on Wisdom 2:23-24 and describing Jesus' equal status with God to be rather "the primal immortality he
would have had from conception." She goes on to add:

---

[33]Elisabeth Schüssler Fiorenza, *Searching the Scriptures* (New York: Crossroad, 1993-1994).
There are as well several examples of much less totalizing interpretation than the examples
I will adduce here, intepretations that are more based on a perspective than a stance to use
the terms as defined above. Examples would be Leila Leah Bronner, *From Eve to Esther:
Rabbinic Reconstructions of Biblical Women* (Louisville: Westminster John Knox, 1994);
Alice Ogden Bellis, *Helpmates, Harlots, and Heroes: Women's Stories in the Hebrew Bible*
(Louisville: Westminster John Knox, 1994); Joyce Hollyday, *Clothed with the Sun: Biblical
Women, Social Justice and Us* (Louisville: Westminster John Knox, 1994).

[34]"In short, this commentary seeks to transgress canonical boundaries in order both to undo the
exclusionary kyriarchical tendencies of the ruling canon and to renew the debate on the limits, functions, and extent of the canon" (Schüssler Fiorenza, *Searching the Scriptures,* 1:5).

[35]Elisabeth Schüssler Fiorenza, *But She Said: Feminist Practices of Biblical Interpretation*
(Boston: Beacon, 1992), p. 7.

[36]Schüssler Fiorenza, *Searching the Scriptures,* 2:237.

> The second interpretation may be more comprehensible to the contemporary femi-
> nist reader, for whom the categories of superior and inferior, transcendent, preexis-
> tent, and exalted are alien and even offensive.[37]

I find this remark puzzling. Is comprehensibility to the "modern feminist reader" the basic category of interpretation? Is the fact that certain
categories may strike some as "alien and even offensive" a reason for
preferring a certain interpretation? The perception underlying this approach seems to be that the "meaning" of the text lies in its acceptability
to a particular liberationist position. This particular text may be difficult,
but it is one thing to acknowledge its difficulty and another to say that
the norm of interpretation is the aptitude of the text to be pressed into
the service of a preestablished agenda. Such a position capitulates to the
very position that is being opposed: how does such an interpretive move
differ from the alleged androcentric and power-based use of language
that necessitates liberation in the first place? If there is no extra-contextu-
al norm by which a preestablished position may be critiqued we are left
with the notion that interpretation is but one more move in a competing
power game, and that "truth" turns out be "success." I am using Carolyn
Osiek's essay as an example of faulty epistemological presuppositions
precisely because it is such a moderate instance of what can only result
in a breakdown of all communication if its bases are not looked into seriously.

There are other examples in *Searching the Scriptures* of the same
moderate approach but which also would require some serious epistemological reflection. Examples would be Elsa Tamez, who finds an intra-
textual basis in James itself for extending concern for the poor and
marginalized to include women (a perfectly valid principle), and Margaret D. Hutaff, who takes the principle of hospitality and generosity in the
Johannine letters to be the basis for a hermeneutics of suspicion which
rejects "the rhetoric of intolerance" also found in the letters. In a more
radical vein, Anne McGuire applies a similar method in her commentary
of a Nag Hammadi gnostic text, "Thunder, Perfect Mind," an address by a
female deity describing herself and instructing her audience. She de-

---

[37]Ibid., 2:44.

scribes the position she adopts by referring to her effort as being that of a "feminist scholar of early Christian literature who seeks to cross boundaries that devalue, silence, or exclude voices from outside the canon" and "to bring to those voices a wider readership as well as a critical feminist perspective."[38] It seems that Professor McGuire considers the gnostic text she is presenting to be an instance of "early Christian literature." But this is surely to extend the content of Christian tradition to the point where it is a different reality. Why continue to call it Christian? The further question to all these commentators would be that already addressed above to Carolyn Osiek: is the feminist interpretive category so absolute that it justifies any interpretation that furthers feminist goals or is there any way that the interpretive category can itself be judged?[39] In terms of the discussion above, would you acknowledge the truth of the position of such divergent thinkers as Habermas, Apel and Gadamer, or do you agree with Rorty and in another way with Adorno and Horkheimer, or in still another way with Stanley Fish that we have only a series of shifting interpretive contexts with nothing transcending them?[40]

Experience as an Interpretive Category

In addition to a feminist liberationist category, one therefore that is directed to *praxis*, there is the interpretive framework of the experience of women. This latter is intimately linked to the former but it moves us along closer to epistemological concerns. I have treated this approach elsewhere; here I wish only to refer to some of its aspects.[41]

An example of how a feminist-consciousness interpretation can form the basis of a feminist sociopragmatic interpretation is provided by San-

---

[38]Ibid., 2:40. A note at this point refers back to the editorial policy of the editor of the volumes to create "a forum and space where different voices can be heard" (1:ix).

[39]Similar remarks are addressed to Elizabeth Schüssler Fiorenza by Ben Witherington III (*The Jesus Quest: The Third Search for the Jew of Nazareth* [Downers Grove, Ill.: InterVarsity Press, 1995], pp. 163-85) in regard to her *Jesus: Miriam's Child, Sophia's Prophet* (New York: Continuum, 1995).

[40]Another kind of question would have to be asked of commentators in this volume such as Deirdre Good who, commenting on *Pistis Sophia*, another gnostic text, reiterates the position of Derrida and the the deconstructionists: "When women interpret texts, several things happen. The text no longer has a fixed meaning" (Schüssler Fiorenza, *Jesus,* p. 678).

[41]Martin, *Feminist Question,* pp. 194-220.

dra Schneiders. At one point she seems to be seeking for a critical principle within the Bible itself:

> The major problem facing feminist interpreters is how to engage the biblical text in
> such a way that the oppressive potential of the Bible is neutralized, while its liberat-
> ing power is invoked on behalf of the victims of church and society.[42]

Earlier she posed the question this way: "How can a text which is
not just accidentally but intrinsically oppressive function normatively
for a faith community?"[43] This problem arises because the text is con-
fronted with feminist consciousness: "Feminism is a comprehensive
theoretical system for analyzing, criticizing, and evaluating ideas, social
structures, procedures and practices, indeed the whole of experienced
reality. . . . Feminism, although it is an ideology, i.e., a theoretical system, does not begin in theory but in experience."[44] Here we have a
clear description of feminism as a totalizing ideology that is able to analyze just about all of reality but, once again, has no reality by which it
itself can be assessed. What is more, it is an ideology that begins in experience, to which of course the answer is, whose experience? Or may
we conclude that there are as many interpretations as there are experiences?

Another type of controlling interpretive context is provided by those
who, following one or other of the reader-dominated theories of interpretation, offer a selection among what is called "multiple competent
readings." This differs somewhat from the approach adopted by most of
the commentators in *Searching the Scriptures* discussed above in that, in
this mode of interpretation, the text is not exploited for its liberating potential as much as it is read from a very particular angle. One illustrative
example of such a reading is provided by the study of Danna Nolan Fewell and David M. Gunn titled "Tipping the Balance: Sternberg's Reader

---

[42]Sandra Schneiders, "The Bible and Feminism: Biblical Theology," in *Freeing Theology: The
Essentials of Theology in Feminist Perspective*, ed. Catherine Mowry LaCugna (San Francisco: Harper, 1993), p. 49.

[43]Sandra Schneiders, "Feminist Ideology Criticism and Biblical Hermeneutics," *Biblical Theology Bulletin* 19 (1989): 4. She poses a similar question in *Beyond Patching* (Mahwah, N.J.:
Paulist, 1989), p. 54.

[44]Schneiders, *Beyond Patching*, p. 16.

and the Rape of Dinah."[45] This article is critical of Meir Sternberg's interpretation of Genesis 34:1-31,[46] which lists this text as one that "by no great exertion you will be making tolerable sense of the world you are in . . . and the point of it all."[47] Fewell and Gunn maintain that Sternberg, by concentrating on the rights, deceit and actions of the men in the story "serves the patriarchy," and they offer another competent reading from Dinah's perspective.

In a subsequent article Sternberg replied to his critics.[48] He remarked first of all that an individual text, such as Genesis 34:1-31, ought to be read in the context of the whole of the Bible with all of the means it employs to transmit a vision of reality and of human conduct. "With all those coordinates of design and signification left unaddressed, the sad apology for a counter argument amounts to tearing the Dinah example out of the poetic system, the part out of the whole."[49] In this Sternberg is contrasting his reading as "poetic," that is, as analyzing the procedures of the author as he/she *communicates* within a context, with a "political" reading which controls the text within a set of preestablished coordinates while ignoring the wider cultural and textual context of the passage. In the approach of Fewell and Gunn, the text is a neutral object open to any number of competent readings. This is not true of any text and it is especially not the case with a biblical text, which is nothing if not wedded to and expressive of a very particular understanding of reality that is born of faith. In the neutral approach "the text comes to figure as a kind of glorified Rorschach ink blot on which to project one's ideology, among other forms of licensed desire."[50]

---

[45]Danna Nolan Fewell and David M. Gunn, "Tipping the Balance: Sternberg's Reader and the Rape of Dinah," *Journal of Biblical Literature* 110 (1991): 193-211.

[46]Meir Sternberg, *The Poetics of Biblical Narrative. Ideological Literature and the Drama of Reading*, (Bloomington: Indiana University Press, 1987), pp. 445-75.

[47]Ibid., p. 51.

[48]Meir Sternberg, "Biblical Poetics and Sexual Politics: From Reading to Counter-Reading," *Journal of Biblical Literature* 111 (1992): 463-88.

[49]Ibid., p. 465. Later he correctly criticizes the fixation of Fewell and Gunn on the individual text with their consequent interpretation that the author (presumably a patriarchalist) does not condemn the rape itself (p. 473). This, of course, ignores the whole biblical context shared by both author and audience. In all of this summary of the article, I am necessarily simplifying a complex argument. For the full argument, see Sternberg's reply itself.

[50]Ibid., p. 470.

Feminist hermeneutics is a varied reality, each type of which is a subset of some broader hermeneutical theory and practice. As such, it inherits the various epistemological positions either explicitly embraced or unconsciously assumed to be characteristic of these theories. Most of these theories take a Kantian bias in favor of a subjectively constructed and interpreted reality. For this reason interpretation becomes interpretation of *words* and why and how they are used. Lost in this is the basic understanding that the unity between communicator and recipient is not merely words but the *reality*, no matter how complex and humanly fashioned, which is mediated by the words. When this is lost, interpretation becomes one more act of knowledge according to the conditions of the subject and communication becomes the art of using words in order to achieve a specific agenda. When language is considered to be only a means of reinforcing power, then we have abandoned not only any possibility of communication but have also embraced a theory of knowledge that traps the thinking subject within her or himself, and we deny that any real knowledge of reality is possible. Unless there is agreement on the nature of the act of knowing, interpretation of how this is communicated cannot but be divided. Once again we see that there is an ineluctable rhythm: we move from interpretation to epistemology to the metaphysics of knowledge. Attempts to deny or short circuit this rhythm only serve to reinforce its necessity. Because this is so, I wish to spend the concluding portion of this essay looking at the question of a specifically feminine way of knowing, and to offer some comments on how such a mode might be described.

Feminist Epistemology

In this last section I wish to indicate another manner in which the faulty linguistic theories discussed earlier can be corrected. This, I suggest, is by a more sensitive study of what is valid in the notion of a feminist epistemology.[51] I will offer two sets of reflections: the first concerns what I will call a

---

[51]In this essay I restrict myself to epistemological issues. For a broader approach to the need for a deeper understanding of women see my essay, "The New Feminism: A New Humanism?" *Josephinum Journal of Theology,* forthcoming.

feminine "point of view"; the second will be an attempt to use this hypothesis as a way out of the impasse in much modern interpretive theory which, knowingly or unknowingly, has set up a series of conflicts between competing foundations for knowledge, whereas, in fact, knowledge is neither an edifice constructed on inhibiting foundations nor a purely subjective creation whose foundation is the self of the thinking subject.

I would like to offer here some reflections on the possibility of understanding what we mean when we speak of a specifically feminine perception of reality and the relation of this to the notion of women and men being related analogically. First, I am speaking of an act of knowing and judging that is intentional. The thinking person is in touch with reality however many times that reality has been transposed or sublated[52] by his or her individual acts of knowing, reflecting and judging, and no matter how many times the perception of reality has become part of a humanized environment, Dilthey's *objectiver Geist*. When this fact is lost sight of, people seek for some sort of foundation for knowledge, some place to stand and to which appeal is made for justification of any assertion which must, for validity, derive from these foundations. The search for foundations derives from a faulty metaphysics of knowledge, one that has misunderstood the true nature of the thinking subject as a *person*, and has restricted the act of knowledge to an isolated function of "the mind" whose role, in one way or another, is not to imitate reality but to represent it, or in Lonergan's terms, to "picture" it.[53] From this point on it makes little difference whether one accepts the immanentist subject of Kant or rebels against it as far as Barthes and Derrida or even Adorno and Horkheimer. The result is the same: there is a war of foundationalisms, with each side striving to impose its foundation on the other. Some feminists, and most feminist hermeneutics, have inherited this war and, as

---

[52]What I mean by sublation is best described in this text of Bernard Lonergan who says he is following Karl Rahner rather than Hegel: "What sublates goes beyond what is sublated, introduces something new and distinct, puts everything on a new basis, yet so far from interfering with the sublated or destroying it, on the contrary needs it, includes it, preserves all its proper features and properties, and carries them forward to a fuller realization within a richer context" (*Method in Theology* [New York: Herder & Herder, 1972], p. 241).

[53]The reader is referred to the discussion earlier concerning the knower and the known, and to Lonergan, "Subject."

we have seen, seek to impose their own type of borrowed epistemological theory, its own foundations, on the rest of the culture. This explains the totalizing tendency of such diverse hermeneutical positions as sociopragmatism, the insistence on woman's experience as a ruling epistemological matrix, and the fixation to find androcentric and patriarchal elements everywhere, with the corresponding license to reinterpret texts from a preestablished hermeneutical framework: these are all foundationalisms deriving from the more theoretical foundationalisms already discussed.

A Feminine "Point of View"

There is an amazing amount of literature that concerns itself with the possibility of there being something specific in a feminine way of knowing, something more basic and more objective than appeals to "women's experience." I will attempt to give here a brief overview of these scholarly efforts.

First of all there are those studies which seek to find a physical basis for this different way of knowing. These studies are extremely important because they are able to respect the fact that feminine and masculine are primarily *physical* characteristics that are then sublated throughout the whole of the human personality. Among philosophers the scholar who has contributed most to an understanding of how physicality enters into the constitution of the human person, male and female, is Prudence Allen.[54] Based on her work, I would propose that we look upon the human person through the image of a tetrahedron. The base of this figure is the fundamental physical reality of the human person, therefore, female or male. The sides are "masculinity" and "femininity," while the whole complex is given its act of relational existence by its personhood. There is thus a male manner of being masculine and feminine and a female manner of being masculine and feminine, and this manner is established by the pervasive fact of male or female physicality modified by cultural interaction and personal decision. An important work that can help in tracing out how this successive sublation of physicality takes place in and through the symbolic

---

[54]See especially her "Fuller's Synergetics and Sex Complementarity," *International Philosophical Quarterly* 32 (1992): 3-16; see also "A Woman and a Man as Prime Analogical Beings," *American Catholic Philosophical Quarterly* 66, no. 4 (1992): 465-82.

and cultural interaction of the "psychic body" is that of Antoine Vergote.[55]

   This line of philosophical thought receives corroboration in the many studies being carried out on the differences between women and men. There are first of all the empirical investigations in regard to physical and psychophysical factors, whose results are now being published.[56] Then there are the studies on women's perceptions and, broader still, analyses of a feminine approach to different areas of thought, sometimes in multi-discipline volumes.[57] Other studies concentrate more on the question of women's way of knowing,[58] and finally others consider the question of religion and gender from an epistemological perspective.[59] The most promising of these studies seek to avoid the extremes of a univocal and reductive understanding of women and men on the one hand—one that restricts the physical differences to "body parts"—and an equivocal understanding that maximizes the differences to such a point that there is really nothing in common. In seeking a point between these poles feminist thought is working toward some form of analogical predication: this is most promising.[60]

[55]Antoine Vergote, "The Body as Understood in Contemporary Thought and Biblical Categories," *Philosophy Today* 35 (1991): 93-105.

[56]Among those studies see Anne Moir and David Jessel, *Brain Sex: The Real Difference Between Men and Women* (New York: Lyle Stuart, 1991); Robert Pool, *Eve's Rib: The Biological Roots of Sex Differences* (New York: Crown, 1994).

[57]Such as Deborah L. Rhode, ed., *Theoretical Perspectives on Sexual Difference* (New Haven, Conn.: Yale University Press, 1990); Toril Moi, ed., *French Feminist Thought: A Reader* (Oxford: Basil Blackwell, 1987), especially the article by Luce Irigaray, "Sexual Difference," pp. 118-30; Seyla Benhabib, Judith Butler et al., eds., *Feminist Contentions. A Philosophical Exchange* (New York: Routledge, 1995).

[58]An early study in feminine ethical perceptions was by Carol Gilligan, *In a Different Voice* (Cambridge, Mass.: Harvard University Press, 1982). More recent examples would be Alison M. Jaggar and Susan R. Bordo, eds., *Gender/Body/Knowledge* (New Brunswick, N.J.: Rutgers University Press, 1989); and Mary McCanney Gergen, ed., *Feminist Thought and the Structure of Knowledge* (New York: New York University Press, 1988).

[59]Ursula King, ed., *Religion and Gender* (Cambridge, Mass.: Blackwell, 1995), especially the valuable introduction by the editor. There are studies particularly from a Lonerganian viewpoint; already noted is Cynthia S. W. Crysdale, ed., *Lonergan and Feminism* (Toronto: University of Toronto Press, 1994), especially the article by Paulette Kidder; also Nancy Ring, "Intentionality Analysis, the Church and Women's Spirituality," in *Lonergan Workshop* 9, ed. Fred Lawrence (Boston: Boston College, 1993), pp. 195-208. In a different vein, Grace M. Jantzen, "Sources of Religious Knowledge," *Literature and Theology* 10, no. 2 (1996): 91-111; Mary McClintockl Fulkerson, "Changing the Subject: Feminist Theology and Discourse," *Literature and Theology* 10, no. 2 (1996): 131-47.

[60]Valuable studies on analogy in general are Gregory P. Rocca, "Aquinas on God Talk: Hover-

Beginning from the position that it is the subject, or better the person, who knows and not merely the mind, I would like to offer a reflection on a possible way of understanding how a body-person, male or female, with a combination of femininity and masculinity, can be said to have a different point of view while knowing the same objective reality. In this attempt I am necessarily going to have to oversimplify and not take into account the many sublated levels within the personality that make up the actual knowing woman or man.

I would like, first of all, to employ a distinction used in phenomenology between *aspect* and *profile*.[61] Let us imagine that we are both looking at a statue, Michelangelo's "Moses" for example, and that we are standing on different sides of the statute. The statue presents an "aspect" of itself to you that is different from what it presents to me. Both of us are able to supply in some way what is "absent" to us, but we are beholding different aspects. Let us suppose that I then come and stand exactly where you are. Then we both receive the same aspect, but, because we are different persons, with all that this means not only metaphysically but also historically, culturally, and so forth, we still have a different *profile* on the statue. Our knowledge is both common and uniquely personal, and we can enrich each other by sharing through dialogue what this statue, even under its various aspects, means to us.

So far I have followed the phenomenological theory as it is currently understood. Now I would like to introduce another dimension, as it were: one that is between aspect and profile. I wish to call this dimension a "point of view" both because the word *perspective* can have foundationalist overtones in some modern discussions and because the expression "point of view" has such a rich history in narratology.[62] While I do not mean to imply that what I

---

ing over the Abyss," *Theological Studies* 54 (1993): 641-61; "*Res Significata* and *Modus Significandi* in Aquinas," *The Thomist* 55 (1991): 173-98; W. Norris Clarke, "Analogy and the Meaningfulness of Language About God: A Reply to Kai Nielsen," *The Thomist* (1976): 61-95. The most apposite study on analogy and men and women is Allen, "Woman and a Man".

[61] I am indebted here to the study by Robert Sokolowski, *Husserlian Meditations,* Northwestern University Studies in Phenomenology and Existential Philosophy (Evanston, Ill.: Northwestern University Press, 1974), especially chap. 4, "Identity in Manifolds."

[62] For a discussion of this expression and some of the relevant literature see Francis Martin, introduction to *Narrative Parallels to the New Testament*, SBL Resources for Biblical Study 22 (Atlanta: Scholars Press, 1988).

am discussing is a point of view in the narratological sense, I do mean that this dimension of the act of knowledge is significant in its own way and needs to be taken into account. Given the fact that we are discussing knowledge as being the result of the interaction between reality and an integral thinking subject, and given the fact that the integrity of the subject includes not only personal history, culture, place in society, and so on, but even more basically gender, we are entitled to try to identify that particular dimension of knowledge which is gendered by a special name. I propose "point of view." All the studies we have discussed up to now, with their analysis of the impact of gender on the thinking body, must be accounted for. Aspects such as the lived experience of body, the manner of relating to physical reality, the difference in capacities to think spatially, to think concretely and personally, to use language well, enter into the point of view of women and men. This is more fundamental than the way cultural norms tend to either foster or inhibit these basic differences, but cultural factors that have become part of gender thinking must be taken into account as well.

What does "point of view" consist in? It is more intimate to the thinking subject than aspect, but it is not as personal, in the metaphysical sense of this word, as is profile. What I am describing has to do with the female manner of being masculine and feminine and the male manner of being masculine and feminine. Philosophically, the difference may be described in terms of modality, but this must be given a "thick description" through the self-appropriation of women and men who begin to be sensitive to this modification of the person and its influence in the act of knowing. As this process continues, and as the dialogue continues, it will be more and more possible to articulate exactly what the "point of view" really is. For now we must be grateful to those who are making the initial attempts to describe this in whatever terms they are using. Equally important to this enterprise is narrative itself where point of view will be operative within its proper domain and be mediated artistically. It is here as well that the distinction between noetic and epistemic discourse has an important application.

It is often said that Western and Eastern Christians must learn from each other, that at the present moment we are looking at reality, especially revealed reality, with only one eye. In order to have true perspective we must have two eyes, and this is more important for the West since we are in a more dominant position. As I read the recent feminist work on epistemology, it occurred to me that we have here as well, and more profoundly, the need to listen to women who are articulating what it means to "think like a woman" and in this way begin to see things with two eyes.[63] This approach, one done in dialogue, will be extremely important for the church and should lead to a genuine development of Christian anthropology. The way is open for such dialogue, and has indeed been followed by several thinkers, men as well as women.

It is hoped that this move from hermeneutics to epistemology will provide the critical norms needed to assess linguistic and sociopragmatic approaches that have not yet emerged from a restrictive foundationalism. Epistemology, considered "with both eyes open," will lead us to a deeper understanding of the metaphysics of knowledge, one that takes account of the whole thinking person, female or male. The achievement of this grasp of intentionality will probably pass through a greater appropriation of the act of experiential faith. This analysis will then provide a basis and a driving motive to articulate how things are known in light of faith.[64] It will not be the first time that faith has protected reason. Where there is knowledge there can be communication, and because of this there can be communion of persons and that profound and mutual conversion that leads to a more authentic presence among us of the kingdom of God.

---

[63]It was at this point that I came across the book edited by Patricia Altenbernd Johnson and Janet Kalven, *With Both Eyes Open: Seeing Beyond Gender* (New York: Pilgrim, 1988), particularly the opening chapter by the editors.

[64]It may be that a theological use of phenomenology can illuminate the way that faith gives certitude about the divine realities and go on from there to develop a metaphysics of knowledge. This would not be unlike the manner in which faith certitude and knowledge regarding the divine and human reality of Jesus Christ finally gave birth to an understanding of person (see John D. Zizioulas, *Being As Communion*, vol. 4 of *Contemporary Greek Theologians* [Crestwood, N.Y.: St. Vladimir's Seminary Press, 1985]). For a discussion of faith as a way of knowing see Martin, *Feminist Question*, chap. 1; for an excellent discussion of this notion in the patristic age see Thomas F. Torrance, *Divine Meaning: Studies in Patristic Hermeneutics* (Edinburgh: T & T Clark, 1995), especially chapter 6, "The Hermeneutics of Clement of Alexandria."

6

LITERAL TALK OF GOD
Its Possibility & Function

William P. Alston

IN THIS ESSAY I WILL DEFEND THE VIEW THAT LITERAL SPEECH ABOUT God is possible and explore the place of literal discourse in theology. I will consider reasons that are offered to show literal talk of God to be impossible; they will be found wanting. Those who reject literal talk of God offer various alternatives. The one I shall be most concerned with is metaphoricity. Though metaphor obviously bulks large in discourse about God, including theology, I shall plump for the position that it is not only possible but crucially important that we also be able to make literal statements about God.

The denial of the possibility of literal speech about God is omnipresent in twentieth-century Christian theology of a revisionist stripe. Here are a few examples. Note that in some cases the position is put in terms of the *application of concepts* rather than in terms of *literal speech*. I take these idioms to be equivalent, for a predicate term's having a meaning amounts to its expressing a concept. Otherwise put, a meaning of a predicate term "correlates" it with a certain property, so that to (literally) apply the predicate to X is to claim that X has that property. And making that claim is equivalent to applying the concept of that property to X. I can literally apply the term *heavy* to X if and only if I can apply the concept of heaviness to X.

John Hick makes the following comments:

None of the concrete descriptions that apply within the realm of human experience can apply literally to the unexperiencable ground of that realm.[1]

Our language can have no purchase on a postulated noumenal reality which is not even partly formed by human concepts. This lies outside the scope of our cognitive capacities.[2]

Though Hick does not use the term *God* here, the "noumenal reality" of which he speaks is conceived by him as the ultimate supreme reality to which our religious responses are directed.

Gordon Kaufman

Somewhat like Hick, Gordon Kaufman in an early book, *God the Problem* (1972), distinguishes between the "real referent" and the "available referent" of "God." The former is the independently existing ultimate reality, while the latter is an "imaginative construct" we devise in our attempts to relate ourselves to the former.

The real referent for "God" is never accessible to us. . . . It must remain always an unknown X, a mere limiting idea with no content. It stands for the fact that God transcends our knowledge in modes and ways of which we can never be aware and of which we have no inkling. . . . The real referent can never be more than a limiting concept for us, a strong reminder that our ideas and experience are far from adequate.[3]

God is ultimately profound Mystery and utterly escapes our every effort to grasp or comprehend him. Our concepts are at best metaphors and symbols of his being, not literally applicable.[4]

But just what are these people denying? The slogan "We cannot speak literally of God," if *it* is construed literally, says that it is impossible for anyone to make a statement with the intention of applying some term literally to God. But that is obviously false. Millions of people have spoken with such an intention. I frequently do so. If the thesis is to be taken seriously, it will have to be construed as denying that such an intention can

---

[1]John Hick, *The Interpretation of Religion* (New Haven, Conn.: Yale University Press, 1989), p. 246.

[2]Ibid, p. 350.

[3]Gordon Kaufman, *God the Problem* (Cambridge, Mass.: Harvard University Press, 1972), p. 85.

[4]Ibid, p. 95.

succeed. What kind of success? The answer would seem to be: "saying something *true*." Look back at our citations. When Hick says that no descriptions can apply literally to God, he is naturally understood as saying that no such descriptions can be *true* of God. When Kaufman says that God "utterly escapes our every effort to grasp or comprehend him" and "our concepts are . . . not literally applicable" he is saying that we can never succeed in *truly* applying a concept to God.[5]

Even though "we can speak literally about God" is to be understood as "we can make *true* literal statements about God," I will not seek to show in this essay that any particular literal statement about God is true. I will confine myself to arguing that we *can* make true literal statements about God, that it is not in principle impossible to do so. There is nothing about God and us and our interrelations that rule this out.

But the antiliterality thesis must be further qualified if it is to be worth discussing. Presumably no one who thinks we can refer to God would deny that some *negative* predicates truly apply to God. These might include "not limited in knowledge," "not possessed of evil intentions" and "not identical with Jesse Helms." Nor would any sensible person deny the literal applicability of all extrinsic, relational predicates like "believed by Aquinas to be atemporal." To accommodate these points, let's formulate the thesis as follows: "No *positive, intrinsic* predicates we can formulate are literally true of God."

One distinction about antiliteralists that is important for this essay is that between *realists* and *nonrealists* about God. I use these terms here to mark the distinction between those who do and those who do not suppose there to be some reality (independent of human thought, talk, activity, feeling, and attitudes) to which we refer with the word *God*. Hick and Tillich, as well as a metaphoricist like McFague, are realists in this minimal sense. But this is by no means true of all those antiliteralists who are concerned to preserve God-talk. In Gordon Kaufman's later works (1981, 1993) the "real referent" drops out of sight. There is no

---

[5]Similarly, to go far back beyond the twentieth century, when Gregory of Nyssa says that God is "incapable of being grasped by any term, or any idea, or any other device of our apprehension," he should be read as saying that we cannot *succeed* in cognitively grasping what God is like in himself.

longer any suggestion that the "available referent" mediates a grasp of a transcendent "real referent." God is now solely *within* an "imaginative construct" or conceptual scheme. Living in relation to God *is* living in the world-view that has God as its focus.[6] "We should, in our attempt to construct conceptions and pictures of humanity, the world, and God, try to speak only in terms of *this world*, of the realities of *this life*."[7] Here we have a full-blooded nonrealism about God. "God-talk" is construed as a particular way of talking about segments of reality that do not include anything identifiable as God. The talk is valued for its expression of attitudes and its orienting function for human life. This represents the most radical alternative to supposing that we can say things that are literally true of God. In this essay I will confine myself to realist antiliteralists (including the earlier Kaufman), those who take it that there is a transcendent reality about which we speak somehow or other.

Literal Language

Before we can usefully consider what to say about the denial of literal speech about God, we must be more explicit about the concept of a literal use of a term. I believe that it can best be explicated in contrast with figurative uses, particularly metaphorical. The first thing to note here is that the distinction concerns *speech* rather than *language*. This crucial but widely neglected distinction was set out in classic form by Ferdinand de Saussure (1916). Briefly, a language is an abstract system, a system of sound types. The systematicity is both "internal" and "external." The phonology, morphology, and syntax of a language constitute its internal system, the ways its elements can be combined to form larger units. The external system is given by the semantics, the way units of the language "represent" aspects of the world, what we talk about. Speech, on the other hand, is the *use* of language in communication.

The fact that a given word or phrase has the *meaning(s)* it has is a fact about the language; it is part of its semantics. Thus it is a semantic

---

[6]Gordon Kaufman, *The Theological Imagination* (Philadelphia: Westminster Press, 1981), p. 38.

[7]Gordon Kaufman, *In Face of Mystery: A Constructive Theology* (Cambridge, Mass.: Harvard University Press, 1993), p. 326.

fact about English that the word *player* has the following meanings:

1. an idler
2. one who plays some (specified) game
3. a gambler
4. an actor[8]

The word *literal*, on the other hand, stands for a certain way of *using* words and other meaningful linguistic units. As such, it stands in contrast with *figurative* uses of terms—"figures of *speech*," as they are appropriately called—the most familiar of which is metaphor.

Since we are specifically interested here in the possibility of literal applications of terms to God, I will confine my explanation of *literal* to uses of predicates in singular subject-predicate statements. As I pointed out above, when I use a predicate term literally in such a statement I make the claim that the property signified by that predicate is possessed by the subject of the statement, what the statement is about. If I make a literal use of "player" in saying "He's one of the players," I am claiming, let's say, that he has the property specified in the fourth definition in the above list. And if my statement is true, if he really does have that property, then we may say that "player" is *literally true* of him, *literally applies* to him.

Then what am I doing when I use a term metaphorically? Shakespeare's Macbeth says, "Life's . . . a poor player that struts and frets his hour upon the stage and then is heard no more." It is clear that life is not really an actor, and that it does not possess any of the other properties signified by *player*. Hence Macbeth, if he has not totally taken leave of his senses, is not claiming that life has any of these properties. Instead, in using the term metaphorically he is doing something like this. He "presents" his hearers with the sort of thing to which the term, in a given meaning, literally applies, in this case an actor: call that the *exemplar*. And he "suggests" that the exemplar can usefully be taken as a model of the *subject*, life. He suggests that by considering a minor actor who plays his part and then disappears from view one will be put in mind of certain features of the subject, life.

As so far characterized, a metaphorical statement would not seem to be making any truth claim about its subject, other than the implicit claim

---

[8]See *Webster's New Collegiate Dictionary* (1959).

that it is enough like the exemplar to make the exemplar a useful model for thinking about it. Now this may sometimes be a complete account of the speaker's intentions; sometimes she is simply suggesting a model that feels right. But more usually the speaker is concerned to exploit the model in a particular way; she will have in mind one or more particular points of resemblance that she means to attribute to the subject. If I say "Religion has been corroded by the acids of modernity," I am not just throwing this image up for grabs, leaving it to my audience to make of it what they will. I mean to assert that certain (unspecified) aspects of modernity have reduced the commitments, influence, or salience of religion in contemporary life.

Literal speech is often confused with quite distinct matters. In philosophical circles one finds people who should know better using "literal meaning" for the meaning of sentences that can be used to make factual claims. But we can use terms just as literally in requests, questions, and expressions of attitudes as in factual statements. I can be speaking as literally when I say "Please hand me the book" as when I say "That is a book." Again, literal speech is sometimes falsely conflated with *precise* speech. But I can use words literally and be speaking vaguely or otherwise indeterminately. The standard meaning of many terms, for example, *bald*, is vague. If I use *bald* literally in saying of Jones that he is bald, I will inevitably be speaking with less than complete precision.

A different set of confusions is characteristic of much contemporary theology.

> On the issue of the truth of religious language, there are continuing, powerful conservative religious movements that insist on the literal reference of language to God. . . . This tendency is linked with fear of relativizing Scripture through historical criticism and a refusal to accept a plurality of interpretive perspectives. The Bible, says this movement, *is* the Word of God; . . . the Bible is inerrant. The Bible is a sacred text, different from all other texts, and not relative and pluralistic as are all other human products. The Bible becomes an idol; the fallible, human words of Scripture are understood as referring correctly and literally to God. . . . If the Bible says that God is "father" then God is literally, really, "father"; the word *father* and the associations of that word truly refer to God's nature.

But there is, I believe, an even deeper reason why religious literalism runs rampant in our time. . . . We do not think in symbols in the way our forebears did. . . . The ancients were less literalistic than we are. . . . Ours is a literalistic mentality; theirs was a symbolical mentality.

Before we leave this preliminary overview of literalism and the truth of religious language, it is necessary to add a word from social anthropology about *why* people cling to religious systems with such fervor. . . . We depend, says Geertz, so deeply on our constructions for our most basic sense of sanity that any threat to them is a threat to our very being. Thus, one can conclude that people will be less open, less imaginative, less flexible during times of threat. They will be more literalistic, absolutist, dogmatic when the construction which orders their world is relativized.[9]

McFague here constructs a gigantic purée in which "literal reference of language to God" is blended with inerrancy about Scripture, rejection of historical criticism, refusal to accept a plurality of interpretive perspectives, bibliolatry, a lack of a "symbolic mentality" and a dogmatic absolutist attitude. We will make no progress at all in discussing the possibility of literal speech about God unless we disengage it from these adventitious associations. I can aspire to make literally true statements about God, and even succeed in doing so, without being idolatrous about the Bible, while recognizing and welcoming historical criticism and a variety of hermeneutic perspectives, while also "thinking symbolically" and while being free from a dogmatic adherence to certain formulations—clinging to them desperately for fear of losing my identity.

Elsewhere McFague suggests that if we understand talk about God to be *literal*, we are *identifying* our talk, our words with God.

Unless one has a sense of mystery surrounding existence, of the profound inadequacy of all our thoughts and words, one will most likely identify God with our words: God *becomes* father, mother, lover, friend.[10]

But this conflation is no better than the ones discussed above. It is absurd to suppose that one cannot speak literally about X without identifying one's speech with X. All of us speak literally of things about us every day. But if I were to identify my house with the word *house* or my wife

[9]Sallie McFague, *Metaphorical Theology* (Philadelphia: Fortress, 1982), pp. 4-7.
[10]Ibid., p. 2.

with the word *wife,* I would be a prime candidate for commitment (not religious commitment!). Why should it be any different with literal speech about God? I don't wish to minimize the danger of bibliolatry or other tendencies to divinize worldly realities. But the idea that engaging in literal speech amounts to such idolatrous identification does not survive a moment's reflection.

So long as we lump all these things together under the rubric of "literalism," our thinking about the issues will be fatally confused. Let us use the term *literal* literally, and when we ask about the possibility of literal speech about God, talk about *that*, rather than these other things with which it gets confused.

The Antiliteralist Position

I now turn to reasons that antiliteralists give for their position. I will begin with the weakest ones and move on to what can be taken more seriously. In this discussion I will use *ineffable* (not unreasonably, I think) to mean "not susceptible to true literal characterization."

The least serious reasons are epistemological ones, which consist in pointing out one or another deficiency in our cognition of God. The line is that since we are unable to acquire knowledge of, or belief about, God that meets certain epistemic standards, the reasonable conclusion is that none of our concepts apply to God. Various epistemic deficiencies are alleged. Kaufman is typical in denying that God can be *directly* experienced or known, saying, "the real referent [of "God] is beyond our direct observation or encounter."[11] And he seems to think that this shows that God is inaccessible to our thought and discourse. "The real referent for "God" must remain always an unknown X, a mere limiting idea with no content." But even if Kaufman is right in denying that we have any *direct* experience of God,[12] that is far from showing that we have no knowledge of God at all. After all, there is indirect as well as direct knowledge. If we could have knowledge only of what is directly observable, we

---

[11]Kaufman, *God the Problem*, p. 85. See also pp. 84, 88, 113, 238.
[12]For an argument to the contrary see William P. Alston, *Perceiving God: The Epistemology of Religious Experience* (Ithaca, N.Y.: Cornell University Press, 1991).

would be in a far worse epistemic position than we are. Among the things we know about that are not given directly to our experience are social institutions, historical movements, nations, the mental states of other persons, the fine structure of matter, the biochemistry of living cells, and the formation of galaxies.

But Kaufman and others deny that we have any knowledge at all of "God." Hence we must scrutinize the second step of the argument—from unknowability to ineffability.

> Any supposed knowledge of God always remains unverifiable and controversial and may be completely mistaken.[13]

> The word "God" . . . designates a transcendent reality never accessible to our observation or even our speculation.[14]

Although I do not agree that we can have no knowledge of God, I will point out that even if we don't, it by no means follows that none of our concepts apply to God.

The basic point is this: Whether a given concept, such as *forgiving*, applies to God is a matter of whether it is ever *true* of God that he forgives someone. And we must be careful not to confuse this question with the question of whether we ever *know*, or can know, that God has forgiven someone. Whether a proposition is *true* depends on whether the relevant segment of reality (the one it is about) is as the proposition says it to be. That is completely independent of whether you or I or any human being, or any other cognitive subject, knows the proposition to be true or false. This is an elementary conceptual distinction that has been widely ignored in the last 150 years or so, during which we have been inundated by a plethora of epistemic conceptions of truth.[15]

I have been conceding for the sake of argument that we have no knowledge of God and arguing that even if that is so, it by no means follows that none of our concepts truly apply to God. But this may seem to be cold comfort. What good is the mere possibility of literal application

---

[13]Kaufman, *God the Problem,* p. 85.

[14]Ibid., p. 96.

[15]In *A Realist Conception of Truth* (Ithaca, N.Y.: Cornell University Press, 1995) I have criticized all these epistemic theories of truth and defended a "realist" conception.

of certain terms to God if we can't know which of them apply? My response is that although knowledge of God would be a fine thing, it is not the only alternative for religious faith. There is, after all, a long tradition according to which although faith, on its cognitive side, does not amount to knowledge, it still amounts to enough of a grasp of the nature of God and our relations thereto to provide sufficient guidance for our lives.[16] Thus even if we should lack knowledge of God, that leaves open the possibility of rational faith that some of our concepts are true of him.

Paul Tillich is famous for arguing that if we accord "ultimate commitment" to anything we are able to conceptualize, we have fallen into idolatry, giving infinite significance to something that is not itself metaphysically ultimate.[17] But however famous this argument, it is an elaborate begging of the question. Consider a being that can be literally characterized as personal, infinite in knowledge, power, and goodness, and who is the source of existence of everything else. Why should we suppose that such a being is less than ultimate? What is the concept of ultimacy involved here, and if there is an unconfused concept being deployed, why should we take ultimacy in this sense as a norm for religious commitment? I think that most sincere Christian, and other theistic, believers will not be impressed by the suggestion that it is *idolatrous* to worship a being that can be literally characterized in the way just specified.

A more important reason for antiliterality is divine *otherness*, the radical difference of God from creatures. Emphasis on this and warnings against assuming similarities between God and creatures have been a persistent theme in the Christian tradition. The focus on otherness has various roots. An important one is mystical experience of the classic sort in which the subject becomes aware of an absolute unity, so absolute as to admit no distinction of parts, components, or aspects. If such experience is taken as our main clue to the divine being, as it commonly has been in the mystical tradition, one is naturally led to antiliterality. Hence the prominence of the *via negativa* in mystical theology. "It [the Divine]

---

[16]See, e.g., Thomas Aquinas *Summa Theologiae* 2.2.1.4.

[17]See, e.g., Paul Tillich, *Systematic Theology* (London: Nisbet & Co., 1953), 1:255; and *Dynamics of Faith* (New York: Harper & Bros., 1957), chap. 1.

is not soul or mind. . . . It is not order or greatness or littleness. . . . It is not immoveable nor in motion nor at rest, and has no power, and is not power or light, and does not live and is not life. . . . Nor is it one, nor is it Godhead or goodness. . . . Nor does it belong to the category of non-existence or to that of existence."[18] And there are other roots as well. In classical Christian theology, from Augustine to Aquinas and beyond, we find the doctrine of divine simplicity, the view that there is no distinction of any kind between parts, aspects, features, properties, attributes or activities in the divine being. These to many have seemed to render literal characterization of God impossible. To truly characterize God as, for example, just, would seem to imply a distinction between his justice and the rest of his nature, and thus to violate the divine simplicity.

I take the argument from divine otherness more seriously than the ones discussed earlier. We cannot deny that God is radically different from any creature, and this is something that must be taken into account in a theory of religious language. But whether that otherness has to be construed after the fashion of the mystical tradition or in terms of the doctrine of divine simplicity is another matter. Those are large questions into which I cannot go within the bounds of this essay. Suffice it to say that we do not find contemporary theological antiliteralists defending their position along these lines.[19]

Indeed, I do not find much in the way of serious argument for the position on the part of recent antiliteralists. What one finds, for the most part, is rather a set of attitudes, senses of the matter, and, not to put too fine a point on it, prejudices, that militate against taking seriously the possibility of literal characterization of God. I have tried hard to find some organization in this territory, some master conviction from which all the rest derives, but these efforts have been unsuccessful. Hence I am thrown back on merely listing what I take to be the main components of the gestalt. Some of these are not made explicit, and here I have tried to divine what lies behind overtly unsupported allegations.

---

[18]Dionysius the Pseudo-Areopagite, *The Divine Names and Mystical Theology*, trans. C. E. Rolt (New York: Macmillan, 1920).

[19]On pages 154-59 I will argue that divine otherness does not prevent any literal application of human concepts to God.

1. There is a considerable emphasis on the sense of mystery, awe in the face of the divine, as in one of the above quotations from McFague. In Kaufman (1993) what he had earlier called the "real referent of 'God'" is replaced by "mystery."

2. There seems to be a deeply rooted reluctance to recognize that God is a reality that is "out there," a being that is what it is, whatever our needs, penchants, conceptual frameworks or imaginative constructions. I sense several sources of this reluctance, which, again, I will just list.

☐ There may be lingering influences of positivism, scientism and naturalism—orientations that are powerful on the contemporary scene even when they are not explicitly acknowledged. This could account for some of the resistance to taking seriously the possibility of the supernatural.

☐ There may be a fear of cognitive failure, of holding false or unwarranted beliefs, of being overly credulous. This can lead to "playing it safe" by taking God to be immune to any characterization that has definite enough truth conditions to make it possible to show that it is false. Whereof we cannot speak we run no risk of error.

☐ I don't regard this last source as a wholly worthy motivation. Still further down on the scale would be a dread of being old-fashioned, out of tune with the times, of kinship with a "prescientific," "mythological" mentality.

If you feel that these suggestions are outrageously defamatory, I can only plead that I put them forward as possibilities only, and that I have been driven to this by the lack of explicit, unconfused support on the part of antiliteralists. Where explicit reasons are so weak, one is driven to look for a hidden agenda.

The Possibility and Necessity of Literal Talk of God

I now turn to my positive part of my agenda—indicating how literal talk about God is possible, and why it is important to engage in it. As a background for the project I will present two aspects of the matter that set the problem for us.

1. Although I do not agree that divine otherness rules out literal predication, it is still a crucial part of the picture. We must not forget that God is of a radically different order of being from any creature, including us. God is infinite in power, knowledge, and goodness; each of us is finite,

and very limited, in these respects. God is dependent on nothing other than himself for his existence, for what he is and for what he does. Or at least he is dependent on others only as much as he freely chooses to be, whereas we are dependent on a variety of natural factors, and ultimately on God, for our existence, our natures, and much else. God is purely spiritual; we are embodied. God is omnipresent; we are severely restricted in spatial location. According to some theologies God enjoys an atemporal mode of being—the simultaneous and complete possession of illimitable life; we live our lives successively, one moment at a time.

These differences have important implications for what it is for God to be or do the various things we believe him to be or do. God's knowledge is a very different thing from human knowledge. It isn't built up by inference from the deliverances of perception. God has no sense organs, and in any event he has no need to infer some truths from others. He knows everything directly—just by being God. I have argued[20] that God does not know by way of forming true beliefs. He is immediately aware of facts; no beliefs stand between him and the facts. Again, since God is immaterial, divine overt action is a very different thing from human overt action, which is mediated by bodily movement. Finally, if God's mode of being is atemporal, the picture will be still more different. Virtually every aspect of our activity is deeply infected with temporality. We acquire information, think, deliberate and act in temporally successive stages. The thought and action of an atemporal being would have to be radically different from ours. Thus it is incumbent on the defender of literal speech about God to show how that is compatible with radical divine-creaturely differences.

2. The difficulty of doing this is exacerbated by another basic feature of the situation: language that we have learned to apply to creatures is our only source for our talk about God. We have no independent purchase on God that would enable us to form concepts (terms) that are in no way derived from concepts (terms) we know how to apply to creatures. At least this is true with respect to public, interpersonally shared language. Our public language for talking about the natural world de-

---

[20]William P. Alston, *Divine Nature and Human Language* (Ithaca, N.Y.: Cornell University Press, 1989), chap. 9.

rives from terms that can be learned *ostensively*. The parent can tell when the child is perceiving a certain object or attending to a certain feature of the object. This enables her to teach the child to associate this object or feature with a certain word; by the same token she can tell whether the child then applies the word to the correct item. But none of this is possible with respect to God. We have no reliable interpersonal ways of determining when a person is aware of some feature or activity of God unless the person tells us. Hence the most basic learning of the meaning of words that apply to God cannot proceed *ostensively*. The obvious alternative is that one learns to apply terms to God by derivation from one's prior understanding of these terms (or other terms) as they are applied to creatures. We first learn what it is for a human being to speak or to know something, and then somehow we get from that to understanding what it is for God to speak or to know. I do not wish to deny that one's experience of the presence and activity of God in one's life provides one with a fuller, deeper understanding of what God is like and what he does. For example, one's understanding of divine grace is enlarged and deepened by experiencing the grace of God. But there is no way of communicating this additional understanding to others except by using terms derived from our common language that was developed to deal with the created world. Hence, so far as publicly shared concepts of God are concerned, the whole structure is based on what we can extract from our repertoire of creaturely concepts.

This means that the question of how we can apply terms literally to God amounts to the question of how terms suitable for doing this can be derived from terms that literally apply to creatures. In dealing with this question I will survey the main modes of derivation available to us and consider which, if any, yield terms that could literally apply to God, keeping in mind throughout the need to give full recognition to divine otherness.

Literal Terms in Talk of God

The simplest way of deriving theological predicates from creaturely predicates is just to transfer the latter to the theological application. This requires *univocal* predication of God and creatures, applying some terms to God and creatures with the same meaning. But it is widely supposed that this is impossible. The divine-human differences adumbrated above would seem to make it impossible for any term to be used in just the same sense of both God and creature. If God's mode of knowledge is so different from ours, how can "know" mean the same in the two applications? And if God is immaterial, and especially if he is atemporal, how can any action term—*forgive, speak, command, punish, create*—mean just the same as applied to God and to humans? Many philosophers and theologians have held that it cannot.

I myself do not agree that no terms can be used univocally of God and creatures. It is plausible to suppose that there are relatively abstract terms like *purpose, power* and *intention* that can be literally applied in just the same sense to God and us, even though the concrete realization of what these terms signify is enormously different. Even though God's power is immeasurably greater than ours, the meaning of *power* could be the same whether we are speaking of God or a human being.

But I do not have the space here to give the possibility of univocal predication (for some terms) the defense it deserves. Hence, for the sake of discussion, I will accept the denial of that possibility and explore other ways of forging terms that can be used literally of God.

This is the place to mention another confusion about literality—its equation with univocity. If they were equivalent, it would make no sense to look for terms that can be used literally of God but not univocally. But a moment's reflection will show that univocity and literality are quite different. *Univocal* is a relational term; it concerns a relation between two or more uses of a term. Hence it makes no sense to ask whether a particular use of a term is univocal. Univocal with what? That would be like asking whether Sam is taller. But *literal* and *metaphorical* are not relational in this way; they can be applied to individual uses of a term. I can ask whether *acid* in "Religion has been corroded by the acids of modernity" is used literally or metaphorically. The conflation of literality and univocity in the case of theological predication undoubtedly stems from the fact that using a term univocally of God and creature is the simplest and most obvious way of employing antecedent linguistic resources to speak literally of God. But it is only if one ignores the other devices I will be discussing that one will suppose this to be the only source of literal theological discourse.

Metaphors in Talk of God

Given that (1) none of the terms we apply to creatures literally apply to God in just the same sense and (2) our talk about God must be ultimately derived from those terms, an obvious suggestion is that in speaking of God we use metaphorically terms that apply literally to creatures. I briefly characterized metaphor at the beginning of this chapter. Metaphorical speech is obviously prominent in religious discourse. Here are just a few samples:

☐ "The LORD is my *shepherd*" (Ps 23:1).

☐ "In his *hand* are the depths of the earth" (Ps 95:4).

☐ "The LORD is my *rock*, my *fortress*" (Ps 18:2).

☐ "The LORD will be your everlasting *light*" (Is 60:19).

☐ "I am the *bread* that came down from heaven" (Jn 6:41).

Nor are metaphors absent from the creeds. In the Nicene Creed Jesus Christ is said to be "eternally *begotten* of the Father," to be "*light* from *light*," to have "*come down* from heaven," to be "*seated at the right hand* of the Father." Clearly metaphorical extension plays a large role in the adaptation of creaturely language for speaking of God.

So long as metaphors remain in their original state, they obviously do not constitute a way of speaking literally about God. But as has been increasingly recognized in this century, what is originally a metaphorical use of a term can develop into (or degenerate into, depending on your point of view) a new established meaning of the term, so that by using the term with that meaning one can be literally predicating it of something. When that happens people speak of a "dead metaphor."[21] The language is rife with senses of terms we can plausibly suppose, and in many cases show by historical research, to have developed out of metaphorical uses. Consider such phrases as "fork in the road," "leg of the table," "mouth of the river," "skyscraper," "eyelids," "hood of the car." In the present state of the language, *leg* has as much an established sense in the above phrase as in "his legs are scrawny." But there was presumably an

---

[21]That appellation is not ideally felicitous. Strictly speaking, a completely "dead metaphor" is not a metaphor at all but an established sense of a term with a metaphorical provenance. But with this caveat I will continue to use the common terminology.

earlier time at which the word was commonly applied only to limbs of animals. People then began using *leg* metaphorically for the supports of tables and chairs. That usage caught on, and later generations learned this use of the term ostensively, without going through the earlier sense and giving it a metaphorical extension. This process is extremely important for the development of language. Most of our terms for mental operations are dead metaphors—*understand, conceive, overlook, deduce, apprehend.* In many cases the metaphorical provenance is hidden from us because the earlier, more concrete senses attached to terms in other languages, especially Latin. Thus *apprehend* is from the Latin verb *prehendere,* to grasp. (We also speak of mentally "grasping" a point.) In other cases the metaphor can easily be recovered on reflection, as in *understand* and *overlook.* It is also salutary to consider the many dead metaphors involving a single word like *cold.* In addition to its primary temperature sense, we speak of a "cold reception," a "cold manner," a "cold decor," "in cold blood" and so on.

The difference between a live and a dead metaphor hangs on the psychological processes involved in using the word. If the user is alive to the earlier sense and is (not necessarily in full and explicit consciousness) using that as a "model" for thinking about that to which it is applied, then the metaphor is alive. If, on the other hand, the earlier sense is not in the picture at all, and the user applies the term "directly" to the subject, without "going through" the earlier sense, we have a dead metaphor. Obviously these are matters of degree; the earlier sense may figure in the usage to a greater or lesser extent. And different speakers may differ on this point. Nevertheless, there are many clear cases on both sides of the divide, in religious discourse and elsewhere. I take it that the religious metaphors I've cited above are all alive, and that the dead metaphors just listed are clear cases. I doubt very much that anyone thinks of scraping the sky when using "skyscraper," and I doubt just as strongly that anyone thinks of seizing anything when using "conceive."

As just indicated, it seems clear that many religious metaphors are fully alive. But it is abstractly possible that dead metaphor plays a significant role in religious discourse, in which case this would be a major source of terms for speaking literally of God. I think it is a serious possi-

LITERAL TALK OF GOD

bility that metaphorical usage plays a role in the provenance of some literal application of terms to God, but not all. With respect to relatively abstract terms like "power," I will suggest below a different etiology that is related to metaphor indirectly, if at all. But with respect to action terms, which, as I will be contending, occupy a central role in our talk and thought about God, a transition from live to dead metaphor is not implausible. It may well be that in the antecedents of our tradition the earliest talk of God as *speaking* (commanding, calling, forgiving, condemning), *creating, protecting,* etc., was metaphorical. The image of a human being doing such things was used as a model, with the suggestion that something (not yet literally specified) like that is true of God. In the course of time people, at least some people, came to grasp the crucial similarities underlying this metaphorical use, or some of them, and were able to attribute these literally to God. In this last section of this essay I will say more about how I think that might go.

Note that religious metaphors cannot metamorphose into literal speech in the way my earlier examples did—by taking on new sense through ostension. As pointed out earlier, we are unable to establish a special theological sense of "speak" in the way an automotive sense of "hood" is established, by associating the word with a certain perceived part of a car. The death and rebirth of theological metaphors will have to be a more discursive, intralinguistic affair. Again, more on this below.

Another important point in this connection is that we should not suppose that a given term has the same status for all users. That there are diachronic differences is implied by the claim that a word can figure as a live metaphor at one time and dead metaphor at a different time. But there are synchronic differences too. For the uninitiated, "electric current" can be a live metaphor, while for the engineer or physicist it is a term with a technical meaning that can be applied literally. In theological discourse it requires a certain facility with abstract thinking to speak non-metaphorically of God as having purposes and doing various things to carry them out. Perhaps for large segments of the population the only way to attach meaning to such talk is via using human purposing and acting as an imaginative model.

The term *father,* about which there has been much discussion of late, fueled especially by feminist concerns, presents an interesting case. Here is a term, it seems clear, that wears its metaphorical provenance on its face. At least in its earliest employments an ideal picture of fathers[22] as loving, providing, caring, protecting and so on was used as a source of suggestions for thinking of God, without all this being spelled out, even partially, in literal terms. In certain sophisticated circles it may have long been used as a technical term for the first person of the Trinity with a meaning something like "*the* ultimate source of being." But what about the vast middle territory? I can't aspire to prove this, but my sense is that the metaphor is very much alive for most people. Instead of having a more or less clearly delimited set of properties that are fixed as the theological meaning of *father*, people generally work with some idealized picture of human fathers (that may well differ for different people) from which they draw various features in thinking of God.

When thinking about the role of metaphor in theological discourse we should take care not to conflate it with other nonliteral construals of that discourse. In particular, it is different from Hick's view of God-talk as being about religious *phenomena*, the ways in which God "appears" to our experience in one or another religious tradition, rather than being about the truly Ultimate itself. Talk about phenomena can be as literal as anything else. I can speak literally in specifying how something appears to me (how it looks, sounds). Metaphor can be used here as elsewhere, of course, but it need not be especially prominent. Again, Kaufman's idea of the "available God" as an "imaginative construct" need not involve metaphorical speech. To be sure, one *can* use the construct as a base for metaphorical speech about the truly Ultimate, but one need not. One can simply rest within the construct and, so to say, live one's religious life there.

Partial Univocity

Leaving aside univocity, and apart from dying metaphors, what possibilities are there for deriving terms from our resources for talking of creatures that can be applied literally to God? A suggestion that immediately

---

[22]In this connection it is worthy of note that it is the rule for metaphors to be based on common stereotypes of what the term literally denotes, rather than on the real nature of the denotatum.

springs to mind is *analogy*. But this all depends on how we think of that. Historically the most influential account of analogy is that of Thomas Aquinas. He has a version of what we can think of as the basic meaning of "analogy" as a semantic term, that is, that two senses of a term can be *similar*, can display a *commonality*, even though they are not exactly the same. But the specific twist he gives to this is based on his doctrine of divine simplicity. This, he holds, makes it impossible that any term can be even partly univocal in divine and creaturely applications. For any term applied to creatures signifies something that is distinct from its subject, but when it is applied to God, in whom there is no distinction between God and his attributes, that difference is lost. And that prevents any part of the meaning from being the same in the two cases.[23]

But if no part of the meaning of "know" as applied to God and humans is the same, how can the two meanings be similar? How can we separate similarity from having something in common? If my house is similar to your house, they must share one or more properties. Therefore I don't take Aquinas' specific version of analogy to be viable. I shall pursue the notion that theological meanings of terms are derived by analogy from creaturely meanings (of those terms or other terms) in a form in which analogy involves what we may call *partial univocity*, sharing some but not all of the meaning of each.

The idea that the meanings of a term in two uses can be partly the same and partly different would seem to be a very simple one. Despite this it has been persistently overlooked in discussion of this issue.[24] My development of it is based on two points. First, the meanings of terms are typically complex; they have parts. Hence some of these parts, and not others, may carry over from one application to another. Second, one way in which concepts are complex is that they include more abstract,

---

[23]For an extended treatment of Aquinas on theological predication see William Alston, "Aquinas on Theological Predication: A Look Backward and a Look Forward," in *Reasoned Faith,* ed. Eleonore Stump (Ithaca, N.Y.: Cornell University Press, 1993).

[24]A notable exception is Richard Swinburne, who develops an account of analogy in terms of partial univocity. In *The Coherence of Theism* (Oxford: Clarendon Press, 1977) he does this in terms of a partial overlap in the semantic and syntactic rules governing the terms. A slightly different formulation is found in *Revelation: From Metaphor to Analogy* (Oxford: Clarendon Press, 1992).

generic aspects and more concrete, specific ones. Perhaps some relatively abstract component of our concept of, e.g., knowledge could be truly applied to God. The inapplicability of the more concrete features (how knowledge is realized in the human case) would then reflect the fact that what it is for God to know something is quite different from what it is for us to know something, while the carry-over of a generic component would still insure that God does know things and that his action can be guided by this knowledge. This partial univocity approach should thus enable us to preserve both sides of the basic contrast—the radical divine-human difference—and enough commonality to make possible the derivation of literally applicable theological terms from creaturely terms.[25]

So the program is to take a concept applicable to human personal agents, extract a certain abstract component thereof, and apply that to God. Since the more concrete component of the human concept is not carried over, we accommodate the fact that the divine realization is quite different from the human realization, while at the same time recognizing a "univocal core" of meaning that can be truly asserted of both God and us. That is the program, stated in the most general terms. To briefly illustrate it I will consider how action terms can be treated along these lines. This is an appropriate area to focus on because of the central place it occupies in our talk about God. The God of theistic religions is preeminently an *agent*, one who acts. Salvation history is largely concerned with what God has done, is doing, and will do vis-à-vis us. And our concepts of divine attributes presuppose divine actions. *Omnipotence* is the power to *do* anything one chooses to *do*. *Providence* consists in *arranging* matters for the good of creatures. *Justice* and *mercy* have to do with ways in which God *does* what he *does*. And so on. Divine action is the hinge on which theology turns in Christianity and other theistic religions.

Immateriality

Earlier I speculated that action terms might originally be applied meta-

---

[25]For Aquinas the doctrine of divine simplicity ensured the radical otherness, while the doctrine that all the perfections of creatures are found in God, in a more eminent mode, ensured a significant degree of divine-creature commonality. But the commonality was dissipated by the denial of even partial univocity.

phorically to God. If so, the question is how, if at all, one can disengage components of the literal meaning of those terms that can also be literally applied to God, thereby crafting theological senses of the term that are analogically related to their creaturely senses. Obviously, this depends both on what those creaturely senses are *and* on what we take the nature of God to be.

As for the latter, the crucial questions here concern the differences between God and creatures that might well affect how much creaturely meaning can be transferred to the divine case. One obvious difference is *immateriality*. Other differences that are clearly relevant, if we accept them, are divine *timelessness* and *simplicity*. In the interest of concision I will ignore the latter two and concentrate on immateriality. What features of the creaturely meaning of "speak," "forgive," "command," "commission," "create" or "protect" must drop out if we are to apply these terms literally to God?

As indicated above, that depends on the constitution of those creaturely senses. In particular, the following issue is crucial. It is a fundamental truth about us that we can perform overt actions, bring about changes outside ourselves, only by moving our bodies in certain ways. Hence, if some bodily movement is part of the meaning of an action term as applied to humans, then the term cannot be literally applied with that meaning to a bodiless agent. Some action terms do clearly have such a component. "Kick open the door," for example, means "bring it about that the door is open by kicking it"; and so that term cannot be literally true of an immaterial agent like God. But what about overt action terms that do not explicitly specify a particular bodily means? What about "open the door," "cure a disease" or "forgive Robinson"? To be sure, I cannot in fact do any of those things without moving my body in some way, but is this part of the *meaning* of those terms, or is it rather a fact about our limitations? Is the meaning of these terms such that we can consistently and intelligibly *say* that a human being cured a disease without moving her body in any way, perhaps by telekinesis, even if this is in fact impossible? If that is the way the cookie crumbles, then these terms, and indefinitely many others, could intelligibly be literally applied to God, even though the way in which God brings them about would be quite different from any way open to us. The meaning of "cure Krasnick's disease" as applied to humans would simply be "bring it about that Krasnick is cured," without any further specification of how this is done.

But since I have already foresworn any assumption of complete univocity, I will not take this route but instead assume that bodily mediation is built into the meaning of human action terms. However, partial univocity is still an option. We simply shear off "by movements of the body" from the human meaning of the term, and that leaves us with the above meaning of "cure Krasnick's disease" which is available for literal application to an immaterial agent.

The human and divine senses will then be partly univocal by virtue of sharing the meaning "bring it about that Krasnick is cured." But since what God does to bring that about will be quite different from anything we do, the otherness of the divine is preserved.

Other cases cannot be handled quite so simply. "Bailey spoke to Henderson" will include in its meaning something about Bailey producing sounds "by using his vocal organs," and we will have to excise "by using his vocal organs" if we are to use "spoke to Henderson" literally of God. But that does not suffice, because divine speech is not necessarily restricted to the medium of sound. God can speak to people by causing them to hear appropriate sounds, but he can also do it by manipulating their stream of thoughts more directly. What we need to do here is to extract the component of the human meaning of "speaks" that neither requires bodily movements nor ties God down to one rather than another mode of communication. Something like "communicates a message" will do the trick. This is involved in the meaning of "speaks" as applied to human beings (in a sense of "communicate" that doesn't imply that the intended recipient receives and understands the message). And this part of the meaning is suitable for literal application to God.

To dig just a bit deeper, if we focus on the basic case of *intentional* human action, to intentionally cure X's disease is to *carry out an intention* to cure X. A reference to the psychological antecedent of the bringing about is involved in the meaning of the term. We want to carry this over to the divine application, since what God does he does intentionally. We can hardly think of God as doing things inadvertently or accidentally or without realizing what he is doing. But this means that we need senses of terms like *intend, know* and *will* which are literally applicable to God. The job of extracting a relatively abstract, theologically usable component of the human meaning of these terms is a complex one into which I cannot enter here.[26] Suffice it to say that the key lies in the way in which action terms and psychological terms enter into an interdependent network, so that we can understand the terms in each group by reference to their functional interrelationships. Roughly speaking, an intention to light a fire is the sort of state that normally (when other prerequisites are satisfied) gives rise to lighting a fire. And lighting a fire is an activity that normally stems from antecedents of those sorts.

The Importance of Literal Speech for Theology

But even if literal speech about God is possible, why should we care? Who needs it? What important function does it perform? What would be lost if it weren't possible?

For the sake of concision I will limit myself to contrasting literal speech about God with metaphorical. I am not at all inclined to deny that metaphor is useful in theology. Quite the contrary. Metaphor has always played, and will continue to play, a large role. I am only concerned to combat the idea that it can take over the whole show. Literal predication is also important for theology.

This importance stems from the features that distinguish literal from metaphorical speech. Chief among these is a greater determinateness. I have already disavowed any claim of a radical difference. Literal speech need not be perfectly determinate, and metaphorical speech often embodies fairly determinate truth claims, as in Churchill's famous 1946 statement, "Russia has dropped an iron curtain across Europe." Nevertheless, there is an important difference in degree. Think of the theological metaphors of *father* and *king*. It is reasonably clear that "king" is intended to imply, inter alia, *power, sovereignty* and *majesty*, while "father" is intended to imply *power, loving care* and *protectiveness*. Nevertheless, if I may assume for the moment that these italicized terms can be applied literally to God, we will be making a much more determinate statement about

---

[26]For an extensive discussion see Alston, *Divine Nature,* chaps. 3, 4.

God if we say that he is powerful, sovereign, and exercises loving care, than if we call him "father" or "king." That is because these metaphors, like any others, are open to other ways of using the models they provide. Figurative speech is essentially open ended, capable of indefinitely varied exploitations. That is both an asset and a defect. Here I am interested in the defect. When we are concerned to make a statement with definite truth conditions, one the reasons for and against which can be set out as explicitly as possible, we are better off speaking literally. By the same token, the theoretical and practical implications of a literal statement will, generally, be more determinate and more specific. We will get clearer guidance of our stance vis-à-vis God from the literal statements that God is all-powerful, loving, concerned to exercise providence over his creatures, than we will from metaphorically characterizing him as "father" and "king." Finally, we can pin down more unambiguously the *reference* of "God" if we can use literal characterizations to do so. If I want you to know of whom I had just been speaking, I will do much better to provide some literal characterization such as "my sister-in-law" or "the woman who lives across the street," than to say "There is a garden in her face where roses and fair lilies grow." Similarly if I can literally characterize God as "the source of being for all other than himself," that will serve to uniquely pin down the reference in a way I can't by saying, in the words of the Gloria, "Lord God, Heavenly King, almighty God and Father."

If my examples of literal talk about God are typical, we can see the limitations as well as the payoffs of the enterprise. Literal speech about God will be abstract. It will not be such as to warm the heart or fire the imagination or move to devotion. For prayer, devotion, liturgy, exhortation, and edification we require metaphor and symbol in addition. There need be no competition between literal and metaphorical talk about God. Each has a crucial place in the total religious response. It behooves us to appreciate the value of one without denigrating the other. In that way we can have the best of both worlds—the imaginative power of the metaphor and the intellectual and practical clarification of the literal characterization.

7

FEMINIST THEOLOGY AS MODERN PROJECT

R. R. Reno

OTH PROPONENTS AND OPPONENTS TAKE FEMINIST THEOLOGY WITH deadly seriousness. This disposition is not mistaken. Feminist theology combines first order moral concerns about human relationality (and not just male-female relations) with an at least partial recognition of the importance and power of language.[1] The former should be the concern of all who seek truth and love justice. The latter is a characteristic insight of late modernity which holds out the promise of freeing Christian theology from its Babylonian captivity to feeling and sensibility. Both are important. Both deserve the sustained attention of any believer, especially those commissioned with responsibility for the corporate life of the church. Neither constitutes the real challenge of feminist theology.

The deepest and most decisive significance of feminist theology is not its uniqueness, but instead what it shares in common with the broader

---

[1]Mary Daly's classic slogan "If God is male, then male is god" captures the insight that the distinctive structure of Christian imagery, language and practice determines not simply our formal religious convictions, but also shapes our vision of the fundamental structures and relations of our lives. This insight gives a twofold vigor to feminist theology. First, recognition of the formative power of language gives a practical urgency to the task of theology. The words matter and so the theologian must attend to them. Second, this recognition motivates a sustained inquiry into the particular warp and woof of the Christian tradition. The theologian is not permitted to glide along the surface—one must grapple with the linguistic texture of the tradition. This vigor is, however, partial. I hope to show that the assumptions of modern theology which feminist theologians such as Elizabeth Johnson and Rosemary Ruether adopt swerve away from particular linguistic fabric of the Christian tradition.

purposes, methods and sensibilities of modern theology.[2] Within the
emerging canon of the feminist theology, one finds the characteristic elements of modern theology: the triumph of ethical criteria over dogmatic,
a distrust of tradition combined with a confidence in the perspicuity of
contemporary experience and a vision of theology as saving the tradition
from both error and irrelevance. The integrity with which feminist theology is loyal to these standard features of modern theology makes it a
compelling voice on the contemporary theological scene.

My goal, then, is to expose the underlying modern structure of the most
influential forms of feminist theology, and in so doing, to achieve three
ends. First, by concentrating on the work of Elizabeth Johnson and Rosemary Ruether, I hope to suggest a reading of feminist theology according
to its modern theological practice rather than its material commitments and
conclusions.[3] The desired result is to convince the reader that the feminist

---

[2]Because I intend to consider feminist theology in light of its continuity with modern theological practice, these remarks apply with equal force to womanist and mujerista theologies.
Important differences obtain among the different stands of modern theological engage-
ments with women's experience within the frame of Christianity; however, those differences
occur in the context of a broad consensus about the basic enabling assumptions of theological analysis, and it is this broad consensus and not particular differences which is the subject of this inquiry.

[3]Some might object to my choice of Johnson and Ruether as representative. In a recent survey of feminist theology, Serene Jones argues for a basic distinction within feminist, womanist and mujerista theologies (*Religious Studies Review* 21, no. 3 [July 1995]: 171-78). Jones
distinguishes between "rock" views of women's experience, that is to say, views which
"employ universalizing and/or ahistorical frames of reference to structure their accounts of
human experience," and "hard place" accounts which "self-consciously avoid universalizing
gestures and opt instead for descriptions of experience which are historically localized and
culturally specific" (pp. 171-72). Such a difference is important and influences the philosophical conceptualities and material conclusions of differing theologies. However, this difference does not map onto differences in basic theological practice. With some exceptions,
postmodern feminists who reject the assumptions of modern epistemology and the concomitant modern conception of the self (the "rock" view) nonetheless continue to engage in
modern theological practice. Whether discussing the biblical text, traditional liturgies or
inherited doctrines, the theological practice of "rock" and "hard place" theologians is sur-
prisingly uniform. It is this practice and the enabling assumptions of this practice (which
Johnson and Ruether exemplify), not the contested question of the appropriate conceptual
tools for interpreting women's experience, that is decisive.

   I may be mistaken in treating Johnson and Ruether as adequately representative of feminist,
womanist and mujerista theological practice. Given my concluding assessment of modern theology, I would like to be convinced that strands within the feminist, womanist, mujerista

theology exemplified by Johnson and Ruether is best grasped as an extension of modern theology (sections one through three). Second, by placing
feminist theology within the context of the modern theological project, I
hope to show the conceptual consistency of feminist theological practice.
As such, a foundational assessment of the prevailing forms of feminist theology must be an assessment of the enabling assumptions of modern theology (section four). Third and finally, to know feminist theology as a
vigorous form of the modern project is to know with a concomitant clarity
the distinctive ethos of modern theology. Sharpening the focus encourages
judgment.[4] I thus conclude with the sketch of an argument why the logic
of modern theology, the feminist theology of the sort exemplified by
Johnson and Ruether, should be rejected (section five).

A warning to the reader: This essay is guided by a heuristic distinction
between the content (feminist) and form (modern) of feminist theology,
with attention directed exclusively toward the latter. This focus on the
modern form of feminist theology may entail arguments against certain
global claims attached to the critique of patriarchy (e.g., that the patriarchal context of Christian language formation and use renders it necessarily and intrinsically defective). However, *in no way* does my concluding
sketch entail arguments either for or against more focused feminist critiques of particular uses of particular elements of the Christian tradition
to reinforce male privilege (e.g., readings of Genesis 2 which legitimate
the treatment of women as intrinsically inferior to men in dignity and
worth). Further, my concluding sketch entails *neither* a rejection of par-

---

movement really are engaged in a theological practice that differs from Johnson and
Ruether. I have no desire for Johnson and Ruether to be representative. It just seems to be
the case.

[4]When one understands a claim with sufficient clarity, then one is in a position to consider
whether that claim is either true or false. Of course, the web of claims which make up the
distinctive practice of modern theology does not admit of anything like the clarity of a single sentence, and so I cannot hope to render the characteristic elements of modern theology transparent to myself, much less the reader. Nonetheless, because the concerns of
feminist theology very quickly and passionately focus on the man Jesus of Nazareth, the
logic of modern theology becomes particularly clear, and that clarity sharpens the difference
between the modern view of faith and the classical alternative. Indeed, that clarity does not
simply sharpen the difference; by force of contrast feminist theology helps bring into focus
the often amorphous outlines of the classical view of faith.

ticular novelties suggested by feminist theologies (e.g., invocations of
God as "Mother") *nor* a dismissal of various present and proposed forms
of gender equality (e.g., the ordination of women). My argument is very
relevant to how one would go about considering such material features
of feminist theology, but this essay will not settle these matters one way
or the other. Instead, my argument throughout focuses on the way in
which feminist theology both develops and uses its material commitments within the modern theological framework, and then turns to suggest a negative assessment of that framework.

The Triumph of the Ethical

Rosemary Ruether provides a clear statement of the fundamental criterion
of feminist theology:

> The critical principle of feminist theology is the promotion of the full humanity of
> women. Whatever denies, diminishes, or distorts the full humanity of women is,
> therefore, appraised as not redemptive. Theologically speaking, whatever diminishes
> or denies the full humanity of women must be presumed not to reflect the divine or
> an authentic relation to the divine, or reflect the authentic nature of things, or to be
> the message or work of an authentic redeemer or a community of redemption.
>
> The negative principle also implies the positive principle: what does promote the
> full humanity of women is of the Holy, it does reflect true relation to the divine, it is
> the true nature of things, the authentic message of redemption and the mission of
> redemptive community.[5]

This criterion is seconded by Elizabeth Johnson. Johnson's feminist summa, *She Who Is*, is a judicious presentation of the basic agenda of feminist
theology, and she has her own, helpful characterization of the fundamental
principle of discernment which makes a theology distinctively feminist:

> In the course of this program [of feminist theology] one criterion recurs as a touch-
> stone for testing the truth and falsity, the adequacy and inadequacy, the coherence
> and incoherence of theological statements and religious structures. This criterion,
> variously enunciated, is the emancipation of women toward human flourishing.[6]

Various feminist theologians dispute the specific nature of the impedi-

---

[5]Rosemary Ruether, *Sexism and God-Talk: Toward a Feminist Theology* (Boston: Beacon, 1983), pp. 18-19.
[6]Elizabeth Johnson, *She Who Is* (New York: Crossroad, 1992), p. 30.

ments to the emancipation of women, as well as dispute the appropriate characterization of full human flourishing. Further, feminist theologians differ regarding the application of this criterion. How much of the tradition is irrecoverably patriarchal? How much is redeemable? How does one go about renewing or revisioning the tradition? Diverse answers abound to these questions, and Johnson argues for her own. Yet, in spite of these disputes and differences, the underlying commitment to women's flourishing remains constant. For feminist theology, the task or method which controls is that of formulating truthful and responsible Christian speech and practice through a foundational commitment to the critical principle or criterion of the full flourishing of women.

Although the content of the feminist critical principle may be distinctive, the role it plays in feminist theology is continuous with earlier, non-feminist modern theologies. The structure is, roughly, this. Moral aspiration X is the unquestionable good of human life. God is good and surely seeks to promote the unquestionable good of human life. Therefore, whatever promotes the unquestionable good of human life is of God, and what does not is not of God. This syllogism exemplifies the theological method of modernity, and it is a method straightforwardly adopted by feminist theology.

Kant's theological work *Religion Within the Limits of Reason Alone* provides a clear illustration of the method employed by feminist theology. Kant's moral interests are somewhat different from those of feminist theologians such as Ruether and Johnson. For example, Kant emphasizes the self-sufficiency of the moral law, and his ideal of conformity to the moral law for its own sake is characteristically rejected by feminists as archetypical of patriarchal neglect of mutuality and community.[7] Nonetheless, Ruether and

---

[7]These differences are less pronounced than feminists often think. Concern for autonomy—critique of tradition—flourishing independent of inherited roles—these are all characteristic Kantian features. To this feminism adds appeals to solidarity and mutuality, but the particular conditions of solidarity and mutuality are freely chosen, and as such fall under the logic of Kantian self-sufficiency. Johnson builds her systematic reconstruction of the doctrine of God around the notion of the trinity as a community of persons united in love (see *She Who Is*, pp. 191-223). Yet, the very logic of the modern theology in which she is fully invested prevents her theology from describing a God who has an irrevocable, tangible and concrete relation with human beings. God is always mediated and never present. Thus, Johnson rejects the symbols of self-sufficiency, but she does not escape the Kantian conceptual framework for self-sufficiency.

Johnson follow the logic, if not the substance, of Kant's approach.

For Kant, the critical principle of morality is the full humanity of persons, and as free and rational creatures we attain our dignity by freely conforming to the practical dictates of reason, the moral law. This means that we should constitute our identity out of a pure respect for the moral law; we should do our duty out of a love of duty and for no other reason. However *materially* defective this might be in feminist eyes, Kant's critical principle has the same *formal* function as the feminist principle of the full humanity of women. Throughout *Religion*, Kant systematically critiques traditional Christian practice according to his critical principle. That which serves to advance our moral dignity as free and rational creatures is affirmed by Kant; that which obscures or retards our moral dignity is denied. For example, the teachings of Jesus which denounce hypocrisy and affirm the necessity of inward virtue are consistent with Kant's moral vision of duty for duty's sake, and as a result these teachings are applauded as the heart of true religion. In contrast, Biblical references to the necessity or efficacy of cultic and ceremonial practices done for the sake of serving God are rejected by Kant. In this way, the whole of *Religion Within the Limits of Reason Alone* is devoted to a careful assessment of Christian belief and practice according to the dictates of Kant's moral vision. Inherited speech about God is subjected to a moral critique.

The parallels are clear. When Elizabeth Johnson turns to the Bible, she applies her moral vision as does Kant. Concerned with patriarchy rather than ceremonialism, Johnson's critical principle leads her away from the *theos-logos* construction of the canonical gospel stories and guides her toward revisioning those stories in terms of a *pneuma-sophia* pattern suggested by the deuterocanonical wisdom literature.[8] Like Kant, then, the text is harnessed to the critical principle; the ethical vision governs a theological reading of the text. As Johnson describes her approach to Scripture,

> When the liberating vision of a community of equal and mutual disciples is endorsed and practiced . . . language generated by women's experience can inter-

[8]See Johnson, *She Who Is*, pp. 150-69: "This chapter respeaks Christology by telling the gospel story of Jesus as the story of Wisdom's child, Sophia incarnate" (p. 154).

weave with [the] ancient symbols [of Scripture] and their hidden recognition of women's creative power and goodness to shape new building blocks for emancipatory discourse about the mystery of God.[9]

As with Kant, the ethical vision is the key that unlocks the hidden truths of the inherited linguistic forms and practices.

This continuity of feminist theology with the fundamental structure of modern theology is exemplified in the characteristic modern assessment of Jesus' salvific significance. For Kant, the matter is straightforward. Jesus' significance is found in "his steadfastness and forthrightness in teaching and example for the sake of the good."[10] Jesus saves as the archetype of pure moral freedom—duty for duty's sake—which awakens within us our own moral freedom. Elizabeth Johnson's account of Jesus' significance is identical in form. Jesus' ministry "unleashes a hope, a vision, and a present experience of liberating relationships" through "his preaching about the reign of God and his inclusive lifestyle."[11] Like Kant, Johnson's Jesus saves because he is archetypical of the moral life. Precisely as such, Johnson pronounces that "Jesus is named the Christ in a paradigmatic way."[12] For both, Jesus is the Christ because he exemplifies our innate sense of human perfection, and he saves by bringing to consciousness the full potential of that innate sense. In this way Christology, like other aspects of modern theology, is recast in terms of a prevenient moral vision.[13]

---

[9]Ibid., p. 103.

[10]Kant, *Religion*, pp. 75-76.

[11]Johnson, *She Who Is*, pp. 157, 160.

[12]Ibid., p. 162.

[13]While I cannot fully explore the logic of modern theology's assessment of Jesus and his role in our salvation, two examples illustrate how characteristic is Johnson's treatment of christology. First, Johnson rejects classical interpretations of Jesus' saving significance which focus upon his atoning death rather than his teaching and "lifestyle." Instead of treating the crucifixion as the decisive event upon which the gospel turns, Johnson reads Jesus' death as a consequence of his teaching which adds nothing new. She observes that Jesus' death "occurred historically in consequence of Jesus' fidelity to the deepest truth he knew, expressed in his message and behavior" (*She Who Is*, p. 158). Kant struggles to give a morally suitable account of the significance of Jesus' death, but out of the muddle Kant is able to say that Jesus' death is significant only as confirmation of his commitment to the moral good for its own sake (see *Religion*, p. 55; see also Kant's extended treatment of the role of suffering in moral exemplars, *Critique of Practical Reason*, trans. L. W. Beck [Indianapolis: Bobbs-Merrill, 1956], pp. 159-60).

This parallel between Johnson and Kant highlights a widespread dogmatic feature of modern

To a greater or lesser extent, one of the defining features of feminist theology is the subordination of the Christian tradition to the ethical priority of the emancipation (variously interpreted) of women. Johnson focuses her attention on the positive task of producing an emancipatory reconstruction of the Christian doctrine of God as participatory love. Other feminist theologians are more interested in excision than revision and enjoy vigorous application of the *negative* function of the critical principle rather than the patient use of its *positive* function. Although this yields quite different rhetorical results, this diversity is encompassed within the same fundamental assumptions about the criterion of theological truthfulness.[14] An ethical truth is the fundamen-

---

theology: its struggle with the centrality of Jesus' passion in the canonical narratives. In Johnson's case, the struggle is especially poignant. When she takes up the question of the suffering God, Johnson affirms a nuanced use of the cross and resurrection as an event which "deepens the mystery of how God's solidarity with the suffering world brings about a future even for the most godforsaken" (*She Who Is*, p. 269). The difficulty, however, is that in this context the cross and resurrection function as empowering *symbols* quite detached from the *events* intrinsic to the life of Jesus of Nazareth as narrated in the gospel stories. Consequently, God is not in solidarity with the suffering world in anything but a symbolic sense. In order to secure the intrinsic and real solidarity with suffering which Johnson seeks, she must shift the cross and resurrection out the metaphorical sensorium of Holy Mystery and back into the narratives of Jesus' fate. However, such a shift entails naming Jesus the Christ unequivocally rather than paradigmatically, a shift blocked by the enabling assumptions of modern theology.

The second example is more easily noted. Both Johnson and Ruether, like many modern theologians, treat the *Jewishness* of Jesus as irrelevant to his saving significance. As Johnson, relying on Ruether, claims, the Christian tradition has "always been clear" that "Jesus' ethnic and social identity" are irrelevant to God's saving purposes (*She Who Is*, pp. 166-67). Here, Johnson and Ruether are mistaken about the tradition (as the fate of Marcion bears witness), but they are certainly right about the *modern* Christian tradition. For Kant and modern theology in his wake, Jesus is the Christ because he is the archetype of an ideal, because he lived in a paradigmatic way, and just this rules out treating Jesus' saving significance as rooted in a messianic fulfillment of the line of Jesse, a fulfillment which makes the Jewishness of Jesus crucial. For a provocative account of the implications of repudiating the salvific significance of Jesus' Jewishness, see Jon D. Levenson, "The God of Abraham & the Enemies of 'Eurocentrism'," *First Things* 16 (October 1991): 15-21; for a sustained account of the dogmatic centrality of Jewishness within Christian theology, see Kendall Soulen, *The God of Israel and Christian Theology* (Minneapolis: Fortress, 1996).

[14]This outline of the parallels between Ruether/Johnson and Kant suggest a wider convergence of feminist theology with much of modern theology since Kant. Pressing this claim home would entail reading other feminist theologians in tandem with a number of signal modern theologians. I cannot pursue such an exposition; however, with respect to the sub-

tal criterion of dogma, and all matters Christian—doctrine, liturgy, ecclesiastical structure, the biblical text—are subordinated to that
foundational moral vision.

Distrust of the Tradition

Feminist theology finds its criterion in the ethical commitment to the
emancipation of women, but its energy and passion emerge out of that
most modern of stances: critique. Elizabeth Johnson states the matter
succinctly: "Theology done from this [feminist] perspective presses a
strong critique against traditional speech about God. It judges it to be
both humanly oppressive and religiously idolatrous."[15] This critique
begins with the observation that the linguistic practice of a religious
community finds its center of gravity in its characterization of the
divine. As Johnson writes, "The symbol of God functions as the primary
symbol of the whole religious system," and in so doing "language
about god implicitly represents what [that faith community] takes to be
the highest good, the profoundest truth, the most appealing beauty."[16]
Precisely because Christian speech about God is dominated by male symbols, the linguistic and conceptual universe of Christianity revolves around
a conception of the male as the highest good, and this "serves in manifold
ways to support an imaginative and structural world that excludes and
subordinates women."[17] By virtue of the imagery and concepts, pronouns

---

ordination of dogma to ethics, I find support in Susan Ross and Elizabeth Johnson's assessment of the basic unity of feminist theology. They observe, "Feminist theologies may be
pluralistic in nature, but they are united by a shared passion for justice for women," and as
they go on to report, that passion leads feminist theologians to the basic consensus that
"the lives and struggles of actual women around the world provide the resources and the
ultimate test of the adequacy of all feminist theologies" ("Feminist Theology: A Review of
the Literature," *Theological Studies* 56, no. 2 [June 1995]: 330). One important exception to
this general observation is Kathryn Tanner's broadly liberationist proposal, *The Politics of
God: Christian Theologies and Social Justice* (Minneapolis: Fortress, 1992). Tanner bases her
analysis on rules for Christian language use which emerge out of the inherited tradition
itself rather than a prevenient moral vision. In this respect, Tanner's proposal diverges from
the characteristic modern approach to dogma, paralleling more nearly the neo-orthodox
and dialectical theologies of the mid-twentieth century.

[15]Johnson, *She Who Is*, p. 18.
[16]Ibid., p. 4.
[17]Ibid., p. 5.

and practices that constitute the concrete particularity of the tradition, Christianity cannot help but reinforce patterns of domination. For Johnson, the "subaqueous pull [of 'the ruling-male-centered partiality'] has shaped all currents of the theological enterprise, so that Christian theory and praxis has been massively distorted."[18] The problem goes all the way down.

This massive distortion is not, at root, merely a matter of male imagery. To the question of *what* the Christian tradition says, Johnson adds the much more important question of *how* the tradition speaks about God. She claims that the tradition not only uses a wrongly narrow and limited set of words, but it also and more importantly uses those words wrongly. She writes, "Insofar as male-dominant language is honored as the only or supremely fitting way to speak about God, it absolutizes a single set of metaphors and obscures the height and depth and length and breadth of divine mystery."[19] The patriarchal defect is deeply and tenaciously embedded within the Christian tradition precisely because this material error has been absolutized, has been presented as obligatory and irreformable. As such, the tradition traffics in the sin of idolatry or, as Johnson sometimes says, the sin of literalism. According to this critique, the tradition is simply and disastrously mistaken about the theological status of inherited speech and practice. The tradition fails to see that all religious speech and practice, including traditional Christian speech about God and liturgical practice, is symbolic rather than literal. In this failure, the patriarchal sin becomes absolutized and frozen into the very bedrock of apostolic teaching. Thus does Johnson level *the* most common modern critique of the Christian tradition: it takes its inherited speech and practice as authoritative.[20]

---

[18]Ibid., p. 29.

[19]Ibid., p. 5.

[20]Johnson does not only depend upon a theory of the symbolic or metaphorical nature of religious language. She also reads the classical theological tradition's treatment of mystery as a warrant for the modern critique of the authoritative form of dogma. This close attention to the theological tradition poses a direct challenge to any who would resist the logic of modern theology. I shall suggest the basis for an alternative reading of the classical tradition in the final section; however, a full reckoning with Johnson's sophisticated form of the

In slightly different language, Rosemary Ruether presents this deeper, structural critique of traditional notions of the authority of the received tradition. In view of a rich modern tradition of phenomenological reflection, Ruether assumes that symbols express human experience. As such, "received symbols, formulas, and laws are either authenticated or not through their ability to illuminate or interpret experience." Since symbols express experience, they are "true" and "false" according to the deeper, more fundamental content of experience. As a feminist, Ruether reports that traditional Christian symbols are false to women's experience; they fail to illuminate or interpret, or more accurately and troublingly, they obscure and efface women's experience and interpret that silence as good. Yet this is not the root of the problem. The difficulty runs more deeply. For Ruether, "systems of authority try to reverse [the relation of experience to symbol] and make received symbols dictate what can be experienced as well as the interpretation of that which is experienced."[21] To be sure, Christian symbols deform because of their patriarchal content, but more importantly, these symbols deform because they are presented to women as *authoritative*. What might be discarded as unhelpful is pressed upon women as necessary. Constituting itself as a system of authority, for Ruether, the apostolic tradition tries to control experience

---

modern critique would require a systematic counter-reading of the sources she uses to support her understanding of the divine mystery. For a counter-reading of Karl Rahner, one of Johnson's important sources, see R. R. Reno, *The Ordinary Transformed: Karl Rahner and the Christian Vision of Transcendence* (Grand Rapids, Mich.: Eerdmans, 1995). In that volume, I attempt to show that for Rahner and the Christian tradition, mystery is not symbolized by but rather transfigures linguistic particularity such that our linguistic finitude takes on the real depth of divine love (see pp. 219-22). For a counter-reading of the Orthodox apophatic tradition, see Verne E. F. Harrison, "The Relationship Between Apophatic and Kataphatic Theology," *Pro ecclesia* 4, no. 3:318-32. Harrison's argument is, at root, an attempt to render explicit Orthodox assumptions which govern the use of the apophatic dimension of theological contemplation in order to prevent misreadings by modern theologians. For a similar attempt to prevent modern misreadings of the Orthodox tradition, see Thomas Hopko, "Apophatic Theology and the Naming of God in Eastern Orthodox Tradition," in *Speaking the Christian God: The Holy Trinity and the Challenge of Feminism,* ed. Alvin Kimel (Grand Rapids, Mich.: Eerdmans, 1992), pp. 144-61. Hopko argues that modern misreadings confuse the Orthodox apophasis with regard to the *ousia* of God with a modern relativization of the *hypostasis* of God in the redemptive economy of Father, Son and Holy Spirit.

[21]Both quotes from Ruether, *Sexism and God-Talk*, pp. 12-13.

and interpretation, subordinating experience, especially *women's* experience, to the purportedly divinely authorized symbols of the tradition. This dogmatism not only oppresses women, but more broadly and fundamentally, by making Christian symbols authoritative it perverts the expressive purpose of religious symbols.

Kant mounts a similar twofold critique of Christianity. For Kant, the material flaw of Christianity is not its patriarchal imagery; rather, the difficulty rests with the "vivid mode of representation"—the language of ceremony, cult, sacrifice and miracle—which dominates the apostolic tradition. In each instance, the archaic historical forms of earlier Jewish attempts to propitiate God through external actions rather than inner virtue, and to seek to guide their lives according to miraculous prophecies rather than the dictates of conscience, subvert the true moral religion of duty for duty's sake. As a consequence, just as the feminist seeks to reinterpret the language which is crippled by the genetic defect of patriarchy, Kant seeks to cleanse the tradition of its offensive "mode of representation." Moreover, like feminist theologians, Kant is well aware that this cleansing requires reading the tradition against the flow of its most basic imagery and structure. Yet this is not only permitted, it is required, "for the final purpose even of reading the holy scriptures, or of investigating their content, is to make men better."[22] Given this foundational moral purpose, Kant expresses a freedom from the tradition that is equal to any feminist proposal. As he says, to make the world better "we can do with [the text] what we like."[23]

---

[22]Kant, *Religion*, p. 102.

[23]Ibid. Kant does indeed do as he pleases with the text. Most chilling is his reading of the New Testament's use of the Old Testament. Because Kant found Judaism such a morally repugnant form of religion (indeed, not a religion at all; see *Religion*, pp. 116-17), the principle of edification requires eliminating the Jewish influences from a proper exegesis of Christian writings. This Kant does by explaining the overwhelming weight of Old Testament quotations, allusions and preoccupations within early Christian texts as itself proof that, for the early Christian authors, "their problem is and was merely the discovery of the most suitable means of *introducing* a purely moral religion in place of the old worship, to which the people were all too well habituated, without directly offending the people's prejudices" (*Religion*, p. 118). In other words, the apparent scriptural emphasis on the continuity between the God of Israel and Jesus of Nazareth is but a technique for extirpating the latter. Such a reading is based upon the following reasoning. Christianity is a vehicle for

This declaration of independence from the constraints of what the Christian linguistic inheritance "actually says" is a hallmark of modern theology, and it is justified by the deeper, structural critique of the tradition which Kant shares with feminist theology. Kant bases this critique upon a distinction between faith and religion. Faith is that constellation of historically particular and culturally specific words and practices that make up the Christian form of life. Left to its own devices, faith treats this constellation of particular words and practices as authoritative. In contrast to faith Kant sets the notion of religion which, for Kant, is the disposition of moral rectitude which acknowledges the relativity of historically conditioned forms of faith and recognizes that the dictates of practical reason (our moral sense), not historical particularities, have final authority. Faith's preoccupations might enliven and accentuate our moral sense (Kant clearly thinks that Christianity, especially the historical particularity of Jesus of Nazareth, does), but those preoccupations are valuable only as aids; they can never be the inner meaning and destiny of the human condition.[24]

---

true moral religion. Judaism is antithetical to true moral religion. Therefore, the preponderance of Jewish themes in the New Testament must be interpreted out as irrelevant to the essence of Christianity. A similar reasoning guides Elizabeth Fiorenza's feminist reconstruction of the original Christian community (see *In Memory of Her* [New York: Crossroad Publishing, 1985]). Her interpretive reasoning changes the material assumptions about what constitutes true moral religion, but otherwise follows Kant's logic. True Christian faith is a vehicle for inclusive religion. The Christian Scriptures are patriarchal. Therefore, the Christian Scriptures are a deformation of a prior, true and inclusive Christian faith. This conclusion then guides a reconstruction of the original community from the fragments of inclusivity remaining in the New Testament.

[24]This is why modern theology has such difficulty digesting the claim that Jesus of Nazareth is the "Son of God" in the sense of being the inner meaning and destiny of the human condition. Most modern theologians affirm that Jesus may *symbolize* our ultimate destiny, but the very logic of the structural critique of the authority of historical particularity requires the modern theologian to deny that Jesus *is* our destiny. Feminist theology is no different from modern theology in its at least implicit repudiation of the tradition's specification of Jesus as the inner purpose and destiny of all human beings, e.g., the creedal affirmation of Jesus as the Son of God. This inability or refusal to digest the "is" which connects the man Jesus with the salvific will of God follows from the logic of distinguishing between faith—the constellation of particularity which, for the Christian tradition, includes the life, death and resurrection of that particular first century Palestinian Jew, Jesus of Nazareth—and religion. Feminist theology differs from most modern theology in questioning the complacent assumption that Jesus can adequately *symbolize* women's inner purpose and ultimate destiny.

On the basis of this distinction Kant is able to formulate quite precisely the structural flaw of traditional Christianity. For the tradition, historical faith is intrinsic to our relation to God. Faith is the whole point. However, given the liberating distinction between faith and religion, we can now see that by absolutizing historically conditioned faith, by making faith the whole point, "the moral order is wholly reversed and what is merely a means is commanded unconditionally (as an end)."[25] This reversal yields the idolatry that Johnson condemns and the system of authority which Ruether rejects as an inversion of the proper, empowering relationship between symbol and experience. For modern theology, the deepest flaw in the apostolic tradition is its confusion of means with ends, its failure to see the symbolic or metaphorical character of the Christian faith. At root, then, the Christian tradition is to be distrusted not simply because it is wrong in its particulars (although for feminist theology, the patriarchy of the tradition is deeply wrong), but more importantly because the tradition presents its particular teachings and practices in the wrong form. Historical particularities are passed on as indispensable, as intrinsically significant, as authoritative, and this form of presentation inevitably obscures the inner essence of religion.

The ascendancy of historically conditioned expressions of transcendence to the status of authoritative truth is perennial. As Kant observes, humans have a "natural need and desire" for "something sensibly tenable" which might outwardly confirm the inner dictates of "the higher concepts and grounds of reason."[26] This need for outward support constantly tempts us to treat the sensible aids, the symbols and metaphors, as the true goal and purpose of religion. Precisely because the Christian tradition *does* offer something "sensibly tenable," it is a source of support but also a temptation. "The words" threaten to entangle us within their particularity, to command our loyalty, and as such, the modern theologian feels the constant undertow of what the words say, the weight of the tradition's sensible presence. Modern theology is in large part defined by its efforts to eliminate the intrinsic authority of the received tradition in order to gain critical independence. These efforts are supported by the basic distinction be-

---

[25]Kant, *Religion*, p. 153.
[26]Ibid., p. 100.

tween outward form (historical faith as symbol and metaphor) and inner essence (true religion as mystery and experience). Through this distinction, modern theology seeks to relativize the authority of the inherited Christian language (the tyranny of the outward form) in order to save the truth of the Christian tradition (the mystery or experience which is its inner essence). This clears the ground for a critique of the dogmatic by the ethical.[27] The structural critique of the linguistic inheritance, which includes not only formal statements of doctrine but also the canonical texts and the ancient liturgical and ecclesiastical practices of the church, clears away the false authority of finite linguistic forms and opens the way for reformulations guided by the moral truths of the Transcendent.

Saving the Tradition

The "problem" of the tradition—its making things of the Spirit routine, its smothering authoritarian institutions, its silencing of dissent, its idolatrous literalism—must be cut away, and the disjointed skeleton of the tradition must be reassembled and a new flesh created according to the truth of the inner essence. Here, the feminist theologian assumes the particularly modern form of the prophetic task.[28] The tradition has prostituted itself

[27]With characteristic economy, Mary Daly links the modern critique of dogmatism to the ethical failures of Christianity. Daly writes, "The various theologies that hypostatize transcendence, that is, those which in one way or another objectify 'God' as *being*, thereby attempt in a self-contradictory way to envisage transcendent reality as finite. 'God' then functions to legitimate the existing social, economic, and political status quo, in which women and other victimized groups are subordinate" (*Beyond God the Father*, p. 19). The order of defect is clear. The structural flaw in Christianity—its belief that finite being (e.g., language itself) is capable of the infinite—reinforces the ethical flaw of patriarchy. Once the flaw is detected and critiqued according to the distinction between inner essence and outward form, the social relations legitimated by the now relativized authority of dogma are desacralized and open to moral critique

[28]A more sustained engagement with feminist theology must come to terms with prevailing modern assumptions about the nature of prophetic witness. I can only draw attention to the call of the prophet Ezekiel when he is told by the likeness of the glory of the Lord to eat a scroll (ezek 3:1-3). Whatever might be the content of Ezekiel's polemic against the clerical status quo, the account of his call suggests that his witness depends upon an immersion in and digestion of the linguistic inheritance of the people of Israel, not personal mystical vision or a universal theory of religious language and practice independent of that inheritance. To swallow the linguistic *concreta* of ancient Israel seems rather far removed from the self-distancing entailed in the structural critique of dogma.

to the sins of the world. It must be cleansed in an act of critical reconstruction. One might be optimistic or pessimistic about how much might
survive the fires of purification, so modern theologians can argue among
themselves quite vigorously. Indeed, feminist theologians divide on precisely this question. But all agree that the gospel cannot come alive
unless the modern theologian frees it from its bondage to the authority of
the tradition. Thus, under the nurturing guidance of the enlightened
theologian is the gospel finally spoken in righteousness and truth.[29]

The Bible is the most widely accepted form of authority within the tradition, and Kant is optimistic about how far a properly moral interpretation of Scripture might be forced. Kant's approach is multi-faceted.
Sometimes he anticipates the use of historical criticism to divest the text
of any relevance at all. Considering the prayer for revenge in Psalm 59,
Kant entertains the hypothesis that the text reflects Jewish notions about
God's purely political regency over earthly affairs, antique notions which
have no moral sense at all for modern readers.[30] Far more often, Kant
uses the distinction between inner and outer to melt away the morally
obscure or troubling passages. The most crucial example is his treatment
of the synoptic gospels, for these texts seem so unequivocally about the
life of a historically conditioned man, Jesus of Nazareth. The "outward"
existence of this man and not a moral ideal appear to be the *whole point*
of the gospel accounts. Kant is quite aware that the heart of the New Testament is a series of narratives deeply immersed in historical detail, details extrinsic to pure religion. Yet the New Testament's scandalous

---

[29]Here feminist theology enjoys a community of interest with a certain species of Reformation traditionalism. See David Yeago, "Gnosticism, Antinomianism and Reformation Theology: Reflections on the Cost of a Construal," *Pro ecclesia* 2, no. 1 (1993): 37-55, for a
discussion of the pervasive modern anxiety about particularity which seems to find a home
in a very determined obedience to an epistemological reading of the traditional Lutheran
distinction between law and gospel. Here, the flaw of investing historical particularities
with unequivocal divine presence is decried not as a threat to modern critical freedom, but
instead as a threat to the freedom of the gospel. In spite of this difference, the results are
the same: our inner destiny and purpose as children of God cannot be vested in any determinate finite form. Thus feminist theologians such as Elizabeth Johnson, who are often
much more serious about the contemplative dimension of the Christian form of life than
are other moderns, are able to critique "literalism" as a threat to divine freedom (holy mystery), as well as the richness of human experience.
[30]See Kant, *Religion,* p. 101n.

emphasis on the merely historical narrative of the life and death of an ancient Jewish man is swept aside with the modern commonplace—the distinction between historical particularity (Kant's notion of faith) and the inner essence of true religion. Here, that distinction is refined into a separation of the outward mode of representation (the historical narrative) from the inward, "rational" meaning (for Kant, the dictates of practical reason). As Kant writes, "Once this mode of representation, which was in its time probably the only *popular* one, is divested of its mystical veil, it is easy to see that, for practical purposes, its spiritual and rational meaning have been valid and binding for the whole world and for all time."[31] Kant then sets about the task of stripping away the "mode of representation." He discards the New Testament's presentation of the life and death of Jesus of Nazareth as the *whole point* of the gospel, and substitutes the assumption that the text uses Jesus in order to make a larger, spiritual and rational point. In this way, Kant is able to save the tradition from its distortion under the burden of a now unnecessary outward form, and to expose, for the first time, the inward, universal truth of the text.

Modern theology since Kant has used the distinction between the outer husk and inner kernel to enact innumerable redemptions of the tradition. Feminist theology may be less sanguine than Kant and his many male followers about how much of the tradition might be redeemed, but the basic moves, the role of the feminist theologian as redeemer of the materially and structurally defective tradition, are the same. For example, Elizabeth Johnson treats the emergence of feminist consciousness as a decisive new resource for speaking truthfully about God. It is "a new experience of God" which is "a new event in the religious history of humankind."[32] Here the feminist movement supplies Christian theology with crucially new material which unlocks salvific truths previously imprisoned in the distortions of a patriarchalism authorized by an uncritical literalism. Inspired by this "new experience of God," Johnson's recovery and redemption of the scriptural tradition follows the modern procedure. Johnson writes, "Since these symbols as they stand are embedded within

---

[31]Ibid., p. 78.
[32]Johnson, *She Who Is*, p. 62.

a text, a culture, and a tradition that are skewed by sexism [echoing Kant: the only mode of representation with any hope of popularity in a patriarchal culture], they cannot be taken and used without passing through the fire of critical feminist principles."[33] The pattern of modern theology repeats itself. The defective inherited form of Christian teachings must be corrected and redeemed by the deeper, more fundamental truths of a "new experience of God." Kant condemns the subjectivism implicit in Johnson's tilt toward experience.[34] A morality of pure reason, not women's experience, drives his critical reconstruction of the Christian faith. Yet, this is a family quarrel. Both are united in their claim that the Christian faith, as received, is inadequate by virtue of its proposal of a finite form as salvifically indispensable and must be saved by the critical efforts of the modern theologian.[35]

As savior of a defective tradition, modern theology displays its distinctive ethos. Sometimes the modern theologian is a lonely voice crying in the wilderness, carrying on a solitary, heroic struggle for the inward truth of the spirit against the outward tyranny of the letter. Other modern theologians speak for a decisive, revolutionary new movement—modern science, existentialism, Marxism, ecological consciousness, women's experience—and the wave of the movement, not the individual theologian, is the heroic actor. More commonly, however, the modern theolo-

---

[33]Ibid., p. 103.

[34]See Kant, *Religion*, pp. 104-5, for his polemic against the use of subjective criteria for theological judgment. Such criteria, he argues, are inscrutable, private mental states which, because exempt from rational criticism, lead to fanaticism.

[35]At times, the modern impulse to see oneself as the harbinger of a New Age, as riding the crest of the New Movement in which the truth is finally unveiled, reaches well beyond the mere renewal of Christianity. In spite of, or rather, because of her exertions to be new and unique, Mary Daly places herself full square within the modern tradition of Rousseau, Emerson, Whitman and Nietzsche when she describes the movement she seeks to serve as a revolutionary new beginning which holds out the possibility of redemption. She writes, "As the women's movement begins to have its effect upon the fabric of society, transforming it from patriarchy into something that never existed before—into a diarchal situation that is radically new—it can become the greatest single challenge to the major religions of the world, Western and Eastern. Beliefs and values that have held sway for thousands of years will be questioned as never before. This revolution may well be the greatest single hope for survival of spiritual consciousness on this planet" (*Beyond God the Father*, pp. 13-14).

gian simply assumes a quality of experience or sensibility, and on the basis of this assumption corrects the defective antiquity of the Christian tradition.[36] Across all these variations, however, the relationship of the theologian to the concrete linguistic form of Christianity is constant. Precisely because the dogmatic form of received formulations is intrinsically defective, the tradition requires the red pencil of the modern theologian.[37] Without the ministrations of the modern theologian, without the critiques and correctives born of the distinctive genius of the present age, the apostolic tradition would be a dead letter. When the day is done, modern theology holds the key that unlocks the gospel.

Seeing the Integrity of Feminist Theology

What does one achieve by seeing feminist theology within the frame of modern theology? At the very least, to see the modern integrity of feminist theology should make clear that no defense of the Christian tradition will be rhetorically successful unless feminist revisions are understood as a part of the larger modern project. For example, to object to the preacher who invokes God with the formula "Creator, Redeemer and Sanctifier" on the grounds that such a formulation is a heterodox deviation from the tradition is to accuse the preacher of something he already affirms as the *very task* of theology. As Kant writes, "We ought even now

---

[36]When considering the classical affirmations of divine impassability and omnipotence, Johnson writes, "Such a God is morally intolerable" (*She Who Is*, p. 249). In defense of her rejection of the classical attributes, she continues, "Large numbers of thoughtful people in the nineteenth and twentieth centuries have rejected the classical idea of the impassable, omnipotent God, finding it both intellectually inadequate and religiously repugnant" (p. 250). Thus, instead of breaking and reforming the metaphysical notions of impassability and omnipotence on the wheel of the passion narratives (as does Cyril of Alexandria), Johnson corrects these classical concerns with the moral sensibility of modernity, a sensibility which she explicates and explains rather than simply assumes, but which is itself above the judgment of the linguistic particularity of the tradition.

[37]Describing his project of revising Christian doctrine to allow for a dynamic, inclusive form of faith, John Hick observes, "If [the original inspiration] can be liberated from the network of [traditional] theories—about Incarnation, Trinity and Atonement—which served once to focus but now only serve to obscure its significance, that lived teaching can continue to be a major source of inspiration for human life" (*The Metaphor of God Incarnate: Christology in a Pluralistic Age* [Louisville: Westminster John Knox, 1993], pp. 12-13). Thus does Hick offer his services as savior of the truth of Christianity "from the mass of ecclesiastical dogmas and practices that have developed over the centuries" (p. 13).

to labor industriously, by way of continuously setting free the pure religion from its present shell, which as yet cannot be spared."[38] The transcendent, our experience of holy mystery, must be freed from its imprisonment in the dogmatic form of the apostolic tradition. Yet, because we shall always need symbols and metaphors, the freedom cannot be pure. We still need the material of the tradition. Hence, we must revise rather than jettison the tradition. We must continue to use the tradition even as we assert our independence from its authority, or more accurately, even as we assert our independence from its outward, literal authority in order to obey its inward, spiritual essence. This disposition toward the tradition—seeking to be free from it but recognizing its symbolic resources as indispensable—explains why modern theologians insist upon reconstructing the tradition rather than simply discarding it. The end result is the situation that drives traditionalists to distraction: modern theologians who repudiate the authority of Christian doctrine but insist upon a role in teaching and proclaiming that doctrine.

The traditionalist must recognize that the revisions of feminists (or any other modern theologians) do not stem from a perverse desire to destroy the Christian faith. Quite the contrary, such revisions grow out of a comprehensive vision of the nature and function of religious language which makes novelty imperative and which rules out traditional ascriptions of authority to particular texts and formulae. For modern theology, preaching against the authority of the tradition is necessary in order to guard against the temptation of literal narrowness, the enticing comfort of what Kant called the sensibly tenable. Vesting unequivocal authority in historically particular linguistic artifacts is a natural response to the human desire for something both intimate and reliable, but, argues modern theology, giving in to this desire generates the structural defect of dogmatizing the outward form. Thus an openness to "heterodox deviation" is the desirable disposition which guards against the temptations of the dogmatizing impulse. Experimenting with novelties such as "Creator, Redeemer and Sanctifier" helps to break the charm of inherited language and the consequent captivity to the mere outward form of faith. The log-

---

[38]Kant, *Religion*, p. 126.

ic of modern theology is able, in this way, to handle sophisticated and highly reasoned objections to modern revision of the Christian tradition as forms of dogmatism. Given the comprehensive quality of modern theology, the defender of the tradition is doomed to frustration and miscommunication, merely trading epithets of "heretic" and "fundamentalist" with the feminist theologian, unless she recognizes the larger modern framework for specific feminist proposals.

Seeing feminist theology as a form of modern theology allows for one to understand how a revision such as "Creator, Redeemer and Sanctifier" might be justified by the speaker as an act of faithfulness. This is crucial if a defender of inherited formulae is to view the revisionist as someone possessing a serious and comprehensive vision of Christian faithfulness. However, the understanding gained by viewing feminist theology as part of the larger project of modern theology extends beyond empathy. In the vigorous and courageous application of the characteristic elements of modern theology to central features of the Christian linguistic inheritance, feminist theology brings modern theology into vivid focus, revealing the structural critique as the key to feminist theology and the modern method it embodies. By relativizing the particular linguistic form of Christianity, the way is open for the subordination of the symbolic dogma to the ethical meaning of religion. Furthermore, by relativizing the authority of the received tradition, the task of theology shifts from second order to first order. Modern theology's structural critique forces the recognition that each age is recasting and renewing its symbolic resources to better evoke and express the sacred. Theology, then, is both a making as well as a making sense of the outward form that symbolizes the inner essence. Theology is itself a creative constituent of the ever-changing metaphorical sensorium of the transcendent. This double function places a creative as well as systematic responsibility upon the theologian, explaining the need for theology to intervene into the inherited language of the church in order to renew and revise. As a result, the integrity of feminist theology is clearest at the point at which it is most publicly controversial and bitterly opposed by traditionalists, for the vigorous drive to introduce both revisions of inherited language and new formulations is testimony to the seriousness with which feminists take the task of modern theology.

Toward an Assessment of Modern Theology

If modern theology and its structural critique are, in fact, the proper form of reflective Christian faithfulness, then far from a threat to Christianity, feminist theology must be viewed as a crucial, perhaps—given its clarity of vision—the crucial voice in renewing the symbolic resources of Christian faith. I would like to conclude by suggesting that though the consequent follows, the inference is unsound because the antecedent is false. Modern theology is not the proper form of reflective Christian faithfulness. To make this suggestion even remotely persuasive, I shall seek to parry one characteristic modern objection and to open up a line of reflection upon the negative consequences of modern theology's crucial feature, the structural critique of dogmatism.

A feminist theologian might object from the very outset that a rejection of that aspect of modern theology cannot be sustained. Modern theology, so the objection continues, must be accepted as the proper form of intellectually responsible Christian faithfulness because its structural critique simply gives clear conceptual expression to an independence from linguistic particularity which Christian reflection has always affirmed and exploited. Paul's use of Jewish Scripture, itself the linguistic anchor of early Christianity, is a sustained declaration of independence from the interpretive tradition of Judaism.[39] Early Christian readings of

---

[39] See Richard B. Hays, *The Echoes of Scripture in the Letters of Paul* (New Haven, Conn.: Yale University Press, 1989). Hays presents Paul's particular exegetical swerves and dodges, and makes a compelling case that Paul's use of the *gramma* of the Septuagint is quite consistent with his comments about the freedom of the *pneuma*. Hays is, however, less convincing when he turns to draw hermeneutical conclusions from Paul's own use of Scripture. Rightly affirming that Paul insists that the letter serves the Spirit, Hays allows the Spirit to drift out of particularity and into "Spirit-experience." Consider Hays's reading of 1 Cor 10. There, Hays allows that Paul's use of the Septuagint flows from a more primitive commitment to the "present datum" of Christian practice, specifically baptism (see pp. 101-2). This is given a gloss by Hays which shifts Paul's hermenuetical anchor out of the "present datum" and into Paul's subjectivity, his experience of God's action. This shift has more to do with the influence of modern assumptions about the relation of spirit and letter than Paul's, and the same influence leads Hays to shift from Paul's insistence that the gospel is an intensification of divine presence which reaches out of the *gramma* of Scripture and into the concrete lives of believers, to an opposition between *gramma* and *pnuema*. Thus, Hays claims that Paul's "gospel is such that it must be written on human hearts rather than in texts," and as a result, Paul's "radical proposal is to reject all text-bound criteria for discerning authenticity" of Christian ministry (p. 149). A great deal hangs on "rather" and "all;" both

the Old Testament are dominated by typological readings of texts that certainly take liberties with the immediate linguistic sense of any number of key texts.[40] One of the most prominent objections to the Nicene Creed was the novelty of the term *homoousion*. Yet, this argument against the creed did not succeed, and one cannot but conclude that an affirmation of the Nicene Creed entails a freedom to use linguistic novelties to express Christian truths. In view of this openness to novelty at the very foundation of what I have been calling "the Christian linguistic inheritance," to reject modern theology on the grounds that it advocates novelty is, then, to break with the tradition itself.

To respond to this challenge, I must simply draw the contrast rather than demonstrate it. The defining feature of modern theology is its enabling assumptions, not its attachment to novelty. The structural critique which funds the critical task of modern theology defines spiritual

---

conflict with Hays's persuasive observation that Paul's quite free use of the *gramma* of Scripture flows from an underlying assumption about the continuity of divine presence. Hays notes that for Paul, "the freedom of intertextual play is grounded in a secure sense of the continuity of God's grace. Paul trusts the same God who spoke through Moses to speak still in his own transformative reading" (p. 156). Surely this is so, but the assumptions of modern theology obscure the fact that the logic of continuity reaches backward as well as forward, and by reaching backward, the *gramma* cannot ever be set against the *pnuema* in any systematic way.

For a feminist appropriation of Hays which seeks to avoid the modern division of spirit from letter, see Amy Plantinga Pauw, "The Word Is Near You: A Feminist Conversation with Lindbeck," *Theology Today* 50, no. 1 (1993): 45-55. Whether one judges Pauw successful depends upon how one reads her conclusion that passages such as Galatians 4 and Romans 8 are "unsuitable for a contemporary social embodiment of God's promises" (p. 55).

[40]See Ignatius's letter to the Philadelphians. That community apparently demanded textual evidence for Ignatius's teaching. Ignatius claims that his teaching is written in the original documents of the community, but the skeptical Philadelphians object that it is precisely Ignatius's ability to read his teachings into seemingly innocent passages of the Septuagint which is in question. The exasperated Ignatius finally insists that his teachings are in the text because Jesus Christ *is* the text. He writes, "To my mind it is Jesus Christ who is the original documents. The inviolable archives are his cross and death and his resurrection and the faith that came by him" (8:2). With such a claim, Ignatius certainly loosens the hold of the inherited *gramma*. The linguistic particularity of the Septuagint is part of a larger whole, and precisely this gives him the interpretive liberty which the Philadelphians call into question. However, any who would view Ignatius as a precursor to modern theology's metaphysical division of the spirit from the letter in the structural critique must pass through Ignatius's identity statement: "Jesus Christ is the text." My contention is that such a passage cannot be effected.

truth in such a way that it cannot be contained in the finite form of human language. For the modern theologian, the innovation of employing the *homoousion*, as innovation, is justified because all language is symbolic of a deeper truth. Therefore, as a matter of principle, inherited canonical language cannot be privileged over other, novel linguistic artifacts. The proper question to ask of an innovation is not whether it is contained within or is even consistent with the linguistic reservoir of the past, but rather whether the innovation is symbolically effective in the present. In contrast (and I am stating a reading of the tradition that requires demonstration), the freedom from the letter expressed by Paul rests in the conviction that the divine can be (because God is) in the finite form of Jesus of Nazareth; similarly, this presence of God in the human finite form both absorbs the words of Scripture (such that Paul finds Christ at every turn) and overflows into the community of eucharistic fellowship (such that Paul takes the language and practice of the Christian community as the proper key to unlock the fullness of the letter). On what I would call the classical view, then, an innovation such as the use of the *homoousion* may be justified because it follows from the concrete presence of God's salvific will in Jesus of Nazareth, a presence which has already overflowed into the writings then coalescing as the New Testament canon, and which shall not rest until it has overflowed into all things. If I am right about the classical view, then its difference from modern theology could not be more basic.[41] The modern independence from the authority of inherited language is based upon a metaphysical judgment about the inability of the finite to contain the infinite. The classical approach to the freedom of the Gospel anticipates novelty because of a christological judgment that the seriousness (unto death upon the cross) of God's redemptive presence in the finite entails a drawing of all

---

[41]One of the most significant challenges to any contrast I might draw is Kathryn Tanner's *Politics of God*. Because she does not rely upon a distinction between experience and symbol to motivate her critique of authoritative social and linguistic forms, her proposal does not rely upon the modern lever of independence, the structural critique. The absence of this crucial feature of modern theology, however, is matched with an equally pronounced absence of the christological affirmation which is central to the classical view. A sustained engagement with Tanner's reading of the linguistic patterns of the divine-human relationship must show the importance and implications of this christological absence.

things, words and persons, into God's transformative love.[42]

I have concentrated on modern theology's structural critique because the question of our proper relation to the Christian linguistic inheritance is much more than a question of theological method and the authority of dogma. The metaphysical judgment and the christological judgment also entail judgments about our relation to God and each other. Are we free from the authority of the Christian linguistic inheritance because all particularity is inherently defective, or is the linguistic particularity itself free because it is not the dead letter of the past but, by virtue of God's love, is in its very particularity the living Spirit? The former is, at root, a denial of the possibility of God's presence in our finite lives.[43] The latter is an

---

[42]If I am right about the classical view of linguistic particularity, then no objection can be made to the linguistic novelties proposed by feminist theology that rules out novelty in itself. For to take a strictly "traditionalist" approach to feminist theology entails mimicking the "traditionalist" objection to the Nicene Creed. Precisely because the christological judgment at the core of the classical view is an affirmation of particularity which is intrinsically dynamic, absolutely nothing can be ruled out on general, metaphysical grounds. To do so would lead to an inversion of rather than alternative to modern theology. Within the classical view, revisions and reformulations must be examined in their particular contexts and along the diverse possible trajectories of Christian language. In these inquiries, then, one may find some novelties wanting while finding others helpful. Thus, although the classical view is antithetical to the modern assumptions of feminist theology, a classical engagement with the particular proposals of feminist theology might yield numerous affirmations and absorptions. For such an engagement, see William C. Placher, *Narratives of a Vulnerable God: Christ, Theology and Scripture* (Louisville: Westminster John Knox, 1994).

[43]Because of the logic of modern theology's metaphysical judgment, Johnson's attempt to give adequate expression to God's participatory love fails. The classical Christian doctrine of God includes trinitarian and incarnational foci, both of which are driven by the conviction that Jesus of Nazareth is the concrete, real and full presence of God in human life. In both instances, theology struggles to give adequate conceptual expression to the fact that God's love fully participates in the condition of the beloved. In contrast, by virtue of the notion of symbolic mediation, the only form of presence permitted by the structural critique of dogmatism, Johnson does not have the conceptual resources for articulating the full participation of God in human life. For example, Johnson insists that "Christ" cannot be reduced to the historical individual Jesus of Nazareth (see *She Who Is*, p. 72). The separation of Christ from Jesus is entailed in the logic of the modern approach. Modern theology must keep God at a distance in order to motivate the structural critique. As such, God is able to participate only symbolically or metaphorically in human life, not concretely and physically. It is precisely at the point of this conceptual failure that a classical engagement with feminist thought might redeem Johnson's desire to give systematic centrality to God's participatory love by making the unequivocal presence of God in Jesus Christ, not the structural critique, the lever for emancipation toward flourishing in mutuality with each other and with God.

extraordinarily optimistic faith that God's presence is continually pouring forth from within the finitude of Christian language into the finitude of our lives.

More is at stake in our judgments about the status of linguistic particularity than a pessimism and optimism about the presence of holiness in our inevitably linguistic and particular lives. The metaphysical judgment which funds the structural critique also entails disturbing consequences for our assessment of our own lives and the lives of others. The structural critique of dogmatism treats the particularity of the other as a source of regret. The fact that we need particularity as a symbolic medium is a misfortune, and the concrete forms we encounter in life, including persons, disfigure the inner essence which is our final destiny. Witness Kant's treatment of Jesus. Kant affirms Jesus as a representative of moral rectitude, but that affirmation is hollow, for the part of Jesus that makes him a person rather than a principle is precisely that part which Kant seeks to excise from his reading of Scripture. The same logic applies to feminist theology. Johnson is able to engage the cross and empty tomb as symbols, but not as part of the man Jesus' intrinsically particular fate. The limitations of modern treatments of Jesus, fem-

---

As a positive proposal consider the following. Johnson's focus upon the motherhood of God seeks to serve a fundamentally participatory vision of God. She writes, "Speaking about God as mother fixes as bedrock the idea that relationship is a constitutive way in which divine freedom enacts itself" (*She Who Is*, p. 185). However, such a claim cannot be made within the modern framework. Precisely because God is present in symbol, and no symbol can be absolutized, *nothing* is fixed as bedrock theologically. To aspire to fix in bedrock is to fall victim to the temptations of literalism. Yet, were Johnson to shift from the metaphysical judgment to the christological judgment, she would have the cross and the empty tomb in the finite form of Jesus of Nazareth as intrinsic to God's identity. There we find the constitutive relationality of God, both *in se* and *ad extra*, fixed in the bedrock of worldly affairs. With such a point of departure, Johnson would be able to tell the story of "She Who Is" as one which pours out of the particularity of Jesus of Nazareth rather than as a metaphorical construction which must itself be "critically relieved of restrictive anthropological and sociological structures" (p. 178), a process which threatens to remove the metaphor from the concrete particularity of our experience of motherhood, since we live in the world of anthropological and sociological structures. In the end, an affirmation that God is revealed in that first century Palestinian Jew, Jesus of Nazareth, is a far more promising place than the metaphysical judgment of modern theology to begin a theology of the Spirit-Sophia's joyful weaving of the intrinsically relational logos of the Mother-Lord into the concrete fabric of human life.

inist theology included, carry over to our treatment of others in their particularity. Regardless of protests about the importance of mutuality and community, to love another with anything like the fullness enjoined by the Christian tradition would entail idolatry, for the holy mystery which is the proper object of our love must be distinguished from the concrete symbols of its presence. In the conceptual universe of modern theology, the concrete other can be but a defective vessel of ultimate significance.

By virtue of these assumptions, modern theology leaves us with no deep defense against the temptations of either nihilism or self-love.[44] Once one awakens from the reveries of transcendence or mystery or being, and one finds oneself living where humans do, in fact, live—amidst linguistic particularity—one either despairs of finding an anchor of abiding significance in the world of particular words and particular persons, or one turns to the inner self as somehow exempt from the prohibition against dogmatism. To the extent that moderns persevere as theologians, the latter seems the most likely path, and so libraries are filled with critiques of the tradition paired with strikingly credulous reports of the dictates of experience or conscience. Elizabeth Johnson is by no means unique when she combines an extended defense of the hidden mystery of God with a confident report of the saving significance of women's experience. What the critiques of modern theology decree as obscured by the outward forms of concrete human interaction (language and ritual) re-emerges within the self. Thus, the anchor

---

[44]For an account of these two temptations in a theological engagement with contemporary literary criticism, see David Dawson, *Literary Theory* (Minneapolis: Augsburg Fortress, 1995). Dawson reads Harold Bloom and Paul de Man as charting opposite paths toward a common anti-incarnational stance. Both Bloom's hyperspiritualization and de Man's opposite hypertextualization of linguistic expression converge in a striking pessimism about the possibility of human mutuality, a pessimism which takes fullest expression in "the violence that seems to haunt both theorists: the violence of the ephebe's struggle with precursors [Bloom's hyperspiritualism] and the violence of the positing power of language [de Man's hypertextualism]" (p. 13). My suggestion is that regardless of the material commitments of modern theology, its formal enabling assumptions point toward either de Man's nihilistic hypertextualism (the assumption that authoritative language is always a deforming expression of power) or Bloom's self-assertive hyperspiritualism (implicit or explicit appeals to some fuller spirit which struggles to escape the intrinsic constraints of the inherited letter).

becomes oneself, and one clings to one's sentiments and experiences with a tenacity born of knowing that otherwise one is adrift.

Out of this temptation toward self-love emerges a violence which marks modern theology, feminist variants included. Recall Kant's observation that in order to interpret the Bible according to the inner essence of religion, one may do with the text what one likes. This disdain for the concrete integrity of what Kant encounters in the Bible is not accidental. Such a disposition follows directly from the modern critique of dogmatism. The linguistic particularities one encounters in the world cannot have intrinsic significance, and as such they are dispensable. Modern theology marches to Kant's orders. What does not fit into the flourishing which is proclaimed as the self-evident good for human beings is cast aside as unusable detritus. Feminist theology does not embody any greater violence to the tradition than other modern precursors; rather, by virtue of the flourishing which feminism identifies as the self-evident good for human beings, compounded with a heightened sensitivity to the features of human language which impede that flourishing, feminist theology brings to fuller expression modern theology's hostility to the tenacious and sensuous particularity of the inherited language of Christianity. However, the tragedy is not the dissected orthodoxy that remains in feminist or any other form of modern theology. The tradition is, after all, the concrete form, not the point of God's love. Human beings are the objects of God's love, and the tragedy of modern theology is that the logic of critique which allows Kant to do with the text as he will easily becomes global. What the metaphysical judgment at the root of the structural critique relativizes as a dispensable symbolic form includes the actual forms of our cohumanity—our shared language, our shared traditions, our interactive gestures—and within the framework of modern theology we are certainly dissuaded from any hope that this linguistic particularity, the very material conditions of our mutuality, might have enduring significance. And worse, in a world in which the concrete forms of human relationality are already deformed by the "necessities" of marketplace, bureaucracy and battlefield, the critique of dogmatism tempts us to think that, like the concrete form of Christian linguistic practice, we may do with persons what we will.[45] That Christian feminism would find its theoretical home in modern theology's violence against particularity, a violence that allows us to fall into the cruel void of modernity, is a sad mystery that calls out for further contemplation.[46]

[45]For a compelling account of the ways in which modernity has stripped humanity of the body (both social and personal) and offered up the particularity of human life to the purposes of the modern state, see William Cavanaugh, " 'A Fire Strong Enough to Consume the House': The Wars of Religion and the Rise of the State," *Modern Theology* 11, no. 4 (1995): 397-420.

[46]I would like to thank David Dawson, Ephraim Radner, Maryanne Stevens and George Sumner for reading drafts of this essay.

8

IS GOD SEXUAL?

Human Embodiment &
the Christian Conception of God

Stanley J. Grenz

CLASSICALLY MINDED CHRISTIAN THINKERS GENERALLY THUNDER A resounding "No!" to any attempt to link God and sexuality. The God Christians worship, they declare, is not only neither male nor female but decidedly nonsexual. Elizabeth Achtemeier speaks for the majority in asserting, "it is universally recognized by biblical scholars that the God of the Bible has no sexuality."[1] Such a sweeping conclusion, however, raises a crucial theological question. One of the strongest theological themes in the Christian tradition is the declaration that humans are created to be the image of God, that is, that God created humans to resemble in some sense their Creator. The *imago Dei* suggests that there is a connection between our essential human nature and the divine reality. As Karl Barth explains, "in God's own sphere and being, there exists a divine and therefore self-grounded prototype to which this being can correspond."[2] But if God and sexuality are dis-

---

[1] Elizabeth Achtemeier, "Exchanging God for 'No Gods': A Discussion of Female Language for God," in *Speaking the Christian God: The Holy Trinity and the Challenge of Feminism*, ed. Alvin F. Kimel Jr. (Grand Rapids, Mich.: Eerdmans, 1992), p. 4. Likewise, Old Testament scholar Phyllis Trible notes that in spite of the strong preponderance of the masculine gender in metaphors and other imagery describing God, "there is a strong consensus that the Old Testament regards Yahweh as nonsexual" ("Depatriarchalizing in Biblical Interpretation," *Journal of the American Academy of Religion* 41 [1973]: 31). Similar conclusions are shared by evangelical feminists. See, for example, Mary J. Evans, *Woman in the Bible* (Downers Grove, Ill.: InterVarsity Press, 1983), p. 21.

[2] Karl Barth, *Church Dogmatics*, trans. J. W. Edwards, O. Bussey, Harold Knight, ed. G. W. Bromiley and T. F. Torrance (Edinburgh: T. & T. Clark, 1958) 3/1:183.

junctive, how can God be the transcendent ground for our human embodiment as sexual creatures? How can human sexuality be "good," if it is an aspect of human existence that makes us unlike, rather than like God? This theological problem is exacerbated when we note that the initial biblical statement asserting the creation of humankind in the divine image links the *imago Dei* to human existence as male and female:

> Then God said, "Let us make human beings in our image, in our likeness, and let them rule over the fish of the sea and the birds of the air, over the livestock, over all the earth, and over all the creatures that move along the ground." So God created human beings in his own image, in the image of God he created him; male and female he created them. (Gen 1:26-27)

The text suggests that human existence as male and female is somehow constitutive for what it means to be the *imago Dei*. Consequently, the creation of humankind as sexual creatures—embodied as male and female—must indicate *something* about the Creator. And our experience of sexuality must have *some* implications for language about God.

The goal of this essay is to explore the connection between sexuality and God in an attempt to show how God is indeed the transcendent foundation for our experience of being sexual creatures. Toward this end, the essay moves through four topics. We look first at the nature of human sexuality, then summarize the use of sexual motifs in biblical descriptions of God before surveying recent theological attempts to speak about God and sexuality. The final, more provocative section invokes the great Christian theme of the triune identity of God as providing the ultimate theological foundation for human sexuality.

The Nature of Human Sexuality

Perhaps nothing about humans is more obvious than that we are sexual beings. To be human means to be an embodied creature, and generally to be embodied means to be either male or female. Indeed, the first observation announced at the birth of a baby is the sex of the newborn. Likewise, the first characteristic we notice in meeting other humans is their sex. And awareness of sex distinctions guides our relationships and social interactions with each other from that point on.

Sexuality is seemingly a universal human reality. But what is sexuality? A growing chorus of voices reminds us that although the differentiation in roles male and female play in reproduction is perhaps its most obvious expression, bodily characteristics do not exhaust what sexuality is. Sexuality is far more than the experience of having, and gratifying, what we call sexual desires.

Instead, sexuality refers to our fundamental existence as embodied persons. This includes the way we relate to the world as male or female, the way we think, and the way we view others and ourselves. The sexuality involved in embodied existence also includes our capacity for sensuality, for enjoying all kinds of bodily sensations as we experience the world around us. Above all, sexuality involves our fundamental incompleteness as embodied creatures. This incompleteness draws us out of our isolation into relationships with others and ultimately with God. James Nelson and Sandra Longfellow offer a succinct summary of these dimensions of sexuality:

> While sexuality may well include our desires for experiencing and sharing genital pleasure, it is far more than this. More fundamentally and inclusively, it is who we are as bodyselves. . . . Sexuality embraces our ways of being in the world as persons embodied with biological femaleness or maleness and with internalized understandings of what these genders mean. . . . Sexuality includes the range of feelings, interpretations, and behaviors through which we express our capacities for sensuous relationships with ourselves, with others, and with the world.
>
> Theologically, we believe that human sexuality, while including God's gift of the procreative capacity, is most fundamentally the divine invitation to find our destinies not in loneliness but in deep connection. . . . We experience our sexuality as the basic eros of our humanness that urges, invites, and lures us out of our loneliness into intimate communication and communion with God and the world.

If human sexuality is more than who does what in the reproductive process—if it is more than being "sexually active," to employ the euphemism of our day—then the sexual dimension does not merely lie on the surface of our being. Rather, as a range of contemporary thinkers from Lewis Smedes[3] to James Nelson[4] has observed, sexuality lies at the core of who we are. We *are* embodied creatures. And being "body-selves" entails being male or female. Our fundamental maleness or femaleness goes to the heart of our being. So pervasive is the acknowledgment of this in contemporary thought that we might safely conclude that "embodiment"—and hence our existence as sexual beings—has become a central concept in theological anthropology. But is there any connection between anthropology and theology? Does human embodiment—being male or female—offer any insight into the divine reality? Is God likewise sexual, even if not in the sense of having sexual desires as we do? This question takes us to the biblical documents.

Sexual Motifs in the Bible

The biblical authors repeatedly use sexual imagery to speak about God, ascribing to God traits that we normally associate with the human sexual distinctions of male and female. Traditionally, exegetes have tended to focus on the male-oriented references, which readily appear to predominate in the Bible. Thus, for example, the primary names the writers use to speak about God are decidedly male in tone. According to the Old Testament, God is the Lord of the universe, the King over all the earth, the Father of humankind,[5] and the husband of Israel. In addition, the biblical writers ascribe to God activities which many human cultures generally associate with the masculine gender. In the act of creation, God appears as an active agent external to the world who *speaks* the universe into existence. ("And God said, 'Let there be. . . . And there was" [Gen 1:3, 6, 14]). In redemption God *sends* the Son into the world (Lk 10:16; Jn 4:34; Gal 4:4; 1 Jn 4:10). And in salvation God *bestows* the Holy Spirit on humans (Lk 11:13; Acts 2:17, 38; 2 Cor 5:5; 1 Jn 4:13), putting the Spirit in the hearts of the

---

[3]Lewis B. Smedes, *Sex for Christians* (Grand Rapids, Mich.: Eerdmans, 1976), p. 28.

[4]See, for example, his pioneering book *Embodiment* (Minneapolis: Augsburg, 1978).

[5]For a helpful discussion of the significance of the dominance of paternal rather than maternal metaphors to speak of the nature of God, see Samuel L. Terrien, *Till the Heart Sings* (Philadelphia: Fortress, 1985), pp. 59-70.

redeemed (2 Cor 1:22).[6] Theologians often connect these seemingly masculine activities with God as the transcendent one and view God's transcendence as lying behind the consistent use of masculine pronouns to refer to God. Yet it would be a mistake to conclude either that the ancient Hebrews perceived of God strictly as transcendent or that they appeal only to what for us appear to be male-oriented or masculine metaphors. Sometimes overlooked, but nevertheless evident in Scripture is indication that God is not only the transcendent one who like a monarch exercises sovereign power, but God is also immanent, present to the universe as one who acts, especially in a nurturing manner, from within creation.

Nurturing does not belong solely to the feminine domain, of course. Nevertheless, to communicate the specific manner in which God nurtures, the biblical authors portray God through female images. Many of these are relational metaphors that draw from the parent-offspring, or more specifically, the mother-child relationship. For example, according to the first creation account at the foundation of the world the Spirit of God hovered or brooded over the primeval waters (Gen 1:2b), hatching, as it were, the "egg" of the world.[7] Likewise, God appears as one who like a mother protects, cares for, and nurtures her offspring. The Old Testament writers view the mother bird as an especially helpful picture for the divine care God's people enjoy. God's care for Israel is like "an eagle that stirs up its nest and hovers over its young, that spreads its wings to catch them and carries them on its pinions" (Deut 32:11). In keeping with this imagery, the Hebrew poets repeatedly speak of the refuge available "in the shadow" of God's "wings" (Ps 17:8; 36:7; 57:1; 61:4; 63:7), although such imagery is not exclusively feminine (hence, Ps 91:4). This Old Testament image adds poignancy to Jesus' lament over Jerusalem: "how often I have longed to gather your

---

[6]The basically masculine orientation of the trinitarian actions is noted by Urban T. Holmes, "The Sexuality of God," in *Male and Female: Christian Approaches to Sexuality*, ed. Ruth Tiffany Barnhouse and Urban T. Holmes III (New York: Seabury, 1976), pp. 264-65.

[7]Yves Congar, *I Believe in the Holy Spirit*, trans. David Smith (New York: Seabury, 1983), 3:161. Congar cites L. Bouyer, *Woman and Man with God* (ET: London and New York, 1960), p. 189.

children together, as a hen gathers her chicks under her wings, but you were not willing" (Mt 23:37).

Old Testament nurture metaphors often highlight God's compassion. The prophets repeatedly borrow maternal images, which build from the idea that God had given birth to Israel (e.g., Deut 32:18). Isaiah offers a poignant example in the vision of the renewal of Israel with which the book ends. Through the prophet God likens this future renewal to the process of giving birth (Is 66:7-9). God promises that the people will once again nurse at Jerusalem's comforting breasts (vv. 11-12); yet it is actually God who will provide this motherly comfort: "As a mother comforts her child, so will I comfort you; and you will be comforted over Jerusalem" (v. 13).

The prophets add that this divine comfort extends toward a people who have forsaken their God. Isaiah, for example, who presents God as lamenting, "I reared children and brought them up, but they have rebelled against me" (Is 1:2), later declares, "For the LORD comforts his people and will have compassion on his afflicted ones" (Is 49:13). The basically maternal character of this compassion is evident in God's subsequent exclamation through the prophet: "Can a mother forget the baby at her breast and have no compassion on the child she has borne? Though she may forget, I will not forget you!" (v. 15).

Parental, perhaps even maternal, compassion in the face of Israel's waywardness forms an important imagery in Hosea as well: "When Israel was a child, I loved him, and out of Egypt I called my son. . . . It was I who taught Ephraim to walk, taking them by the arms. . . . I led them with cords of human kindness, with ties of love; I lifted the yoke from their neck and bent down to feed them" (Hos 11:1-4). Parental and conjugal imagery unite in the opening chapters of the prophecy. The child of the prophet's unfaithful wife is Lo-Ruhamah, a name which Samuel Terrien claims means "the one for whom there is no motherly love."[8] In contrast to this present unloved state, in the coming renewal God will extend compassion—"motherly compassion," Terrien suggests—to Lo-Ruhamah (2:23). Terrien, standing in a tradition of

---

[8]Terrien, *Till the Heart Sings*, p. 57.

scholars that includes Phyllis Trible[9] and Yves Congar,[10] draws from a
supposed etymological link between the Hebrew terms for *compassion*
and *womb*. He also claims that the word for *grace* originally meant
"maternal yearning."[11] While we must be careful not to put too much
stock in conclusions from word rootage, Terrien is surely correct in seeing at least a parental, if not a specifically maternal, aspect of the Hebrew understanding of God at work in the Old Testament reflections on
experiences of the gracious compassion of God. God's actions reveal a
parental heart, which the prophets often describe in maternal images.
As Jesus' lament over Jerusalem indicates, the maternal character of
God's parental heart is not lost in the New Testament. Even Paul, who
as a male could never have experienced the maternal dimension of
parenting, speaks of his relationship to his converts in imagery reminiscent of the Old Testament metaphor of divine maternal compassion:
"but we were gentle among you, like a mother caring for her little children" (1 Thess 2:7). Images such as these illumine God's tender care for
us.[12] The prevalence in biblical declarations about God of imagery
which draws from our human experience as sexual creatures raises a
crucial theological question: Is all this merely metaphor, or is God actually sexual?

Recent Theological Proposals

Demythologizing the images. Christian theologians offer various
responses to the question of God's sexuality. The most common
approach is the one to which we alluded in the opening paragraph,
namely, that of "demythologizing" the imagery. Proponents declare that
rather than being either male or female, God is not only beyond sexual
distinctions, God is decidedly non-nonsexual. Demythologizers acknowl-

---

[9]Phyllis Trible, *God and the Rhetoric of Sexuality* (Philadelphia: Fortress, 1978), p. 33.

[10]Congar, *I Believe in the Holy Spirit*, 3:156.

[11]Terrien, *Till the Heart Sings*, p. 57.

[12]The feminine images of the divine has been the subject of several studies. For a short summary of these images, see Aída Besançon Spencer, *Beyond the Curse: Women Called to
Ministry* (Peabody, Mass.: Hendrickson, 1985), pp. 122-31. One feminine motif is foreign to
the Bible, however. In contrast to metaphors that speak of Yahweh as husband to Israel,
the biblical writers never refer to God as wife.

edge that the biblical authors do attribute sexual characteristics to God. But they resolutely assert that these attributions are simply anthropomorphisms; we ought not to view them as declaring that God is essentially sexual.

Advocates of this approach often appeal to a central difference between the Old Testament faith and the religions of the surrounding nations. In contrast to other ancient peoples, the Hebrews desacralized sexuality. According to the prophets, for example, Yahweh is not a male deity who has a goddess at his side, as in other ancient religions. Yahweh alone is God; there simply are no other gods (or goddesses).[13] In addition, proponents point out that the Old Testament doctrine of creation precludes Yahweh from being a "sexually active" God. Rather than needing to infuse the earth with fertility each spring, which would involve some type of repeated divine sexual activity, God gave fertility to the earth in the beginning. In fact, the fertility of creation finds its source in God's primal creative command. It derives from God's word (e.g., Gen 1:11, 20) and God's blessing ("be fruitful and increase in number" [Gen 1:22, 28]), not from any sexual cohabiting among the gods, as in other ancient religions. Pamela J. Scalise explains the implications of this understanding of God's creation of the world for worship in Israel: "Sexuality is a means by which fertility has been granted by God from the beginning (Gen 1:28). In Israelite faith, therefore, fertility did not depend on the sexuality of the gods, so Israel did not represent sexual consorting among the gods in her worship."[14] The intent of such demythologizing the sexual motifs in the Bible is surely laudable. It reminds us that this process, as well as the "secularization" of sexuality, began early in the Old Testament era. The biblical God who "speaks and it is so" differs cat-

---

[13]The significance of the Hebrew assertion of the celibacy of God in contrast to the outlook of the surrounding religions is put forth by Joseph Blenkinsopp, *Sexuality and the Christian Tradition* (Dayton, Ohio: Pflaum, 1969), pp. 24-27. See also Tikva Frymer-Kensky, "Law and Philosophy: The Case of Sex in the Bible," *Semeia* 45 (1989): 90-91. Nevertheless, the situation may not have been so simple, as is argued by Mark S. Smith, "God Male and Female in the Old Testament: Yahweh and His 'Asherah,' " *Theological Studies* 48 (1987): 333-40.

[14]Pamela J. Scalise, "Women in Ministry: Reclaiming Our Old Testament Heritage," *Review and Expositor* 83, no. 1 (1986): 8.

egorically from the gods and goddesses who in the myths of ancient peoples consort with each other.

Yet despite Israel's radical departure from the religious ideas of the surrounding peoples, in both creation narratives when the Creator chooses to make creatures who would mirror the divine being, what God creates is male and female. This aspect of the Genesis stories indicates that our sexuality (including human sexual distinctions) is somehow grounded in the divine reality and that our experience of being sexually differentiated is important for our understanding of God.

Therefore, to conclude that God is non-nonsexual risks disengaging human sexuality from the *imago Dei*. Thereby human sexuality loses all transcendent foundation. We are left with nothing in the divine "self-grounded prototype" (to allude to Barth's language) to which this dimension of our being can "correspond." Rather than belonging to our exalted status as God's image, our sexuality comes to be relegated to the periphery of our humanness.

Literalizing the images. Perhaps this difficulty suggests that we follow a second approach, namely, to take the biblical metaphors literally and thereby view God as being inherently gendered. In the past, this option has generally led to a masculine, if not even a male God. Indeed, because God could only be masculine or feminine, the predominance of masculine imagery in the Bible seems to tip the scale toward the former.[15] Some Christians seem to move from the idea that God is masculine to the assumption that God is male. They appeal to the biblical material I noted earlier—the masculine imagery and names for God, the ascription of seemingly masculine activities to God and the consistent use of masculine pronouns to refer to God. Proponents also read certain Scripture references as indicating that females cannot bear the divine im-

---

[15]Many "traditionalists" argue that God is masculine but not male. Some note that part of the problem is the recent blurring between linguistic gender and sexuality (being male or female) in the English language. The result is that using masculine pronouns of God has come to imply that God is of the male sex. For a discussion, see Donald D. Hook and Alvin F. Kimel Jr., "Is God 'He'?" *Worship* 68, no. 2 (1994): 145-57. See also George H. Tavard, "Sexist Language in Theology?" in *Woman: New Dimensions*, ed. Walter J. Burghardt (New York: Paulist, 1977), pp. 130-32.

age to the same degree as males (e.g., 1 Cor. 11:7).[16] And they find God's maleness confirmed by the incarnation. For them, the incontestable fact that Jesus was male, not female, carries theological significance. The incarnation of the Word of God as a man—not a woman—indicates that God too is male.[17] Feminist theologians have launched a much-needed critique of this position. They claim that viewing God as male has devastating effects, for it serves to deify the male gender among humans. Mary Daly's often quoted statement succinctly states the point: "If God is male, then the male is god."[18] Feminists argue that viewing God as male provides a cosmic sanction for patriarchy, leading to the enslavement of women. In addition to its debilitating social ramifications, many theologians conclude that the idea of a male God runs counter to the biblical documents. The move from masculine imagery to a male God is illfounded, they argue, because it goes beyond the intent of the authors of Scripture. As I indicated earlier, these scholars point out how the Bible actually demythologizes the sexual deities of the ancient peoples.

But why the use of masculine motifs in the Bible? Some feminists look to the social conditions of the ancient world to explain why the masculine took precedence over the feminine. They argue that a patriarchal society will naturally develop a view of God that confirms patriarchy. Stephen C. Barton, for example, states, "The predominance of masculine images of God in both Scripture and tradition has to do with the patriar-

---

[16]Actually, this view may be as old as Augustine, who suggests that men possessed the image of God to a greater degree than women. See Augustine *On the Trinity* 7.7.10, trans. Stephen McKenna, vol. 45 of *Fathers of the Church*, ed. Hermigild Dressler et al. (Washington, D.C.: Catholic University of America Press, 1963), pp. 351-52. For a discussion of Luther's ambiguity on the subject, see Jane Dempsey Douglass, "The Image of God in Women as Seen by Luther and Calvin," in *The Image of God: Gender Models in Judaeo-Christian Tradition*, ed. Kari Elizabeth Borresen (Minneapolis: Fortress, 1991), pp. 236-66.

[17]For representatives of the various viewpoints listed here, see C. S. Lewis, "Priestesses in the Church?" in *God in the Dock*, ed. Walter Hooper (Grand Rapids, Mich.: Eerdmans, 1970), p. 236; Roger Beckwith, "The Bearing of Holy Scripture," in *Man, Woman and Priesthood*, ed. Peter Moore (London: SPCK, 1978), p. 57; John M. Frame, "Men and Women in the Image of God," in *Recovering Biblical Manhood and Womanhood: A Response to Evangelical Feminism*, ed. John Piper and Wayne Grudem (Wheaton, Ill.: Crossway, 1991), p. 231; Michael Novak, "Women, Ordination and Angels," *First Things* 32 (April 1993): 32.

[18]Mary Daly, *Beyond God the Father: Toward a Philosophy of Women's Liberation* (Boston: Beacon, 1973), p. 19.

chal structure of the societies in and for which those images were developed, not with the gender of God."[19] While the social setting of the Bible ought not to be overlooked, interpretations such as Barton's are ultimately unsatisfying. All too often sociological explanations cut too deeply, as their proponents find irresistible the temptation to move from observation to application. Once we know why male imagery came to be used, they declare, we are awakened to the fact that it was a misguided development in the tradition; this, in turn, moves us to eradicate that development.

In their desire to avoid the radical revisionist tendencies of much contemporary feminist theology, some thinkers have developed a more nuanced understanding of God's maleness. In their view, the use of predominately masculine imagery to refer to God was not a misguided development in the biblical tradition. Instead it was part of God's chosen means of communicating to us.[20] With this in view, these theologians seek to discover the theological importance of masculine metaphors, while avoiding the faulty conclusion that God is literally male. A widely held approach focuses on the use of masculine pronouns to speak about God. Proponents argue that biblical talk about God as "he" carries personal, rather than sexual significance. At the heart of the Christian understanding, they declare, is the assertion that God is personal, rather than impersonal. This central truth about the nature of God can only be maintained through personal pronouns, for the use of the neuter term "it" when speaking of God would reduce God to an impersonal reality. Because personal pronouns come in only two types, the personal dimension, and not the gender-specific aspect, is the chief focus of the use of such pronouns.[21] Paul Jewett speaks for many who hold this position: "We construe the masculine language about God analogically, not literally, when we interpret Scripture. The univocal element in the analogy is the *personal*, not the *sexual*, mean-

---

[19]Stephen C. Barton, "Impatient for Justice: Five Reasons Why the Church of England Should Ordain Women to the Priesthood," *Theology* 92 (September 1989): 404.

[20]See, for example, Alvin F. Kimel Jr., "The God Who Likes His Name: Holy Trinity, Feminism, and the Language of Faith," in *Speaking the Christian God*, pp. 188-208.

[21]See, for example, Hook and Kimel, "Is God 'He'?" pp. 151-52.

ing of the language."[22] He then draws the obvious conclusion: "Because the language about God is analogical, the personal pronouns used of God—he, his, him, himself—in Scripture, theology, and devotion are to be understood *generically* not specifically."[23] Jewett's explanation would be persuasive if pronouns were the only issue. But the male-orientation of the biblical designations for God runs deeper than the predominance of masculine personal pronouns. Repeatedly, the biblical authors use masculine images and concepts to describe God. In Christian history, the most vital—and controversial—of these is the designation of God as Father (to which could be added the dominant description of the Second Person of the Trinity as God the Son).

Most theologians reject the idea that the designation "Father" means that God is literally a male deity. Rather, they argue that the word is merely the best image available for conveying certain dimensions of the divine reality that God wants us to understand. Paralleling their treatment of the use of masculine pronouns, proponents argue that rather than carrying sexual connotations masculine images speak of God's personhood. Above all, calling God "Father" is a reminder of the close relationship Jesus enjoyed with God and of his invitation to us to share in that special filial bond. This points to the similar conclusion that "Son" is also a personal metaphor.

Madeleine Boucher claims that the personal understanding of the male imagery of Father and Son has been the dominant understanding from the beginning of the Christian tradition:

> The early Christian theologians understood perfectly well that names such as "Father" and "Son" were metaphors, and inadequate for describing God. For the theologians of the late first and second centuries, the metaphor "Father" simply referred to God considered as creator and author of all things. . . . For the early theologians, the metaphor "Son" was intended to assert only two points; that the Second Person is "like" the First, and that the Second Person is "from" the First rather than "from" nothing (that is, uncreated). The metaphors were not pressed beyond this. They were not

---

[22]Paul King Jewett, "Why I Favor the Ordination of Women," *Christianity Today,* June 6, 1975, p. 10.
[23]Ibid.

taken to express sexual character whether in the divine Nature or in any of the Persons.[24]

Despite valiant attempts to reinterpret the use of masculine pronouns, as well as the designations "Father" and "Son," the claim that all such language *merely* carries personal, and not sexual significance seems overdrawn. The richness of the biblical use of sexual imagery to speak about God indicates that we must take these metaphors seriously, even if not literally. Hence, it would seem that the widespread presence of male-oriented metaphors must carry greater importance than is exhausted in the conclusion that they simply designate God as personal.

Certain contemporary scholars *are* finding greater significance in these images. One typical proposal discovers in the widespread use of male images an indication of the way God relates to the world. Specifically, proponents argue that God interacts with creation primarily in a manner analogous to the human male. God is ultimately transcendent; God creates and cares for the world as a reality outside himself—hence, in what proponents see as a typically masculine manner. Stephen Barton explains: "The Christian doctrine of God as 'Father' is an analogical way of describing the providence of God and our sense of God's care for the whole of creation."[25] In this view, the Old Testament choice of masculine rather than feminine images does carry theological significance. In emphasizing male-oriented images, the ancient Hebrews set their understanding of God apart from that of the surrounding nations. Rather than a mother goddess who brings forth creation as a child is brought forth from the womb, the Old Testament writers teach that God created by fiat an external universe.[26] Classically theologians have spoken of this as *creatio ex nihilo*. This explanation of the foundational maleness of God would be compelling if the biblical authors had limited their conception of God and the world to what we interpret as masculine motifs. As we noted earlier, however, Scripture also contains feminine images. Vis-à-vis

[24]Madeleine Boucher, "Ecumenical Documents: Authority-in-Community" *Midstream* 21, no. 3 (July 1982): 409.

[25]Barton, "Impatient for Justice," p. 404.

[26]See, for example, Achtemeier, "Exchanging God for 'No Gods,' " pp. 1-16.

creation, God is both transcendent (hence what some see as malelike) and immanent (femalelike). God's relationship to creation—even the manner in which God nurtures God's people—takes on both masculine and feminine dimensions. Consequently, while God may be spoken of in masculine ways, the masculine does not exhaust the divine reality.

Compartmentalizing the divine: This conclusion suggests a third way of responding to the sexual imagery of the Bible. Some theologians advocate compartmentalizing God into male and female components. The most widely proposed manner of accomplishing this feat builds from the Christian doctrine of God as triune—as Father, Son and Holy Spirit. The doctrine of the Trinity seems to provide a way of viewing God as beyond sexual distinctions, while finding both the masculine and the feminine dimensions within God, namely, as focused on the three persons individually.

Traditional trinitarian language facilitates the task of placing masculinity within the triune God. The search for the bearer of the feminine dimension is more complicated. Although some theologians look to the second person,[27] the third trinitarian member looms as the obvious candidate.[28] Not only is the word *Spirit* devoid of the overtly masculine sense found in "Father" and "Son," the Hebrew term for "spirit" (*ruach*) is grammatically feminine.[29] In addition, the Bible sometimes symbolizes the Spirit by feminine images, such as fire or a dove. And the New Testament writers speak of the Spirit as the agent of the new birth (e.g., John 3:1-10). A historically more important link between the feminine and the Spirit lies in the Hebrew concept of wisdom.[30] Wisdom is personified in a feminine form in the great hymn of Proverbs 8—9. The deuterocanonical

---

[27]Margaret Farley, "New Patterns of Relationship: Beginnings of a Moral Revolution," *Theological Studies* 36, no. 4 (1975): 641-43.

[28]Joan Chamberlain Engelsman anticipates that focusing on the Spirit is likely to gain prominence as a way of expressing the feminine dimension of the divine (*The Feminine Dimension of the Divine* [Philadelphia: Westminster Press, 1979], p. 152).

[29]Many scholars claim that there is no necessary correlation between grammatical gender and actual gender. Hence Donald Bloesch, *The Battle for the Trinity: The Debate over Inclusive God-Language* (Ann Arbor, Mich.: Servant, 1985), p. 33.

[30]For a discussion of the development (and suppression) of wisdom as a feminine concept in the biblical era, see Engelsman, *Feminine Dimension of the Divine*, pp. 74-120.

literature pushes the analogy farther, presenting wisdom as a mother and a bride (Wis 8:2; Sir 15:2; cf. 14:23-27). Whereas the New Testament links wisdom to Christ, the Jewish tradition places it in close affinity with God's Spirit (Wis 9:17). Perhaps as a result, the idea of the Spirit as "mother" entered the Christian tradition through Judaism and the Syriac world.[31] Some ancient thinkers even posited a family model of the Trinity, consisting of Father, Mother and Son, an idea that is currently being revived by certain Asian theologians.[32] Several attempts have been made in recent years to provide a theological understanding of the connection between the feminine and the Holy Spirit. Yves Congar describes two Roman Catholic proposals. The first derives the link through the church. Because the church is the new Eve, the Spirit in a human existence, woman is the symbol of the response of love given to God, which within God is the Holy Spirit.[33] A second attempt forges a link through the three tasks of love particular to a woman—virgin (welcoming and receiving), spouse (uniting) and mother (communicating life).[34] Congar himself prefers the image of mother: The Spirit is "mother" to creation, to Christ and to the church.[35] While it may boast a long pedigree in Christian tradition, picturing the Holy Spirit as feminine is problematic. It does not achieve what its feminist proponents anticipate. A feminine Spirit does not eliminate the religious foundation of patriarchy, for the Spirit too readily retains the lowly position of "third member" in a divine hierarchy headed by the male Father.[36] Theologically more problematic is the compartmentalization of God that this proposal entails. We simply cannot localize the

---

[31]For several historical examples, see Congar, *I Believe in the Holy Spirit*, 3:157.

[32]See, for example, Jung Young Lee, *The Trinity in Asian Perspective* (Nashville: Abingdon, 1996).

[33]Congar ascribes this proposal to Maura Boeckeler (see *I Believe in the Holy Spirit*, 3:160).

[34]For this characterization of the position of Willi Moll, see Congar, *I Believe in the Holy Spirit*, 3:161.

[35]In our lives, Congar explains, the Spirit plays the part of "a mother who enables us to know our Father, God, and our brother, Jesus. The Spirit also enables us to invoke God as our Father and he reveals to us Jesus our Lord, introducing us gradually to his inheritance of grace and truth. Finally, he teaches us how to practice the virtues and how to use the gifts of a son of God by grace. All this is part of a mother's function" (ibid., 3:161).

[36]For this critique see, for example, Rosemary Radford Ruether, *Sexism and God-talk* (Boston: Beacon, 1983), p. 60.

feminine dimension of God in the Holy Spirit. The biblical texts will not allow such a limitation in the *economic* Trinity. The compassionate, mothering God of the Old Testament cannot be limited to the Spirit, understood as the feminine dimension of the divine. On the contrary, the same God who will comfort Israel as a mother comforts her child (Is 66:13) will also mete out wrath and judgment to the wicked, which in our culture is seen to be a more masculine image:

> When you see this, your heart will rejoice and you will flourish like grass; the hand of the LORD will be made known to his servants, but his fury will be shown to his foes. See, the LORD is coming with fire, and his chariots are like a whirlwind; he will bring down his anger with fury, and his rebuke with flames of fire. For with fire and with his sword the LORD will execute judgment upon all men, and many will be those slain by the LORD. (Is 66:14-16)

Consequently, whenever we encounter the nurturing God, we are not faced merely with the feminine dimension of the divine localized in the third trinitarian person. We have come face to face with none other than Yahweh; we have encountered the one God, the one whom Christians know as the triune God.[37] Nor can we localize the feminine dimension in the Spirit within the *immanent* Trinity. Such a compartmentalization is inconsistent with the idea of *perichoresis.*[38] The personal indwelling of each person in the other two, to which this term refers, precludes seeing the Father (and the Son) as exclusively masculine and the Spirit as exclusively feminine. Rather, whatever masculinity and femininity are present within any trinitarian person are likewise shared by the other two.

Re-imaging the divine. The problems posed by the attempt to relegate the feminine dimension to the Holy Spirit have led several feminist theologians to propose a fourth alternative, namely, the structuring of a

---

[37]Elizabeth Johnson makes this point concerning the feminine image of wisdom, "Sophia is a female personification of God's own being in creative and saving involvement with the world. . . . Sophia is Israel's God in female imagery" (Elizabeth A. Johnson, *She Who Is: The Mystery of God in Feminist Theological Discourse* [New York: Crossroad, 1992], p. 91).

[38]See, for example, Jürgen Moltmann, *The Trinity and the Kingdom,* trans. Margaret Kohl (San Francisco: Harper & Row, 1981), p. 175.

composite feminine image of the divine. Perhaps no proposal has been more influential in recent years than Rosemary Radford Ruether's reimaging of the divine reality. Ruether claims that the most ancient human image of the divine was female, the "Primal Matrix," the great womb within which all things are generated. In light of this discovery, she calls for a move beyond merely the incorporation of feminine aspects into an otherwise male God. Her theological vision is that of a truly inclusive deity, whom she names God/ess.[39] Elizabeth Johnson offers what appears to be a less radical re-imaging of the God of the Christian tradition. To this end, she draws from the wisdom theme, which has played such a prominent role in feminist reflections, to provide a specifically female conception of the Trinity.[40] Following a theological method that moves from the economic Trinity to the immanent Trinity, Johnson begins with the third person, rather than the first. "God is God as Spirit-Sophia,"[41] she declares. This Sophia-God "dwells in the world at its center and at its edges." As an active vitality crying out in labor, the Spirit gives birth to the new creation.[42] "God is God again," Johnson then adds, "as Jesus Christ, Sophia's child and prophet, and yes, Sophia herself personally pitching her tent in the flesh of humanity."[43] Jesus' historical life reveals the shape of Wisdom's love for the world. Finally, "God is God again as unimaginable abyss of livingness, Holy Wisdom unknown and unknowable."[44] Reminiscent of Ruether's language, Johnson speaks of this God as "the matrix of all that exists, mother and fashioner of all things."[45] The feminist quest to re-image the divine reality presents the most thoroughgoing attempt to incorporate the human experience of embodiment—specifically, women's experience—into theological language. And it has sparked a fledgling, parallel attempt to

---

[39]Ruether, *Sexism and God-talk*, pp. 67-71.

[40]Johnson is convinced that Christians "need a strong dose of explicitly female imagery to break the unconscious sway that male trinitarian imagery holds over the imaginations of even the most sophisticated thinkers" (*She Who Is*, p. 212).

[41]Ibid., p. 213.

[42]Ibid.

[43]Ibid.

[44]Ibid., p. 214.

[45]Ibid.

re-image God on the basis of the male experience.[46] Despite its positive features, the feminist enterprise is not free from problems. For example, re-imaging the Christian God along feminine lines runs the same risk of literalizing the biblical language that critics find so abhorrent in the older "God is male" tradition. What is to prevent women from concluding that the divine reality truly is female? What will guard feminists against replacing the discredited male God with an equally one-sided female Goddess?

This question points to a deeper theological problem. Those who would re-image the divine reality risk losing continuity with the Christian tradition and thereby placing themselves outside the historic church. For some feminists, continuity with the tradition is not a high priority. Rather than drawing solely from biblical sources, they consciously reappropriate pre-Judeo-Christian traditions.[47] However, by resurrecting aspects of the worldview of the ancient Canaanite and Mesopotamian religions against which the Hebrew prophets struggled, these theologians may actually be transforming Christianity into another religion.[48] Certain radical feminist thinkers readily perceive the theological shift involved in the renewal of ancient extrabiblical traditions. As Starhawk admits:

> The symbolism of the Goddess is not a parallel structure to the symbolism of God the Father. The Goddess does not rule the world; She *is* the world. Manifest in each of us, She can be known internally be every individual, in all her magnificent diversity.[49]

No wonder the re-imaging path has led some theologians to repudiate the Christian tradition entirely in the quest to construct a new post-Christian, feminist religion. Less radical feminist theologians make a more conscious effort to remain within the Christian tradition. To facilitate this

---

[46]See, for example, James B. Nelson, *The Intimate Connection: Male Sexuality, Masculine Spirituality* (Philadelphia: Westminster Press, 1988), pp. 85-111; Nelson, *Body Theology* (Louisville: Westminster John Knox, 1992), pp. 93-104.

[47]E.g., Rosemary Radford Ruether, *Women-Church: Theology and Practice* (San Francisco: Harper & Row, 1985), p. 104.

[48]This is the point Bloesch is making in his *Battle for the Trinity.*

[49]Starhawk, *The Spiral Dance: A Rebirth of the Ancient Religion of the Great Goddess,* 2nd ed. (San Francisco: Harper, 1989), p. 23.

goal, many—including Elizabeth Johnson—appropriate the panentheistic conception of God developed by process theologians.[50] In their estimation, panentheism stands within the broader Christian tradition, while offering a basis from which to launch a feminist critique of classical Christian theism with its seemingly masculine understanding of God. Of course, the extent to which panentheism actually is compatible with the Christian tradition is a hotly debated issue.

Sexuality and the Triune God

The use of sexual metaphors in the Bible suggests that although God is neither strictly male nor female—at this point the demythologizers are correct—God somehow encompasses what to us are the sexual distinctions of male and female. And sexuality, which is an integral part of our humanness, derives its significance from the divine reality. But how?

We have noted examples of how the biblical literature depicts God's relationship to the world in both masculine and feminine ways, and how God's relationship to humans includes both maternal and paternal characteristics. In addition, the biblical writers appeal to a specifically sexual bond—marriage—to speak about the relationship God desires to have with God's people, both Old Testament Israel (e.g., Jer 2:2; Is 62:5) and the New Testament church (Eph 5:22-32). In this manner, in relationship to humankind God emerges in the Bible as the foundation for human sexuality, insofar as God is the transcendent basis for the distinctively masculine and feminine dimensions of human existence.

Hence, the "sexuality" of God's relationship to creation provides a promising means of bringing human sexuality and theological language together. Yet it does not point the way as to how sexuality can be thought to be present within the *eternal* divine reality. There remains, however, a more explicit link between humans as the *imago Dei* and the eternal God, a link forged through the *social* nature of both human and divine life.

Much of Christian history has been dominated by an emphasis on the oneness of the transcendent God. According to this view, God is

---

[50]Johnson declares that God is "in the world" and the world is "in God"; yet "each remains radically distinct" (*She Who Is*, p. 231).

the powerful sovereign over the world. God is Father, Lord and King over all. This focus led historically to the conclusion that God is a male deity. One great gain of recent theological reflection, however, has been a renewal of trinitarian thought, which lies at the foundation of the Christian tradition but which was eventually overshadowed by the monarchial view of God. According to trinitarian theology, God is one, of course, but God's oneness is not the solitary aloneness of an exalted monarch. The eternal God is not an undifferentiated essence. Rather, God is triune, a unity-in-diversity. And rather than being characterized by solitude, the divine life is fundamentally social. The triune God is relational, the fellowship of the three trinitarian persons. In short, God is the social Trinity.

Human life is also social; we are created for community. This theme lies at the heart of the biblical vision, beginning with the creation narratives and climaxing in the expectations for the new creation. Genesis 2 begins the narrative. God creates the first human pair to enjoy community with each other. More specifically, the creation of the woman is God's antidote for the man's aloneness. The primal community of male and female then becomes expansive, as the sexual union of husband and wife produces children and eventually gives rise to tribe and nation. But God's purpose finds its consummation only in the eschatological new creation. Only then will the redeemed humanity live within the renewed creation and enjoy perfect fellowship with the Creator (Rev 21:1—22:5).

While Genesis 2 indicates that God created humans for community, Genesis 1 suggests that the human social reality finds its source in the divine social dynamic. The bridge between creature and Creator lies in the creation of humankind to be the bearer of the *imago Dei* as male and female. This is evident in the statement of the divine intent to create humankind (Gen 1:26-27). God announces, "Let us make human beings in our image." The use of the plural forms ("Let us . . . our") ought not to be interpreted as indicating that the writer was a proto-trinitarian (as many exegetes since Tertullian have erroneously argued). Yet at the very least these pronouns suggest, in the words of Derrick Bailey, that the narrator

envisaged God as associating others with himself in some mysterious way as partners in the act of creation, and that he regarded Man as constituted in some sense after the pattern of a plurality of supernatural beings.[51]

The fuller divine self-disclosure found in the New Testament retroactively places a more profound meaning in the words in Genesis 1. "They express," to follow through with the conclusion of Bailey, "the Creator's resolve to crown his works by making a creature in whom, subject to the limitations of finitude, his own nature should be mirrored."[52]

The plural self-reference of the Creator then finds its outworking in the creation of humankind as male and female, that is, as a plural sexual creation. In this manner, the narrator explicitly links the plurality of human sexes to a plurality articulated already in the divine self-reference. Indeed, it is not surprising that when the triune God fashions the highest creation, a unity-in-diversity is formed—humankind as male and female. This theological connection in the first creation narrative forms the background for the narrative of the formation of Eve from Adam in Genesis 2. The second account explains the significance of the creation of humankind as male and female disclosed in the first. The second narrative climaxes as the interaction of sameness and difference between the man and the woman gives rise to a unique relationship—a social, sexual bond—between them. The man sees in the woman a creature like himself, in contrast to the animals who are unlike him. At the same time, the two are different, for he is male and she is female. For the narrator, this sameness and difference—this mutuality within a plurality—explains the mystery of the two forming the unity of "one flesh," a unity held together by the attraction (love) they sense for each other.

Read in the light of the first creation narrative, Genesis 2 suggests that the same principle that forms the genius of the human social dynamic is present in a prior way in God. The Creator's words, "Let us make human beings in our image," provide a hint that the plurality of humanity as male and female is to be viewed as an expression of a foundational plurality within the unity of the divine reality. Indeed, the Christian conception of God understands

---

[51]Derrick Sherwin Bailey, *The Man-Woman Relation in Christian Thought* (New York: Harper & Brothers, 1959), p. 267.

[52]Ibid.

the divine reality as a living relationship, a social dynamic.

Mutuality, or unity-in-diversity, inheres within the eternal God. Mutuality is evident in the traditional description of the dynamic relationship between the Father and the Son within the one God. As the early-third-century thinker Origen declared, from all eternity the Father begets the Son in one eternal act (the eternal generation of the Son). But as other church theologians including Athanasius[53] added, this dynamic not only generates the Son, it also constitutes the Father. Just as the second trinitarian person is the Son of the Father, so also the first person is the Father of the Son. The *unity* within this diversity, however, the sameness in the midst of difference, arises from the interplay of another principle, the central divine attribute of love (e.g., 1 Jn 4:16). Jesus described the bond he shares as the Son with his Father in terms of love: The Father loves the Son, and the Son reciprocates the Father's love. Although this love characterizes the divine nature as a whole, it emerges as a separate hypostasis in the third person, the Holy Spirit, who (according to the Western tradition) is the Spirit of the relationship between the Father and the Son. The Spirit who proceeds from the Father and the Son comprises the "sameness" they share, namely, the one divine nature—love. Yet just as the Father is not the Son, so also the Spirit is neither the Father nor the Son.

The Genesis creation narratives suggest that the phenomenon of male-female bonding provides a window into the dynamic within the divine Trinity. This occurs because unity-in-diversity characterizes the divine dynamic throughout all eternity apart from creation. The bonding that characterizes the divine life is similar to the interaction of sameness and difference found in human sexuality. The persons of the Trinity share in the one divine essence, love, for there is but one God. Yet they differ from one another, for each is a distinct person who cannot simply be equated with the others. In this manner, God stands as the foundation for human sexual bonding. The triune God is the "self-grounded prototype," of which Barth speaks, to whom this dimension of human life "corresponds."

Yet the foundational connection between the triune God and human sexuality does not occur because God is either male or female or be-

---

[53]Athanasius *Contra Arian* 3.6.

cause God is both male and female. Rather, God is the foundation of human sexual bonding, insofar as the dynamic that characterizes the social Trinity (unity-in-diversity, mutuality of distinct persons, the interaction of sameness and difference) is reflected in the dynamic of relationships to which our existence as embodied (and hence sexual) creatures leads.

Contrary to what we might at first conclude, however, the theological use of the male-female marital relationship leading to "one flesh" does not mean that the image of God is present only in the marital union of male and female.[54] The unity-in-diversity that arises out of the bond that brings male and female together in marriage offers an obvious picture of the unity-in-diversity present within the triune God. But it is not the only picture. Indeed, it is not the most significant picture. According to the New Testament, ultimately the *imago Dei* is Christ (2 Cor 4:4; Col 1:15; Heb 1:3). By extension, those who are united to Christ share in Christ's relationship to God and consequently are being transformed into the image of God in Christ (1 Cor 15:49; 2 Cor 3:18; Col 3:10). For this reason the church emerges in the New Testament as an even more foundational exemplar of the *imago Dei*. Indeed, the fellowship of Christ's disciples becomes the primary expression of community, having replaced the Old Testament emphasis on family and tribe (Mt 12:50; Mk 10:29-30; Acts 4:32-35).

In the final analysis, then, the "image of God" is corporate; the nature of the triune God comes to expression through humans-in-community. And wherever community emerges, human sexuality understood in its foundational sense—the incompleteness bound up with embodied existence that draws us out of our isolation into fellowship—is at work. This sexuality gives rise to the primal male-female relationship, the bond of marriage. But sexuality likewise brings us into community with Christ and with one another in the fellowship of the church. It is this connection that will eternally draw us into participation in the very life of the triune God, as the Spirit molds us into one great chorus of praise to the Father through the Son, which in turn will mark the Father's eternal glorification of us in the Son.

---

[54]This is a weakness in several recent statements. See, for example, Dwight Hervey Small's otherwise helpful treatment of this theme in *Christian: Celebrate Your Sexuality* (Old Tappan, N.J.: Revell, 1974), pp. 130-40. Jewett criticizes Barth at this point (*Man as Male and Female*, pp. 46-47).

9

SECULAR & ESCHATOLOGICAL CONCEPTIONS OF SALVATION IN THE CONTROVERSY OVER THE INVOCATION OF GOD

Paul R. Hinlicky

ACCORDING TO ALL THE TRADITIONS OF CHRISTIAN ORTHODOXY, THE canonical narrative of human salvation tells of the gift of God's reign which comes mercifully to lost and perishing children of Adam from the heavenly Father through the missions of Christ and the Spirit. Elect Israel was trained by God to expect salvation as the coming of the reign, which would bring about the divine judgment and redemption of human history. In the fullness of time, Jesus, a son of Israel endowed with the Spirit of God, came proclaiming the advent of the reign. He called upon that coming king, the God of Israel, as his own Father and freely invited others, especially sinners, to join him in this same invocation of God. For this two-sided act of self-identification, at once with the Father as his own Son, and at the same time with the godless, Jesus was at length condemned and executed as a messianic pretender. The One whom Jesus called on as his Father, however, revealed the nearness of his kingly power by raising the Crucified from death and exalting him as Lord over all. In this very act, God re-cognized the crucified Jesus as his own beloved Son and validated his mission of mercy to sinners. The Father and the exalted Son sent their Spirit, creating the church to be the body of the Christ in the drama of the history of salvation till every contra-divine power is subdued and God becomes all things to all people.

The State of the Question

Reflection on the foregoing primary theology of the biblical narrative reveals that the trinitarian structure is integral and inalienable. The message of salvation tells of the Father who bestows his Spirit on lost humanity in Christ so that with the Son a new humanity returns lives of loving praise and service to the Father, now and forever. This trinitarian structure of salvation is not amenable to thoroughgoing conceptual translation; it rather presses for the on-going conversion of believers, not least in their thinking about who and what deity must be. The form of biblical language and the content of salvation as communion in the triune God are at best distinguishable in the abstract. Concretely they coinhere and are inseparable: salvation as communion with God is inconceivable apart from the particular relations made known to us in the canonical story of Jesus and his Father and their Spirit. Apart from trinitarianism, on the other hand, the biblical narrative quickly fragments into a collection of ancient Near Eastern texts which have lost sight of the unifying subject, the triune God at work in the history of salvation. Consequently, orthodox language about God articulates the intrinsically trinitarian structure of the God who appears in the biblical narrative, at the center of which appears Jesus the Christ, his mission, death and resurrection, hidden reign and final glory. Thus contemporary orthodox theology has come to speak of the "narrative identification of God."[1] It is critical to grasp that the evangelical salvation-event so apprehended does not conform to preconceived notions of God, humanity or salvation, but rather challenges believers to think in a new way about the reality of God: trinitarianism.[2]

---

[1]George Lindbeck, "Reflections on Trinitarian Language," *Pro ecclesia* 4, no. 3 (1995): 261-64. See the present volume's predecessor, *Speaking the Christian God: The Holy Trinity and the Challenge of Feminism,* ed. Alvin F. Kimel Jr. (Grand Rapids, Mich.: Eerdmans, 1992).

[2]I am instructed in the contemporary trinitarian revival chiefly by three texts: Robert W. Jenson, *The Triune Identity* (Philadelphia: Fortress, 1982); Wolfhart Pannenberg, *Systematic Theology* 1, trans. G. W. Bromiley (Grand Rapids, Mich.: Eerdmans, 1991) and Eberhard Jüngel, *God as the Mystery of the World,* trans. D. L. Guder (Grand Rapids, Mich.: Eerdmans, 1983). It is instructive to compare these with Catherine Mowry LaCugna, *God for Us: The Trinity and the Christian Life* (San Francisco: Harper, 1991), a book that suffers from a certain Roman Catholic parochialism (one cannot properly understand Rahner without also reading all the Barth and Bultmann that Rahner read!), but is nonetheless important because

It is admittedly a great offense to the human heart that its true good should depend utterly on another's free act of love, for which no other ground or necessity can be determined than the other's freedom to love. Yet this healing offense of ultimately unmerited love, not some mathematical riddle about the three and the one, is the gravamen of the church's doctrinal exposition of the gospel's talk about God.[3] Divine *agape* is what the church's doctrine of the Trinity seeks to make intelligible to us. The ground of God's love, manifest in the providential acts of the creation of the world from nothing, the justification of the ungodly, and the resurrection of the dead, is the superabundance of God's own eternal life as the Father, the Son and the Holy Spirit. Ultimate reality is not, as Westerners have been long tempted to think, a "God beyond God," the ineffable, nameless One beyond the "one and the many," who is "the ground of being" of an eternally undulating but essentially static

---

it recognizes the sympathy of trinitarianism with at least some of feminism's most cherished values, such as the ultimate value of relationships of love constituted in history. As a Lutheran theologian who has consistently supported the ordination of women (see my "Afterword: Why Women May Be Ordained" in *Different Voices/Shared Vision: Male and Female in the Trinitarian Community* [Delhi, N.Y.: ALPB Books, 1992]; and " 'Women in the Church:' A Theological Critique of the Missouri Synod Report," *Dialog* 25, no. 4 [1986]: 303-6), it is difficult to know how to engage fruitfully with Roman Catholic feminist theologians who are reacting against a tradition whose criticism (but not rejection!) my own tradition has long taken for granted. It is worth noting that Roman Catholic feminist theologians vary considerably among themselves; see only, for instance, the collection edited by LaCugna, *Freeing Theology: The Essentials of Theology in Feminist Perspective* (San Francisco: Harper, 1993). At this point, I should simply make one comment about the ordination of women: the question is not whether women may be ordained, but whether the ministry to which they are ordained is in fact the ministry of Jesus Christ and the Triune God. I include my own ordination, both in principle and in its public solidarity with ordained women, in the same questionableness that I just articulated; indeed, I consider the question of women's ordination to be quite analogous to that of Lutheran orders. The issue is not whether Lutherans can ordain, but whether their orders are in fact those willed by God. What I mean by that question is that it is not difficult to argue that women should have positions of leadership in a religious institution. What is a question, both theoretically and empirically, is whether the ordination of women can be justified for specifically Christian reasons. I believe that the answer to that question is yes. But I acknowledge that the case has not yet convinced the vast majority of the world's Christians, and that the jury is still out, empirically, on whether the ordination of women will strengthen the church in the gospel of Jesus Christ, or be an occasion of falling away from the specific hope of the reign which is ours in Christ alone, by grace alone, through faith alone.

[3]Jüngel, *Mystery,* pp.376-96.

cosmic order.[4] Ultimate reality is rather the personal Will who will prevail in the freedom of his love to have mercy on all, the Father, the Son and the Holy Spirit, blessed forever, amen.

All true talk of God concludes in such a doxology. The naming of God serves several important purposes, such as identifying the God on whom faith relies, proclaiming his Word, and so on. But the praise of God is the final end and lends order to these others. Doxology is the concrete end of trinitarian theology. "Because you are children, God has sent the Spirit of his Son into our hearts, crying, 'Abba! Father!'" (Gal 4:6).[5] Thus human beings become the eucharistic community that they were created to be, just as the triune God reigns in the loving praises of the redeemed. For this reason, participation in the reign of God is not some abnegating submission to heteronomous force but the very fulfillment of the human creature's being, who is called to its own true life in the life of the Creator: in the Spirit, with the Son, to the Father, now and forever.[6]

In contemporary feminist theologies, by contrast (generalizing now as in the foregoing with regard to orthodox theologies), salvation is envisioned as the social, political and cultural task of overcoming the historical oppression of women. As a result, language about God must articulate itself anthropologically (i.e., with regard to the immediate consciousness of believers, withholding reflection on what God is for God, as in trinitarianism).[7] Speech

---

[4]It is a noteworthy result of the century of historical research since the great Adolph von Harnack that it has virtually reversed his famous thesis about the "Hellenization of the gospel," in the sense that today fault for the uncritical reception of the Plotinian notion of God as immutable substance is laid to the door, not of any Easterner after the crisis of Origenism which led to the victory of trinitarianism in 381 at Constantinople, but of no less significant a Western theologian than Augustine.

[5]All citations from the NRSV unless noted otherwise.

[6]The roots of such a correlation of anthropology and trinitarianism are to be found in Irenaeus. For the notion of eucharistic humanity, I am especially indebted to Alexander Schmemann, *The Eucharist* (New York: St Vladimir's Seminary Press, 1987), and more generally John Meyendorff, *Byzantine Theology: Historical Trends and Doctrinal Themes* (New York: Fordham University Press, 1974).

[7]"Who could venture to say that the impression made by the divine in Christ obliges us to conceive such an eternal distinction as its basis?" asked Schleiermacher, who then answered his own question in the way that has proven fateful for Protestantism ever since: "the main pivots of the ecclesiastical doctrine—the being of God in Christ and in the Christian Church—are

about God in feminist theology expresses women's struggle for liberation in the present and projects hope of liberation into the future. Feminist theology is thus a theology of salvation, but it conceives of
salvation in light of the critical principle and ethical commitment of the
liberation of women from patriarchy. Feminist theology correlates the
liberation of women to broader, global concerns for economic justice
and the ecological well-being of the earth. Consequently feminist theology identifies the divine mission in the world with movements for
liberation, justice, peace and ecological healing. It works to redirect
the religious institutions of Christianity to participation in such movements.

From the perspective of this vision and praxis of liberation, the revisionist invocation or naming of God follows cogently. The need for
a spirituality which can empower the foregoing commitments is keen-
ly felt, just as is the need to overcome the power of spiritualities
which entrench or cultivate patriarchy. The very act of naming God
constitutes a bold breach with patriarchical thought structures and the
religious mystification of women's oppression. Women liberate themselves from interiorized inferiority, dualistic construals of reality and
the authoritarianism of the traditional doctrine of revelation in the
very religious act of naming God as the power of their own embattled
being on the way to liberation: "I found God in myself and loved her
fiercely," as one powerful sample of such revisionism has it. Such language, inasmuch as it expresses and presents a vision of global liberation, can hardly keep to itself. It must sound out publicly. It must
become the liturgy of the people of God, which will give birth to new

---

independent of the doctrine of the Trinity." Friedrich Schleiermacher, *The Christian Faith*, ed.
H. R. Mackintosh and J. S. Stewart (New York: Harper Torchbooks, 1963), 2:739, 741. Schleiermacher of course saw that the point of the doctrine is precisely to say how the "God *for us*" is
also "God *for God*," and so "really" able to be "*God* for us," a consideration that LaCugna (see
note 2 above) does not adequately grasp. It is no genuine retrieval of trinitarianism to reiterate
Schleiermacher's odd blend of Sabbellianism and Arianism. Ironically, in the strict sense, that
would amount to something that could seriously be designated "patriarchal theology"—as
Schleiermacher himself shrewdly noted when he accused the orthodox trinitarians of in fact
being (like himself!) crypto-Origenists, i.e., for whom God the Father is God absolutely, but
the Son and Spirit only by participation in the Father's being.

and liberating forms of community on the way to the reconciliation of all life.

Thus profound controversy over the naming of God has broken out. The contradiction, which is rooted in varying conceptions of salvation, is so sweeping that it is difficult to know how to proceed. Some perspective is needed.

If we call to mind the early Christian theology of the martyrs, we are reminded that controversy about the naming of God has always characterized the encounter of biblical faith with the nations. The invocation of God has always demarcated the distinctive new community of the Christians over against predominant civic pieties and the loyalties which they inspire.

> The magistrate persisted and said, "Swear the oath, and I will release you; revile Christ!" Polycarp replied, "For eighty-six years I have been his servant, and he has done me no wrong. How can I blaspheme my King who saved me? . . . If you vainly suppose that I will swear by the Genius of Caesar, as you request, and pretend not to know who I am, listen carefully: I am a Christian."[8]

Here we witness a collision between mutually exclusive invocations of God, that of a civic and secular theology on one side, and that of an ecclesiastical and eschatological theology on the other. Polycarp's naming of God—through Christ as King, not Caesar—and act of self-incrimination—"Make no mistake, I am a Christian"—correspond to the offensive notion of salvation through the cross, first of all Christ's own, but then, by virtue of sharing in Christ's Spirit, also the martyr's.[9] A little later, the anonymous author of *The Martyrdom of Polycarp* added the further comment about his community:

> We will never be able either to abandon the Christ who suffered for the salvation of the whole world of those who are saved, the blameless on behalf of sinners, or to worship anyone else. For this one, who is the Son of God, we

---

[8]"The Martyrdom of Polycarp," in *The Apostolic Fathers*, 2nd ed., trans. J. B. Lightfoot and J. R. Harmer, ed. and rev. M. W. Holmes (Grand Rapids, Mich.: Baker, 1992), p. 235.

[9]A theology Polycarp could have learned from Ignatius. See my series "Ignatius, Bishop and Martyr," *Lutheran Forum* 28, no. 2 (1994): 58-62; "Luther and Ignatius on the History of Salvation," *Lutheran Forum* 28, no. 3 (1994): 56-62; "The Church as the Kingdom of Christ," *Lutheran Forum* 28, no. 4 (1994): 58-62.

worship, but the martyrs we love as disciples and imitators of the Lord.[10]

I recall this second-century sample from the theology of the martyrs in part to indicate why it should not surprise or shock today that contention over the naming of God re-erupts. In the present-day controversy, the same issues of the identity and solidity of the Christian community and the authenticity of its witness to God's reign in the world are at stake as are visible in *The Martyrdom of Polycarp*. Christians might even recognize such a turn of events as a return to normalcy after centuries of Constantinian captivity. In any case, the current controversy surely gives opportunity to clarify what the gospel is. We should be warned, however, by the same theology of the martyrs that in the light of the pure divine fire which they knew, we shall ourselves be judged for our sectarian disunity, for our obsequiousness before worldly power, for our apathy in mission, for the dullness of our consciences, for our theological sloth, and not least, for our failure in questions of sexuality and gender relations.

Before addressing directly the controversy associated with proposals from feminist theologies for the revision of language about God, I want to explore in brief the question of what the gospel is. There is an important reason for proceeding this way. In the absence of clarification about the gospel as a message of salvation through the cross of Jesus, orthodox objections to the revisionist feminist proposals, chiefly made on the grounds of the doctrine of revelation, are difficult to communicate.[11] At the very least, the orthodox objection sounds abstract: does not "a rose by any other name smell sweet the same?" At worst, the orthodox objection sounds authoritarian, arbitrary, a mystification which conceals patriarchal power. In that case, the damning appearance of *fundamentalism*—"God said it, I believe it, that settles it!"—subverts the orthodox case for the retrieval of trinitarianism. On the other hand, answering the question adequately about the sense of the gospel as a message about the Christ "who suffered for the whole world, the blameless on behalf of

---

[10]"Martyrdom of Polycarp" 241. I have studied the tension between secular and eschatological theologies in "What if the 'Real World' Is the Coming Reign of God?" *Dialog* 26, no. 3 (1987): 180-83; and "Theocentrism," *Dialog* 26, no. 4 (1987): 258-63.

[11]Lindbeck, "Reflections."

sinners," is admittedly the task of an entire dogmatics. Of necessity then I have something drastically more modest in mind.

Can We Say What the Gospel Is?

Christianity has never expressly dogmatized the soteriological sense of the biblical narrative (though we may take the third article on the Holy Spirit from the Council of Constantinople, 381, as expressing an implicit doctrine of salvation). This ecumenical failure haunts us today. Even among those who regard the canonical salvation history as bearing ultimate significance, we experience significant, perhaps church-dividing variance at just this juncture. Is salvation a question of being "born-again," of justification by faith, the liberation of the oppressed, divinization, going to heaven when we die? Does not *that confusion* reveal the depth of the present crisis? On the other hand, were there doctrinal agreement in the strong sense about the meaning of biblical salvation as eternal communion in the life of God, the Father, Son and Holy Spirit, could we not tolerate significant diversity in theological conceptualization of that final reality and its relation to the church's mission in any given time and place?

George Lindbeck's significant but somewhat different suggestion, that "the present crisis" lies in the diverse understandings of what reality the biblical narrative refers to,[12] has in mind the havoc that has been wreaked by the attempt of the past several centuries to criticize the dogmas of the church, and the biblical narrative which those dogmas parse, by reconstruction of "what really happened" in history. This quest has rarely led to a sufficiently strong base of historical knowledge that would be able to settle theological questions. But it has succeeded in making any naive appropriation of the biblical narrative impossible. It has rendered the very determination of "canon" dubious. Above all, it has profoundly unsettled traditional conceptions of salvation. Consequently many theologians today

---

[12]With this question I am taking up the important issue raised by George Lindbeck, who suggested something slightly other when he wrote: "The depth of the present crisis is best seen when one considers that even those who doctrinally agree the story of Jesus is the key to the understanding of reality are often in fundamental theological disagreement over what the story is really about, over its normative or literal sense" (*The Nature of Doctrine: Religion and Theology in a Post-Liberal Age* [Philadelphia: Westminster Press, 1984], p. 119).

are unsure that Christian dogmatics is possible at all. Of course, without the discipline that teaches what Christians believe and confess on the basis of the Word of God, the identification and criticism of false teaching also becomes impossible. It is not difficult on, say, purely historical, psychological or aesthetic grounds to detect the magnitude of the liturgical innovation being proposed by feminist theologies. But it is difficult in the present environment to say that it is wrong merely on account of the innovation involved. On the contrary, the towering figure of Rudolf Bultmann represents the predominant conclusion drawn from the critical study of dogma and Bible in the twentieth century: theology has to become hermeneutical reflection on texts which will give contemporary voice to a message of salvation in the sense of a new, existentially liberating understanding of the self. Such a new way of "bringing God to speech" has to replace the old mythological "objectifying" language about God which is in any case historically incredible and offensive to modern sensibilities.

This deconstruction of Christian dogma and the biblical narrative of the past two centuries is one of the central presuppositions of current feminist theology, even though the movement inadequately acknowledges its dependence on nineteenth-century liberal theology and twentieth-century existentialist theology. The old passion for ascertaining "what really happened" in history has been taken up anew by an explicit "hermeneutic of suspicion" which intends to unveil the silencing of women which lies behind the placid surface of the canonical text (e.g., Schüssler Fiorenza).[13] This claim that the lineage of today's feminist theology lies in existentialism also holds true in spite of the interest much feminist theology shows in remythologizing (here we can think beyond Bultmann to the influence of Tillich and the various Whiteheadians), since it is explicitly acknowledged in leading feminist theologies (e.g., Sallie McFague, Elizabeth Johnson)[14] that the pursuit of new metaphors for God is not to

---

[13]Elisabeth Schüssler Fiorenza, *But She Said: Feminist Practices of Biblical Interpretation* (Boston: Beacon Press, 1992), is a sophisticated exercise in the "hermeneutic of suspicion" supplemented by proposals for a "transformative discursive practice which must position itself within the public space created by the logic of democracy" (p. 179).

[14]Elizabeth A. Johnson, *She Who Is: The Mystery of God in Feminist Theological Discourse* (New York: Crossroad, 1994), pp. 33ff.

be understood as one authoritarianism replacing another, or one claim for "revelation" over against another. Rather the new naming of God is meant as an avowedly human act set against the backdrop of the radical otherness and incomprehensibility of divine being. The offense of mythical speech about God, in other words, is construed to lie only in taking such worldly talk about the transcendent literally, and by means of that construal, privileging one set of (supposedly "true," that is, "literal") images of divinity over against others which are in turn devalued as false and idolatrous projections.

Bultmann himself tacitly continued to privilege the ecclesiastical canon of the Bible, even as his own theological method propelled him to a paradoxical search for a "canon within the canon." But increasingly the canonical delimitation of the textual sources of theology seemed arbitrary vis-à-vis the variety of early Christian voices. In fact the canon itself came more and more to appear to be the very essence of the retrospective imposition of a dogmatic framework, the founding act of orthodoxy. But this imposition distorts even our reading of the authorized texts since it deprives them also of their own historical specificity.[15] As such considerations gained ground, Bultmann's restraint in holding on to the unsurpassability of Jesus as the Christ, and in declining to speculate about God for fear of newly "objectifying" the transcendent, would not survive. The search for a "canon within the canon" disintegrated into a free-for-all. But the powerful idea of creative theology, which brings "God to utterance" in a liberating contemporaneous word of transformed human self-understanding, flourished, though it could be hardly be constrained any longer within the cramped walls of the New Testament. The pluralistic needs for new self-understanding of contemporary people living in the closed universe of secularism had to breach those old canonical barriers. Manifestly, feminist theology stands squarely in this development. Orthodox protestations that so much of feminist theology today is *Gnosticism redivivus* fall on deaf

---

[15]I have treated the Bultmann-Käsemann discussion of canonicity within the framework of my own proposal in "Evangelical Authority," *Lutheran Forum* 27, no. 4 (1993): 58-62, and "Evangelical Authority, Part Two," *Lutheran Forum* 28, no. 1 (1994): 58-62.

ears for this very reason. For the protagonists of the new naming of God, the Gnostics of old were unjustly silenced by the orthodox triumph and their voices ruled out of the church's conversation by the construction of the biblical canon—this to the profound impoverishment of the possibilities for Christian self-understanding for succeeding generations.[16]

Thus for significant Christian thinkers today in the liberal tradition, including contemporary feminist theologians, the biblical narrative is *literally impossible*, and for others it is *impossibly constrictive*. In either case, it cannot serve canonically as the primary rule of faith that identifies God in the economy of salvation.

In spite of these weighty considerations, one should not concede that the regnant confusion about the soteriological sense of the biblical narrative today is justified. Quests to ascertain "what really happened," in the strong sense required to deconstruct dogmatic Christianity, have repeatedly come to grief. As historical science, the scholarship today of celebrity figures like John Dominic Crossan, the Jesus Seminar or Elaine Pagels is painfully remiss. More importantly, one can better describe the same phenomena of Christian origins under another aegis. I am referring to the hermeneutical supposition of the primacy of any text's grammatical-historical meaning. That is to say, one could seek critical-historical understanding by trying to stand *before* the text (rather than seeking to penetrate *behind* it). In this case one wants to discipline one's own reading by hearing the text (primarily, not exclusively) as would have its first audience. This serves as a check against present day assimilations which may exploit texts merely to buttress present arrangements. Indeed it would serve as a means of qualifying the present

---

[16]See the sharply-worded "introduction" by editor James M. Robinson and the acute "Afterword: The Modern Relevance of Gnosticism" by Richard Smith in *The Nag Hammadi Library* (New York: Harper & Row, 1988). Smith rightly traces the lineage of Gnosticism in Voltaire and the French Enlightenment through the Existentialists to today's literary deconstructionism. He concludes, "the traditional codes no longer determine our meaning. The traditional canon of texts no longer has authority. . . . This most modern appreciation of Gnosticism seems indeed to have an affinity with ancient sectarianism and revisionary mythologizing" (p. 548). See also my essay (with Ellen Hinlicky) "Gnosticism: New and Old," *Dialog* 28, no. 1 (1989): 12-17.

through encounter with the text's original message.[17]

Proceeding in this fashion, we discover something quite remarkable. As we stand *before the text*, we stand *within a certain community* of faith that continually transcends its own time and space. That is to say, we discover a community of faith which preserves and extends the Word of God which it has received in written form, as Scripture.[18] In that very act of writing down and passing on the historically concrete words of prophets or apostles, sages or scribes, the Word of God is made to transcend its immediate occasion and to extend its meaning into the projected future of the community—yet without ever abandoning the primacy of the historically specific occasion which is preserved and handed on in just this fashion. In this light, we can say that a scriptural community exists in the world in that it stands before (what come to be assembled in time as) canonical texts in disciplined listening to their distinctive, historically specific and precisely as such untranslatable witnesses of the Word of God. Thus—and this is the critical point—this community exists by relying on the Spirit, who once spoke by these prophets, to speak to today's community anew. The community survives and flourishes if, and only if, this reliance on the same Spirit to speak anew is justified. So far as such confidence is justified, the canonical biblical narrative and the eschatological community of the *ecclesia* imply one another, "for whatever was written in former days was written for our instruction, so that by steadfastness and by the encouragement of the scriptures we might have hope" (Rom 15:4).

It follows from the foregoing analysis that it is necessary to distinguish but not separate the gospel and the Scripture.[19] The gospel is the divine

---

[17]I should stress that there is nothing uncritical or intrinsically monolithic about this approach to historical understanding. It would be more interesting and more fruitful were scholars imaginatively to reconstruct how differently, for instance, the men and women of the first audience might have heard the message of the text—and also how, in spite of such difference, the message unified them.

[18]See my review of *The Old Testament of the Old Testament* by R. W. L. Moberly, *Pro ecclesia* 2, no. 4 (1993): 493-97, and the studies cited above in note 14.

[19]"What is the New Testament but a public preaching and proclamation of Christ, set forth through the sayings of the Old Testament and fulfilled through Christ?" (Martin Luther, "Preface to the Old Testament" [1523, revised 1545], in *Luther's Works: The American Edition*, ed. J. Pelikan [Minneapolis: Fortress], 35:236). See also my exegetical argument from the Gospel of John on this point, "Resurrection and the Knowledge of God," *Pro ecclesia* 4,

proclamation of Easter morning that in Christ, the crucified and risen One, the Scriptures of Israel are fulfilled. By his death and resurrection, the reign of God has shown its power and pledged its victory for all those poor and helpless on whose behalf Jesus came, for whom he lived and in whose God-forsaken place he died, "the blameless for sinners." So it follows that in Christ such confident reliance on the Spirit to speak anew is justified, for the very Spirit with which Christ is fully endowed is also imparted to the community of those who believe in him. In that evangelical light, the function of Scripture is to lend a specific hope to the community in its sorrows and struggles, so that it does not despair and fall away from its hope. Concretely, the community taught by Scripture may not settle for a lesser salvation than the reign which Israel expects in all its fullness (cf. Mk 13:21-27).[20] At the same time the gospel,

---

no. 2 (1995): 226-32.

[20]In this way the historical appropriateness of early Christianity's theological development becomes intelligible, including the remarkable fact of the canonical construction of the sweeping biblical narrative stretching from the day of creation to the eschatological vision of God and the Lamb on the throne and the coming thence of the new heaven and earth. We have to note here the serious objection that George Lindbeck alluded to (see note 11 above). How is the acknowledgement that the biblical narrative is a *construction* to be taken? What reality status has this appeal to a " 'history-like' narrative" (Frei) of the biblical canon, which is not a literal denotation of "what really happened" but neither is it meant as, nor can it be taken as, sheer fiction? The biblical narrative is, so to say, "prophetic history" which is written from the divine perspective of destiny, from the perspective of the triumphant coming of the reign of God—which is the only non-magical way of understanding its inspiration by the Spirit. That much can be affirmed simply as a critical observation about biblical narrative, which constructs and synthesizes accounts of God's embattled reign in and ultimately over human history. In spiritual rapture (inspiration), the biblical narrators anticipated in the fragmentary fulfillments of divine promise which were already visible to them the eternal peace, righteousness and freedom of the divine victory. They ordered their narrative description of events in that divine light. The question of the truth of the Christian narrative in this connection is a very serious one and cannot be evaded, but it would take us far afield to pursue the matter here. It suffices to acknowledge the problem, for it would in any case constitute a considerable clarification in the current controversy over the naming of God, if only those today who reject "the narrative identification of God," would acknowledge that in fact they have come to the prior conclusion (on the basis of the hermeneutic of suspicion which I have criticized above) that the Christian narrative is not and cannot be taken as true. Precisely as an orthodox theologian, I want to acknowledge that Christianity may be false just because its claim to truth is untranslatably articulated by means of the biblical narrative. It is an aspect of the truthfulness of orthodox theological statements that they acknowledge their questionableness vis-à-vis the truth of God which must confirm them eschatologically.

comprehended in this canonical framework, is not, and never was, infinitely malleable. In fact, the gospel of salvation in the reign of God through the cross of Jesus has been from the beginning the substance of the Eucharistic institution narrative, which was (and remains) the liturgical center around which the explosive trajectories in early Christianity eventually gravitated.[21] The very same apostolic preaching of the cross was offense and folly to the present order of things, then, just because it was definitely intelligible and unmistakably communicable. "God on a cross," Nietzsche once exclaimed, "the transvaluation of all hitherto existing values!"

Consequently the question about what the gospel really is can be asked and answered succinctly. The gospel is the message in which the God of Israel is mercifully seeking and finding us godless Gentiles and bringing us by his Spirit to new life, to a share in his own divine life, life within his gracious reign. Precisely as such the gospel message is about Jesus the Christ, that is, about salvation by virtue of his cross and resurrection, as the apostle (here drawing on the earliest Christian traditions) states in Romans 1:1-4,[22] "the gospel of God, which [God] promised beforehand through his prophets in the holy scriptures [is] *the gospel concerning his Son*, who was descended from David according to the flesh and was declared to be Son of God with power according to the spirit of holiness by resurrection from the dead, Jesus Christ our Lord." The gospel then is not any titillating contemporary word of salvation which may or may not have a role for Jesus, which may or may not share in Israel's messianic hope. Any attempt to "translate" the gospel into another idiom to make it more readily communicable would only set one down a false path that does not need nor rely on the Spirit. All such attempts are in fact regressive. They miss the point entirely. It is rather we who have to

---

[21]See above, note 15.

[22]This was of course Luther's key text, which did not mean, however, that he made out of an existentialized Paulinism a "canon within the canon!" Precisely here in Rom 1:1-4 Paul—and Luther in his time—is appealing to the normative tradition. Luther defines on the basis of Rom 1:1-4: "the gospel is a discourse about Christ that he is the Son of God and became man for us, that he died and was raised, that he has been established Lord over all things" in "A Brief Instruction on What to Look for and Expect in the Gospels" (1521) in *Luther's Works* 35:118.

be converted, lose our old identities, and enter the new world of scriptural hope.

Christian doctrine, on the other hand, develops in history in the very event of the community's attending to the Word of God borne by Scripture and understood in the light of the gospel. Orthodoxy has nothing to do with theological reaction. It has its sights set forward toward the revolution of revolutions. Just so, the church has a history of progress and regress which is theologically relevant, in which the Spirit continues to make God known in spite of the church's failures. But in fact the church lives faithfully in that it expects constantly, as the Puritans said so wonderfully, that "God has yet more truth to break out of his Holy Word." Knowledge of the living God has to expect progress in doctrine. Precisely this expectation was recognized and established in the crowning achievement of the early dogmatic development: the trinitarian faith in the coequal divinity of the person of the Spirit (Council of Constantinople, 381), who is the very Spirit imparted to believers, who leads the church in her pilgrimage into all truth by bringing to remembrance Jesus' word.

The faith in the divine personhood of the Holy Spirit in the trinitarian context means faith in the Spirit as the third concrete existence of the mutually related life of the God of Israel and Jesus his Son. Historically, this faith in the personal existence of the divine Spirit, who proceeds from the Father of the Son, broke the metaphysical spell of middle Platonism's vertical, static scheme of God-Logos-Kosmos. It implied instead that our world exists as a history which is divinely determined by the God who from all eternity has fullness of life as the Spirit of the Father and the Son. In that case we have to view our reality strictly as creation which exists in order to be included through a unique historical journey in God's life. With this theological comprehension of eschatology in the doctrine of the divine personhood of the Spirit of the Father and the Son, all the originative elements fall into historical coherence: the primitive Christian gospel of salvation through the cross of Jesus, the centrality of eucharistic worship, the mission to the nations, the canonical expansion and consolidation of the biblical narrative, the rejection of Gnosticism, and the witness of the martyrs to the lordship of Jesus the crucified. The dogmatic development of early Christianity, culminating in the trinitarian conviction about the deity of the Spirit, constitutes a logical clarification and elucidation of the primitive Christian message that the God of Israel has reconciled the world in the cross of Christ and sent the Spirit in his Name to actualize the peace of the approaching reign.

Yet it also represents a new apprehension of truth. Trinitarian faith in the Spirit is both the basis for the expectation of progress in doctrine and itself the prime instance of such doctrinal progress. Believers therefore have to learn who and what the word *God* means by a double immersion, of body and soul in the waters of baptism (and daily return to baptism), and of the mind in the pages of Scripture. Such learning is the business of the dogmatic theology of a real, physical community on this earth, the body of Christ. Because Christianity is the church, it has always had to be a dogmatic (i.e., a teaching) faith which says yes and no amid the maelstrom of voices who at any moment are claiming saving authority over human souls. Certainly this very teaching activity in Christianity is eschatologically qualified or reserved; it paradoxically teaches that God alone teaches in the person of the Holy Spirit. But that is to say that in faith dogmatic theology audaciously ventures its own (derivative but real) inspiration. Dogmatic theology must assert that without dancing dialectical jigs of self-cancellation. "Take away assertions and you take away Christianity."[23] Theology which locates itself in the church can teach with evangelical authority because the very Spirit of God was manifested without reserve in Jesus the Christ. This same Spirit is bestowed on his community, not, of course, like some impersonal fluid mechanically injected into the ecclesiastical machinery but rather as the final Person, whose self-impartation consists in calling believers forward "to the glorious liberty of the children of God."

The transcendence of God to which believers infinitely advance is designated this way, not as something beyond or behind the triune God's life but within this very life of the Spirit, the Son and the Father, which life is alone eternal. Because of this, the gospel's doctrinal meaning can

---

[23]Martin Luther, *The Bondage of the Will*, trans. J. I. Packer and O. R. Johnston (Grand Rapids, Mich.: Revell, 1957), p. 67.

be by no means immediately obvious to any individual, nor has it been fully articulated in any hitherto existing form of the community's life, which is still underway. The fullness of the gospel's light does not and cannot shine until all that it promises is fulfilled in the uninterrupted joy of God's victory. Consequently, faith always has to see in the dark and wait eagerly for the dawn. Nevertheless on the basis of the concrete hope which is promised in the Scriptures and attested by the Spirit to the eucharistic community, faith does see and bear witness, both teaches and judges.

Salvation and the Doctrine of Revelation

The way has now been prepared for the central contention of this essay. It is because of the notion of salvation *as communion with God*, a notion that the doctrine of the Trinity explicates, that the predominant understanding of the naming of God in feminist theology has to be rejected. Specifically what must be rejected is "projectionism," along the lines of Feuerbach's theory[24] that in religious language alienated human beings project onto the empty screen of infinity, as it were, an idealized image of their estranged being and then worship that objectification as "God" in a kind of compensatory act. The chief modern theologian of revelation, Karl Barth, accepted Feuerbach's theory—as an acute description of idolatry! He contended that inasmuch as human beings are inclined in their sinful alienation to exchange "the truth about God for a lie" and worship and serve "the creature rather than the Creator" (Rom 1:24-25), only God can name God. Consequently any true human naming of God can only be derivative. Our naming of God can only be an act of faith that ventures itself on the supposition of God's self-revelation. Our speech about God can exist only as a participation in God's self-revealing communication. Karl Barth pressed this thought so thoroughly and so consequently that he even tried to uncover the root of the doctrine of the Trinity by logical analysis of the three aspects of the one event stipulated in the state-

---

[24]Ludwig Feuerbach, *The Essence of Christianity,* with an introduction by Karl Barth, trans. G. Eliot (New York: Harper Torchbooks, 1957).

ment, "God reveals himself as Lord."[25] The artificiality and abstractness of this attempt should not conceal Barth's profound insight, that in the complex, narrative unity of the Father's sendings of the Son and the Spirit, the one saving event of the coming of God's reign occurs and becomes revealed. Thus it is hardly accidental that the triune Name and the doctrine of revelation should align themselves against feminist revisionism in language for God, and the projectionist, "experiential-expressive" theory of religious language[26] which it presupposes.

As a response to the challenge of feminist theology, the Barthian contradiction on the grounds of the doctrine of revelation is well-taken. Yet it amounts to little more than a flat contradiction of feminist theology which misses in crucial respects both the depth of a common crisis of faith and the paradoxical opportunity its challenge offers to the beleaguered and disunited forces of Christian orthodoxy in post-Christian America today. That is the opportunity to clarify for our times the sense of salvation through the cross, not simply or even primarily as a negation of idolatry but primarily and positively as the power to establish the new human community—new in that it anticipates final salvation as communion with God. It is one thing to smash the idols iconoclastically; it is quite another to build up the living temple of the Lord in the true image of God, Jesus Christ.

At its best, the challenge of feminist theology to those who would be orthodox is the categorical demand for the church to become in our time that community which, precisely by virtue of baptism into Christ's death, is promised in Galatians 3:28: "There is no longer Jew or Greek, there is no longer slave or free, there is no longer male and female; for all of you are one in Christ Jesus." The attractiveness of this text is apparent enough; what needs to be clearly recognized and elucidated is the fact that this radiant vision is nothing but a gloss on the message of salvation through the cross of Jesus, and therewith recognition of the trinitarian differentiation and relation of the Father and the Son in the life of God

---

[25]Karl Barth, *Church Dogmatics,* ed. G. W. Bromiley & T. F. Torrance, I/1, *The Doctrine of the Word of God* (Edinburgh: T & T Clark, 1975), pp. 304-33.

[26]Lindbeck, *Doctrine,* pp. 30-45.

which the central, saving event of the cross of the Son demands of all future theology. It is through the cross of Jesus, the apostle concludes in this very epistle, that he is crucified to the world and world to him (6:14), so that those old roles determined by life in this present order have lost their definitive power over the human person. These have been supplanted by the new identification with Jesus, the Son of God. "As many of you as were baptized into Christ have clothed yourselves with Christ" (3:27). All become united in the personhood of Christ, in that they are assumed into Christ's own relation to God as Son to Father. It is "in Christ Jesus you are all *sons of God* through faith" (3:26, correcting the NRSV of Galatians 3:26, in that the NRSV's translation, *children of God*, obscures the christological basis of the believer's adoption in Jesus' sonship).

These soteriological and ecclesiastical dimensions, which bring out unmistakably the integral and inalienable place of biblical language of the Father and the Son, define the issue of the invocation of God with greater depth and precision. In this light the question becomes, "How do we come to recognize the transcendence of the true God, who can in no wise be controlled, manipulated or predicted, even on the basis of true theological assertions?" Is the transcendence of God a general presupposition of revelation or is it something we first truly come to acknowledge in consequence of revelation? Is "God the Father" the idolatrous expression of patriarchal power, or the revelation of the very God whom we can only fear, love and trust—or flee in all eternity? The problems of the naming of God, the distinctive identity and witness of the church in the world, and the nature of human salvation constitute a whole complex of concerns. I see no controversy on this abstract level between defenders of the traditional Christian language for God and feminist revisionists. In the response to feminist theology, however, most attention has been focused one-sidedly on the epistemological aspect of the problem, namely, the apparent contradiction of the proposed revisionism to the doctrine of revelation. As already indicated, this response stands in need of further elucidation by uncovering the soteriological and ecclesiastical dimensions of it. Attending to that helps us see that the issue of substance before us is the godliness of God, how that is conceived and how we communally relate to it and what path to salvation it presents us with.

The reason for the emphasis on the doctrine of revelation as a response to revisionist proposals, of course, lies in the unique content of theological statements as statements *about God* which, if they are to be true, must always also demonstrate themselves as statements *of God*. All statements about God (especially "orthodox" ones), then, stand under the proviso of awaiting God's own confirmation. That bears no little ethical implication: "Not everyone who says to me, 'Lord, Lord,' will enter the kingdom of heaven, but only the one who does the will of my Father in heaven" (Mt 7:21). Whoever dares to speak about God does so in fear and trembling, for that one above all must answer to God! "You shall not make wrongful use of the name of the LORD your God, for the LORD will not acquit anyone who misuses his name" (Ex 20:7). Of course, this ethical stipulation does not preclude the possibility of sin. It merely identifies the possibility of using God's name falsely, and warns against it. In fact, nothing further can be secured. No one can prematurely bring the contest of history to an end by eliminating the possibility of sin, nor can any amount of theological revisionism solve the real problem we have in using God's name. Faced with the feeling that any attempt to speak of God must fail, not a few people today follow Wittgenstein's attractive dictum and chose silence, "That whereof we cannot speak we must remain silent." But that too is no solution. Silence about God is no less an abuse of God's name. The proper use of God's name has intrinsically and essentially to do with the deliverance of all humanity from sin and death. To be silent about that is to take the side of the devil.

Not by accident, then, the commandment about the proper use of God's name is introduced in the soteriological context of the Lord's rescue of his people from bondage in Egypt, just as God has revealed his name in these saving acts. God gives his name as a pledge of his saving help, on which alone the people are to rely, lest they turn back, hankering after the flesh-pots of Egypt. The etymology of the divine name revealed to Israel denotes the freedom of the Lord, who will be who he will be, who is free to elect the lowly Hebrews (yet also free to hand over these very people who bear his name into the apparent power of other nations and their gods). This free God, whose will determines all things, whose name denotes the One who cannot be manipulated but only feared, loved and trusted—this one true God gives himself over into human language in the form of a concrete, personal name upon which Israel can call, even though as a "name" God himself now becomes vulnerable, in contradiction to his own transcendent being, to human abuse and manipulation.

So anew and anew by the Spirit, God himself must demonstrate what word *about God* is in fact the word *of God*. Second Isaiah speaks in God's name,

> To whom will you liken me and make me equal, and compare me, as though we were alike? Those who lavish gold from the purse, and weigh out silver in the scales—they hire a goldsmith, who makes it into a god; then they fall down and worship! They lift it to their shoulders, they carry it, they set it in its place, and it stands there; it cannot move from its place. *If one cries out to it, it does not answer or save anyone from trouble.* Remember this and consider, recall it to mind, you transgressors, remember the former things of old; for I am God, and there is no other; I am God, and there is no one like me. (Is 46:5-9, emphasis mine)

At this pinnacle of scriptural theology what we see is that the incomparable One, who is alone worthy of all our fear and love, in fact wills to be the Savior. The free God declares himself in his word of promise to be worthy of all our trust. Abstract dialectics of transcendence and immanence have long misled Western theology, obscuring the soteriological and eschatological context in which the God of the Bible manifests incomparable freedom precisely in, and not apart from, the historically rendered promise of salvation. The hallowing of God's name to which Jesus summoned his disciples belongs in the same soteriological context of imploring the coming of the heavenly Father's reign. While Jesus' invocation of God his heavenly Father is uniquely his own, Jesus' usage of God's name stands in the same prophetic stream of biblical speech about God. Such speech names the only One whom people can trust to save, not in spite of, but just because this very God is alone beyond the reach of all manipulation and his love is grounded in his free commitment. Knowing this God in his self-declaration, his word of promise, people can be freed from the service of vain and helpless idols; they can begin instead to live by hope in the salvation of God's reign which surely comes.

Thus the incomparable God is the God who makes and keeps his promises; the God whose being is freedom becomes manifest in love; the authentic transcendence of God is the imminence of his saving reign; the truth of God will be demonstrated by his power to redeem all that he has made. All these statements come together and culminate in the biblical perception that God has made the human person for himself, for communion with God, for eternal life which is participation in that life which the Father, the Son and the Holy Spirit live. From this final horizon of soteriology, it is clear that statements about God self-destruct when we think to reduce them to thematizations of human intentions. In this way the real transcendence of the God who can and will save is obliterated. Such thematizations, moreover, are no less "graven images," because they take the (apparently!) nonliteral form of metaphors, tropes or metaphysical conceptions for that matter. Nor does it help that we are intending to speak of God in connection with some human benefit, whether that be going to heaven when we die, liberation from patriarchal oppression, or whatever. Literally, as Second Isaiah insists, the idols we manufacture do not help. They leave us at the mercy of our own illusions, secular or religious, or to perish in despair. They do not challenge us, change us or convert us, and they can never heal us.

What makes an idol then is not in the first place a literal or arbitrary representation of the unknowable God but turning to a false savior who draws our love away from the only One who is worthy of all our love, the incomparable Lord, the Father of Jesus Christ who pours out his Spirit on perishing humanity and gives of his own life to the dead. It will be in loving wholly and forever the One who has loved us incomparably in Christ that we are saved. We recognize with joy and thanksgiving the transcendence of the true God, the real godliness of God the heavenly Father, when we come to live by faith, that is, in the ecstatic openness of the Spirit to reign. That means here and now sharing daily in the Son's death, living here and now such a life which spiritually, ethically, culturally, indeed physically depends wholly upon the promise of the resurrection of the dead.

The Redemption of the Body

Contemporary traditions of Christian orthodoxy have no interest whatsoever in aiding or abetting the oppression of women, and to the extent that they have consciously or unconsciously participated in that oppression the only response worthy of the gospel is repentance. Important as that is, it is not directly a theological issue, unless one has come to the post-Christian decision that Christianity is so intrinsically hostile to the liberation of women that one must repudiate it. In that case, no depth of repentance could ever suffice, because the very terms in which sin, repentance and the works of love are understood are in question. We have a theological issue, as I have sought to show, when we encounter just such contending narratives of sin, righteousness and salvation. Short of that, the question of the oppression of women and the historical record of Christianity becomes urgent, complex, and often baffling. This history, as I alluded above, matters theologically. Elsewhere I have made explorations in this direction.[27] Such historical theology is an enormous task before us, and in conclusion I can only point in the direction in which orthodox theology is obligated to go in this connection.

With a view to the ambiguity that attends all human history, the role of Christianity in history has to be comprehended as a positive force in elevating of the status of women (and children), indeed in affirming women (and children) as such. If we were not operating with a Manichaean philosophy of history, we would in fact see that it was Christianity from its beginnings, and often against the inherited prejudices of its own adherents, which made audible to the world the cry of Rachel weeping. If we are not forgetting the premodern facts of life which cast (and still cast in the two-thirds world) a universal shadow of pain and heartbreak over women's sexuality, we can perceive what a monumental ethical transformation in the institution of marriage is already visible in the deutero-Pauline writings (or in Jesus' prohibition of divorce). We would appreciate the evangelical authenticity of the "resurrection ethics" of early Christian sexual renunciation that liberated so many from the civic duty to reproduce in a world without medicine, contraception or pain-

---

[27]See my "Luther Against the Contempt of Women," *Lutheran Quarterly* 2, no. 4 (1989): 515-30; for what follows, see also my "Havens from the Heartless Home," *Dialog* 28, no. 3 (1989): 175-82.

control.[28] If we did not with the epithet *patriarchy* descend into a night in which all cats are gray, we would recall for example that Martin Luther once invoked as a reason for civil defense the fear that the conquering Turks would institute a legal order which treats women as property. We might thereby become freshly aware of the tension and inevitable "compromises" which attend every attempt to put the eschatological message of the gospel into a simple, positive relation to "this world." We might be equally instructed by the fact that this same reformer railed against the influence of the Aristotelian doctrine of woman as maimed man on the church's theological anthropology. We would discover that Luther's recovery of biblical anthropology represented an emphatic endorsement of the heterosexual norm. It is man and woman in life's partnership who are together, and only together, the image of the Creator, the stewards of this earth and caretakers of life on it.[29] If we could disenchant ourselves from the spell which "democratic" ideology holds over us,[30] finally, we would consider that Protestant evangelicalism in nineteenth-century America was the seedbed of the original women's movement whose leaders invariably understood themselves to be on the forefront of the progress of Christian civilization—and we would ask far more critically about what continuity exists between that movement and today's dominant forms of aggressively secularizing feminism.[31]

This superficial sampling, skimming across the major epochs of Christian history, suffices to challenge fundamentally undifferentiated and propagandistically bleak portraits of Christianity's role in history. What is really in question is what kind of account of the variegated and complex oppression of women is made and thus also the tacit, often hidden norms employed. What counts as progress? Secular feminist scholars acknowledge an irreducible pluralism of perspectives: liberal, Marxist, les-

[28]Peter Brown, *The Body and Society: Men, Women and Sexual Renunciation in Early Christianity* (New York: Columbia University Press, 1988).

[29]Hinlicky, "Luther Against the Contempt of Women."

[30]See my "War of Worlds: Re-Visioning the Abortion Dilemma," *Pro ecclesia* 2, no. 2 (1993): 187-207.

[31]See the study, unjustly neglected by American theologians, of Jean Bethke Elshtain, *Public Man, Private Woman: Women in Social and Political Thought* (Princeton, N.J.: Princeton University Press, 1981).

bian, and those of persons of color. This acknowledged pluralism in itself gives lie to the conceit of pretending to speak in the name of women as such. Far more problematic is the striking lack of a perspective which would articulate and affirm the aspirations of the vast majority of women for good marriages, healthy children, relief from domestic drudgery, a flexible labor system, but above all a meaningful relationship with God. Yet if a critic today is presupposing a fundamentally secularist perspective, all the human past too easily appears as but shifting fogs of mystification obscuring the dreary uniform reality of comprehensive patriarchal oppression. Likewise the role of eschatological faith will appear more as a collaborator in perpetuating the false consciousness of religion as such rather than as a liberator in exposing ideologies which silenced women. But orthodox traditions of Christian theology today have to challenge precisely the adequacy of the fundamentally secularist perspective.[32]

So it is finally important to place the tensions with feminist theology in the context of a larger conflict. What we witness today is a conflict not unlike that in the first Christian centuries, between secularizing civic theologies and eschatologically oriented ecclesiastical theologies. Christianity is essentially an eschatology, a message promising the coming of God's saving reign. The "real world" is the coming reign of God, to which "the suffering of this present age is not worthy to be compared." "The form of this world is passing away," and so we live by faith in the promise of "God who gives life to the dead and calls into being things which are not." Living in the tension of a history of salvation, the one fundamental heresy, the apostasy which falls away from the hope of the reign, is to make an "ism" out of the present order of reality, secular*ism*. But God in Christ has "chosen what is weak and foolish in this world, indeed, what is nothing at all in order to bring to naught the things that are." Not that this Christian eschatology devalues the present creation whatsoever, but rather strains for its redemption from the powers of sin and death. Christian eschatology, whose chief symbol is the resurrection

---

[32]John Milbank, *Theology and Social Theory: Beyond Secular Reason* (Cambridge, Mass.: Blackwell, 1997).

of the body, values this present reality eternally.[33] Indeed, it regards eternity as nothing but the divine redemption of the body, *pars pro toto*, of all that God has made.

For that reason the conflict between secular theology and eschatological theology becomes acute at the level of ethical life, where the claims of civic and ecclesiastical communities overlap. In connection with this central conviction about the "redemption of our bodies," Christianity singles out human sexuality as an especially significant arena of the conflict between the saving power of God's Spirit and the destructive force of human self-reliance. The Spirit makes of marriage a living, sacramental sign of the future consummation, sees in celibacy a charism for single-minded devotion to the work of the kingdom. From this eschatological and redemptive perspective, Christianity thus insists upon what can only appear to secularist perspectives, which do not reckon on the Spirit as the power of the coming kingdom, as an inhumanly rigorous ethic. *But in fact precisely what is human and what is inhuman is at question.* In view of God's faithfulness to humanity manifest in Christ's love for the church and the church's Spirit-wrought love for Christ, the standard which reflects a humanity renewed in the image of God is fidelity in the marriage of one man and one woman and celibacy in singleness. Without hope in the resurrection, by contrast, secularism is seen to license, not the vaunted sexual freedom that it claims, but the ugly reality of sexual predation, the victims of which are almost universally women and children.[34]

Much work lies ahead of us, both ecclesiastically and theologically, if the church in America is to become again the church of the gospel, the *ecclesia* of the reign. At least the radicalness of the present controversy

---

[33]It is secularism which finds its egalitarian illusions regularly dashed by the pressures of competition in the closed universe which it has posited. Secularism is constrained to erect hierarchies—a system of triage on spaceship Earth—which devalue some kinds or aspects of human life. One only has to reflect on rationalizations of the nonpersonhood of human fetal life, by those who allegedly value and affirm women's experience in its particularity, in order to witness the sad spectacle of this new secular hierarchicalism playing itself out.

[34]A stance already articulated with great coherence and insight by the second-century apologist Athenagoras in explicit dependence on the resurrection faith. See "A Plea for the Christians" 34, in *Fathers of the Second Century*, ed. A. Cleveland Coxe (reprint, Peabody, Mass.: Hendrikson, 1995).

makes that unavoidably clear. Do we have grounds, in the gospel of Jesus Christ, to entrust ourselves to the saving God freely, joyfully—which means to live here and now on the basis of the promise of "one holy catholic and apostolic church . . . one baptism for the forgiveness of sins . . . the resurrection of the dead and the life of the world to come"? Or does our speech about God finally end in silence, leaving us to the task of self-imagined liberations? That is the real choice before us in the controversy about the naming of God.

Contributors

William P. Alston is an emeritus professor of philosophy at Syracuse University, Syracuse, New York.

Gary W. Deddo is an associate editor at InterVarsity Press, Downers Grove, Illinois.

Stanely J. Grenz is the Pioneer McDonald Professor of Theology and Ethics at Carey Theological College and Regent College, Vancouver, British Columbia.

Paul R. Hinlicky is the Jordan-Trexler Professor of Religion at Roanoke College, Salem, Virginia.

Donald D. Hook is an emeritus professor of linguistics at Trinity College, Hartford, Connecticut.

Alvin F. Kimel Jr. is rector of the Church of the Holy Communion, Charleston, South Carolina.

Paul Mankowski is a lector in biblical Hebrew at the Pontifical Biblical Institute in Rome.

Francis Martin is a priest of the Archdiocese of Washington, D.C., and professor of biblical studies at the John Paul II Institute for Studies on Marriage and Family, Washington, D.C.

R. R. Reno is an associate professor of theology at Creighton University, Omaha, Nebraska.

Thomas E. Schmidt is director of the Westminster Institute, an educational nonprofit serving students at the University of California, Santa Barbara.

Christopher R. Seitz is a professor of Old Testament and theological studies at the University of St Andrews, Scotland.